Stay in the Fight!!

Warrior's Guide to the Combat Pistol

By Kyle E. Lamb

Edited by MSG Kevin P. Dorsh

Trample & Hurdle Publishers

WARNING

The practices, methods, and techniques described in this book are not for beginners. This book is designed for persons with background, knowledge, and experience in firearms and firearm handling. If you do not have substantial background, knowledge, and experience with firearms and firearm handling, seek instruction before attempting to utilize or implement the practices, methods, and techniques described in this book.

Shooting and handling of firearms involves inherent and unavoidable risks. Firearms are dangerous. If you are not willing and able to take responsibility for your actions, do not handle firearms. Whenever handling a firearm, remove the magazine (if applicable) and visually check the chamber before handling, cleaning or working on the firearm to verify that it is not loaded. Always use appropriate eye and ear protection whenever shooting. Know how to fire and otherwise operate any firearm you are handling. Refer to the applicable owner's manual for specific instructions. Many firearms are different, even if they appear to be similar. Your firearm may not operate in the same manner as the firearms described in this book. Never handle a firearm except in an appropriate location, such as a shooting range.

ALWAYS OBSERVE THE FOUR (4) PRIMARY RULES OF GUN SAFETY:

1. **Treat all firearms as if they were loaded.**
2. **Never point a firearm at anyone or anything you are not willing to put a bullet through.**
3. **Keep your finger off the trigger and out of the trigger guard until you are ready to fire.**
4. **Know your target and what is behind it.**

This book is not intended to be a complete or exclusive guide to firearm operation, and it particularly does not purport to give complete instructions with regard to any particular firearm. This book must be used in conjunction with adequate prior experience and other resources.

***Disclaimer:** No one associated with this book, including its author, is or will be responsible for death, injury, loss or damage to property due to the use or misuse of firearms.*

SHOOT SAFE!

This book is dedicated to my Dad, Lyle E. Lamb.

Good Cowboy

Great Shooter

The Finest Father any Warrior could ask for.

"I wish I could show you what I've learned."

ACKNOWLEDGEMENTS

This book has truly been a team effort. I hope I have presented a finished product that you will be proud of.

Melynda, she has been my biggest fan, and to keep me grounded, my biggest critic. She has done her best to keep me focused. When all was said and done, she still allows me to hunt more than I should, shoot more than I need, and travel enough to make Diamond level with Delta. Not something to be proud of but it puts this all in perspective. For those of you who know my wife, she is absolutely the best example of what we all should aspire to be.

Thanks as well to Kelsey and Lukas for what they do to keep me pointed in the right direction.

As a U.S. Army Special Forces Soldier and VTAC student, Master Sergeant Kevin Dorsh was the perfect choice as the editor for this book. As a former English Teacher gone rogue, Kevin is what most would call the Citizen Soldier. His insight to my training style and fighting system made this project a breeze.

When a crazy German and a Gun-slinging American get together, watch out. Oliver Falk was the photographer for 99% of the pictures in this book. Not only is he a great photographer, but a talented shooter as well. We have become great friends over the years and his help is much appreciated.

This book wouldn't be as much fun to look at if it weren't for our Supermodels. MSG Dan Brokos, U.S. Army Special Forces, and Sergeant Jason Teague, Gwinnett County Police Department S.W.A.T. Special Thanks to Officer Bryan Bailey and Fayetteville, North Carolina Police Department.

Taking a break from singing lead vocals for a well-known Heavy Metal Band to help design this book, Matt Frederick. He is the hardest workingman in show business and I appreciate his dedication and friendship.

The normal list of vagabonds grows with every passing day. Mike Laut, John Waters and Dave Vandenberg, they only laugh when I don't know how to dress myself. Thanks guys. Dave, don't laugh, you aren't a very snappy dresser either....

To a few special folks that always look out for me, no matter how bad I am about getting back to them or how many balls I drop. These men are a special breed. John Cone, Tim Sellars, Gravy, Todd, Bob Mc, Butch, Joe B., Dan Fay and his N.J. Posse.

Thanks to all of the "Honcho's" I served with for teaching me a few tricks here and there. Thanks as well to all of the great shooters who have taken the time to help me over the years and continue to mentor me yet today.

Thanks to all of my students. You are truly what this is all about. Thanks for keeping an open mind when I ask you to do something out of the ordinary. I learn from you every time I step on the range. And thanks especially for what you do on a daily basis, putting yourselves in harms way to keep us free and protected. This book is for you.

Kyle

Lastly, thanks to the Warriors who helped me get where I am today. The Warriors who will continue the fight, and the Warriors who will build their skills and test their temper against enemies, foreign and domestic, now and during the upcoming fight.

Kyle E. Lamb

Part I Core Skills

Part II Tools of the Trade

Part III Intermediate/Advanced Skills

INTRODUCTION

After writing "Green Eyes and Black Rifles: The Warriors Guide to the Combat Carbine", I received numerous calls and emails from friends as well as folks we had never met, asking for a Combat Pistol book as well. This book is another step in trying to get information out to those who need it but have not been able to get into one of our classes, and is also intended to be a reference for those that have attended our courses.

We will discuss several techniques, which I classify as ***A WAY*** to accomplish the task at hand, not ***THEE WAY***, you will have to determine what works best for you.

This book is intended to be about shooting, not the arms race. If you are looking for the latest and greatest gadgets you will be disappointed. If you are looking for hard core Combat shooting techniques this book is for you.

Keep an open mind and enjoy the book, as I said in "Green Eyes and Black Rifles" I am not an English Professor, simply a Soldier who decided to share my skills and experiences with all of you.

The training we conduct with the Combat pistol is just that, for those that intend to use the pistol for Combat purposes. I am a big fan of Competitive shooting; I always have been and always will be. I think competition is a great place to hone your skills for Combat Shooting, however you must not have a mindset that these two disciplines are one in the same. Don't confuse competition with combat. Certain competition skills and styles may or may not have a place in the Combat world. As Tactical Shooters we must not forget why we are training and what we are planning to accomplish with these skills. We are training to KILL; this cannot be taken lightly. We are planning to WIN a Gunfight, not a competition. This is for real, the consequences of poor planning for the fight are serious. If we don't WIN this real world competition, you still get to go home, the only difference is you will be in a wooden box.

Stay in the Fight!!

Kyle E. Lamb

Chapter 1, Safety

The techniques we will discuss and demonstrate throughout this book will be basic to some and advanced to others. No matter what your skill level is, it is crucial that you conduct all drills dry before going hot on the range. Be absolutely sure that all weapons and magazines are unloaded before trying these new skills.

There are several techniques that we will discuss that cause you to bring the muzzle of the weapon close to your body. At no time should you cover or point the weapon at your body or anyone around you while conducting these maneuvers.

When you are using your support hand to conduct shooting drills, malfunction clearances, or new positions, be extremely careful to ensure that you have control of your weapon at all times.

No matter the type of target, always wear eye protection.

Train hard, train often, but always train safe.

Always observe the four (4) primary rules of gun safety.

1. Treat all firearms as though they are loaded.

2. Never point a firearm at anyone or anything you are not willing to destroy.

3. Keep your finger off of the trigger and out of the trigger guard until you are ready to fire.

4. Know your target and what is behind it.

When you head to the range it never hurts to conduct a safety brief for those that you are training. There may be shooters in the crowd that are not aware of certain rules that apply to sharing a range with others. May sound goofy to you, but we have seen shooters who didn't understand what "in a safe direction" actually meant.

Chapter 2, Dry Fire

2. DRY FIRE

Before we get into the meat of Combat Pistol shooting, you must understand the building block process that I have grown to believe in. This process takes years and must be taken very serious. You never know when a threat will present itself and you will be called on to use your tools.

But how do we get there?

Practice, practice, practice. Does this all have to be live fire? Definitely not. In the next several chapters we will discuss and depict techniques that may be foreign to you. If these techniques are different than what you have used in the past, or they are techniques that are radically different than your current techniques, you must dry fire. Dry fire is the practice of practicing with your unloaded weapon or even a soft air or training weapon, to get familiar with certain techniques before wasting ammo. I say wasting, because if all you ever do is live fire, you will not notice some of the nuances that dry fire may help eliminate.

Make sure you are using an unloaded weapon, and also ensure that you are training in an area that is safe. Do not point your weapon at anything you are not willing to destroy. Be sure of not only your target but what is beyond your target. These are basic safety rules but we must always adhere to them.

I believe you will have better luck if you read until you get to a point that is new, then take the time and dry fire that technique. See what you think and move on. We have also added hundreds of illustrations to help get our points across. Hopefully it will all make sense by the end of each chapter.

Some shooters don't believe dry fire is for them. I have been shooting since I was a young kid and I still dry fire several days a week. Maybe not for extended periods of time, but I constantly am making sure I practice new and old techniques.

Give the techniques a shot and see what you think. You may know a better way, or hopefully you may just pick up something new to add to your toolbox.

Chapter 3, Stance

3. STANCE

"Your shooting stance is a fighting stance and your fighting stance is a shooting stance."

Some of the misconceptions about the shooting stance drive me crazy. I have had shooters say, "I shoot more accurately from this straight up stance." That is fine, but it takes you five minutes to fire one round. This book is not about competition shooting, or putting holes in paper, it is about Gunfighting and that implies that the enemy may be shooting back at you.

Your stance must be one that allows for quick movement, quick follow through, quick reengagement of the threat, and if possible, lowers your silhouette. Your stance should also transition nicely to shooting while moving, as well as working around cover, inside a building, or in the street. We want to have a system that works naturally and does not require changing everything about the grip or stance because you decide to wear assault kit, body armor, or shoot while moving.

Isosceles vs. Weaver

If you want to shoot extremely fast, while moving, around cover, or while wearing assault kit, Isosceles or Modified Isosceles is for you. The fastest shooters in the world use the Modified Isosceles shooting stance. It is asinine that we even have this discussion, but there are still a few enclaves holding onto the Weaver shooting stance.

3.1 Jack Weaver shooting his original Weaver Stance

3.2 Weaver Stance

Jack Weaver developed the Weaver shooting stance in 1959, and it really worked well for the competitions he was shooting at the time. It has since been made obsolete by the introduction of the Modified Isosceles stance. I shouldn't say the introduction, just the education of the shooting community. The Isosceles shooting stance was used in WW II by the fellas in the picture below, they were the

Founding Fathers of the United States Special Forces; and yet we have to endure discussion about a stance that was developed to shoot balloons. Enough said.

3.3 WWII Special Operations Soldiers firing from Isoceles Stance.

Be Aggressive

When shooting the Isosceles stance, you must remember what I said at the beginning of this chapter, "your fighting stance is your shooting stance." What this means is this: shoot like you are in a fight, or waiting to get punched. How would you stand if I said I was going to punch you in the chest? You would lean into it to keep from getting knocked over by the punch. The same is true of the shooting stance; we want to lean into the punch that the pistol is delivering to us. Aggression will get you through most problems in life, at least it has for me, and shooting is no different. In order to

3.4 Fighting Stance

3.5 Aggressive Shooting Stance

3.6 Aggressive Fighting Stance *3.7 Poor Fighting Stance*

3.8 *Weaver Stance*

3.9 Weight on balls of feet.

3.10 Bad Stance (weight not forward).

3.11 Lifting support foot starts immediate movement.

deliver a huge amount of lead onto the threat, in a short amount of time, you must be aggressive.

When you stand in your shooting stance, you should be pushed or leaning forward on your toes. Not standing on your tip toes, but most of the weight should be forward. If you offset your stance slightly, with the support side foot forward, you should be able to lift the support foot off the ground and immediately start to move forward. That is aggressive. If you watch your partner shoot and their toes move every time they shoot, tell them to get aggressive. If they don't understand, push on their chest to send the point home. If that doesn't work, just punch them in the chest. Might not fix the problem, but it is entertaining.

Bend your knees

It is important that the knees are slightly bent. I try to bend the support knee enough to allow the kneecap to ride over the ball of the support foot. This will put you in the aggressive position that will allow for extreme recoil management, as well as quick movement. You will not have to bend your knee to start your movement, just pick up the foot and start moving, as I stated earlier.

3.12 Knee not over toe, leg too straight.

3.13 Aggressive knee bend, knee over toe.

3.14 Knee not over toe, leg too straight.

3.15 Aggressive knee bend, knee over toe.

Arm Positioning

Who can say what the perfect position for your arms are? Really only you will know what is perfect. Two things to think about with regard to arm positioning. First, if the arms are too straight, all of the weapons recoil will be delivered to the shoulders of the shooter, pushing the body back as they shoot. You must allow the shoulders and arms to work together as giant shock absorbers. This will also cause you to be stiff when trying to push your speed. I have also noticed some shooters who have extremely stiff arms also reach for the target. Leaning too far forward is not more aggressive, it has a tendency to slow you down, and make your stance unstable. Secondly, if your arms are bent too far, you will not be able to control recoil either. My rule of

3.17 Arms too Straight

3.18 Arms Bent Too Far.

3.16 Good Arm Positioning

3.19 Good grip with support hand.

3.20 Arms pushed too far forward, degrading support hand grip.

3.21 Reaching for the targets as seen here is not more aggressive.

thumb is this: I push my arms out until my shooting grip starts to degrade. You will notice as you push your hands farther from your body, you will get to a point where the support hand will start to be pulled from the perfect grip. Normally, it feels like your fingers are sliding across the back of your firing hand. This should be an indicator that you need to stop pressing forward and stay in this position. As you shoot more and more the position will come to you. It is also very helpful to video yourself to see what you look like when you shoot. This is not being vain, if it is done for the right reason. If there is no training value to the video, and you are just looking at yourself, you might just have the potential to become a Navy SEAL….. just checking to see if you were still reading. Don't get excited.

Head Positioning

As you push the weapon forward and get more aggressive, it is also natural to drop the head. Some say this is the natural position to get into if you feel threatened, I disagree. Normally what I see is the dropping of the head, not the craning of the neck forward. So if you want to drop your head slightly, just know this has no effect on the shooting position, with the exception of possibly making your shoulders a little more tight, which will also degrade speed and quick mobility.

3.22 Good head positioning. Head straight up and down allowing for good peripheral vision.

3.23 Head craned too far forward

3.24 Head craned too far back, non-aggressive

As you crane your neck forward, which is the less desirable position, here is what also happens. You start to look through the tops of your eyes, not through the center of your eye socket. This can start to distort your vision and will also limit peripheral vision above you. Definitely not a good thing. If you are a tactical shooter on a special team, or in the military, you more than likely are also wearing eye protection. This could be wrap around shooting glasses or ballistic goggles. Either way, as you crane your neck forward you will begin to distort your vision more and more as you look through the less perfect portion of the glass, the edges. Some crane their neck so far that the edge of the helmet actually becomes visible, not the desired head positioning when engaging a threat.

Heads Up

I like to tell students to keep their head up, keep looking through the center of their eye socket. Stay aware of your total surroundings by having the largest peripheral vision of the environment as possible. Don't confuse heads up with standing straight up, which is not what we are pushing for.

Checking your stance

If you want to confirm that your stance is working, you should try to accomplish tasks that will be performed in your line of work. If you had to shoot until a threat was eliminated, how many rounds would that be? It could be a whole magazine worth of ammunition. Will your stance support this amount of blasting? Are you back on your heels after 6-10 rounds? What about multiple targets? Your stance must work no matter what the scenario.

Stance Checklist

- *Fighting Stance*
- *Knees Slightly Bent*
- *Weight on the balls of your feet*
- *Don't lock your elbows*
- *Push the weapon out until your grip starts to break*
- *Keep your head up*

3.25 Keep your head up

3.26 Good elbow positioning

3.30 Elbows slightly bent

3.31 Good fighting stance

3.27 Push weapon out until your grip starts to break

3.29 Knees slightly bent

3.28 Weight on balls of your feet

Chapter 4, Grip

4. GRIP

While shooting a pistol is not rocket science, there are some tricks to the trade. One huge trick that is often ignored is the shooting grip. Maybe ignored is a bad word, misunderstood is a better term for the grip on the Combat pistol.

I have heard terms such as Push/Pull, 50/50, and squeeze as hard as you can. This completely defeats what is needed to get a shooter to shoot extremely quick, while maintaining accuracy.

Percentage

The first misunderstanding is the percentage of grip in relation to the firing or strong hand and non-firing or support hand. Saying 50/50, or 50% with each hand, or equal squeeze with both hands is a sign of misunderstanding. In order to squeeze the trigger without disturbing our sights, and to shoot quickly, the trigger finger and hand must be slightly more relaxed than the support hand. Make a fist, squeeze as hard as you can, now try to move your trigger finger quickly. Of course it can't be done. So why would we do this when we grip the pistol?

70/30

When I teach the grip, I try to teach 70 percent of the grip with the support hand, 30 percent with the strong hand. If it makes you feel better to say 60/40, then go with that. I use 70/30 because it is an extreme difference; it cannot be measured, but it will get the point across that the difference is not negligible, it is significant. When you start to relax the firing hand, the trigger finger will be able to manipulate the trigger easily without disturbing the sight picture or the rest of the shooting grip.

Push/Pull

Push/Pull is another technique that is taught, mostly when using the Weaver Stance. The Push/Pull technique requires the shooter to pull back with the support hand, while pushing forward with the firing hand, it is a technique, but I think you will be pleasantly surprised how much better the 70/30 technique will work. The Push/Pull may work if you are forced to use a Weaver stance. Hopefully in the Stance Chapter we were able to convince you otherwise, however the Push/Pull won't work for the Modified Isosceles Shooting Stance.

Firing Hand

Place the firing hand as high on the pistol as possible, choke up like you are playing Little League baseball, every little bit counts. As you slide your hand higher, you immediately take away the leverage that the pistol has against you while you fire. If you have a thumb safety, such as the 1911 or some M&P Pistols, place the firing hand thumb on that safety. This will also give you leverage to further control recoil and muzzle rise. The thumb must stay on the safety, not just for leverage.

4.1 Firing hand as high as possible.

4.2 Low grip, poor recoil control.

4.3 Thumb on safety.

4.4 Low thumb may knock safety on during firing sequence.

4.5 Thumb not on safety, no leverage.

If you don't place your thumb in this position, you may accidentally knock the weapon on safe with one hand or the other. Not a good thing to have happen in a gunfight.

Support Hand Positioning

There are several techniques that I have been exposed to over the years. Cup and Saucer, a technique that looks as though you are resting the firing hand on the palm of the support hand. Another common technique is the thumb trap technique, where the firing thumb is trapped to the side of the pistol with the support hand.

These may work for you at your current level of proficiency, but if you want to push to the next level, and attain extreme recoil management and follow through, you will need to use a different technique.

4.6 Cup and saucer.

4.7 Thumb trap technique. Used with Weaver Stance.

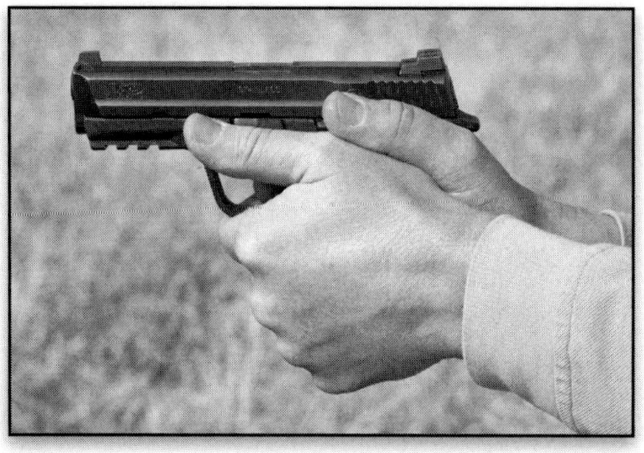

4.8 Thumbs forward grip.

4.9 Firing hand as high as possible.

Thumb Forward or Canted Hand

This is absolutely the most important point that can be made about the firing grip. This technique will improve your grip and vastly improve your shooting ability. If you want to shoot both quick and accurate, this will be the technique for you.

Place the support hand with as much of the meaty portion of the palm on the pistol grip as possible. The palm of the support hand should actually use the fingertips of the firing hand as a ledge to grip against. The support hand should be canted as far forward as you can, naturally that is. Don't force the hand down farther than it will go comfortably. Point the support thumb down range at your target, or let it fall naturally against the side of the pistol. Do not push against the side of the slide or frame with this thumb, it will cause shots to be thrown left and right if too much pressure is applied. If you are using a weapon mounted light, let the thumb rest where it will be able to activate the switch at the rear of the light. If you are using a pressure pad for your light, still allow the thumb to rest near the rear of the frame mounted light. You should also ensure that you don't end up with a gap between your hands; if you have a gap, fill the gap by pushing the palm of the non-firing hand into the space. Do not let your index finger of the support hand slide over the front of the trigger guard. If you are using a weapon mounted light this can't happen anyway,

4.10 Support hand with as much of meaty portion of palm on weapon as possible.

4.11 Thumb on switch of flashlight.

4.12 Fingers at a 45 degree angle to ground.

4.13 Thumb on switch of flashlight.

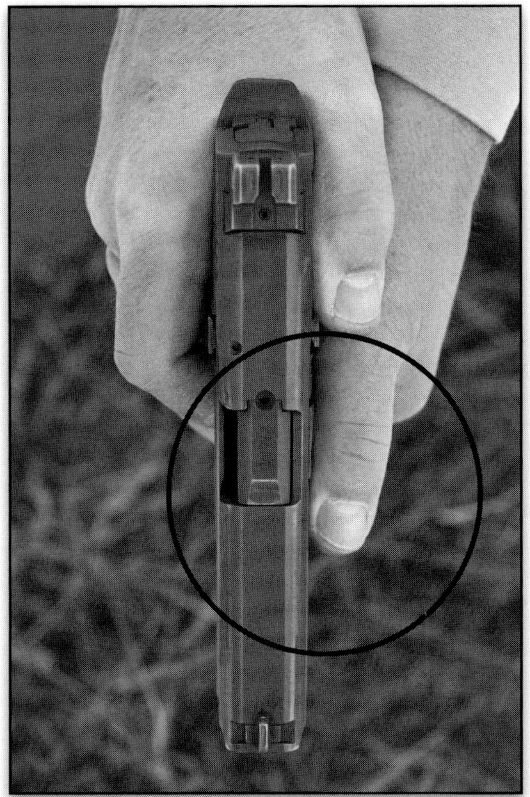

4.14 Thumb touching frame will disturb accuracy.

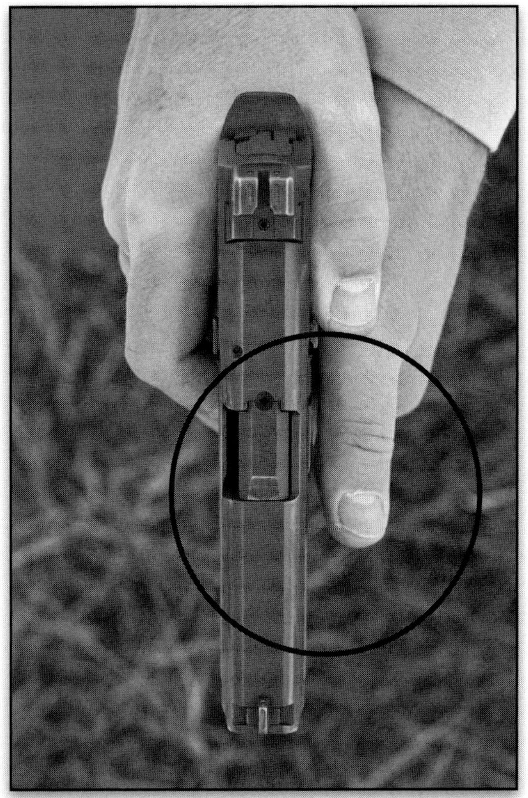

4.15 Thumb not touching frame

but you will be better off if you use the same technique with or without the light mounted.

If you use this technique you will immediately see your sights return to the center of the target much quicker than ever before. Applying this technique with the 70/30 grip ratio will definitely take you to the next level.

4.16 Do not let support side trigger finger ride on the front of the trigger guard.

4.17 Do not let support side trigger finger ride on the front of the trigger guard.

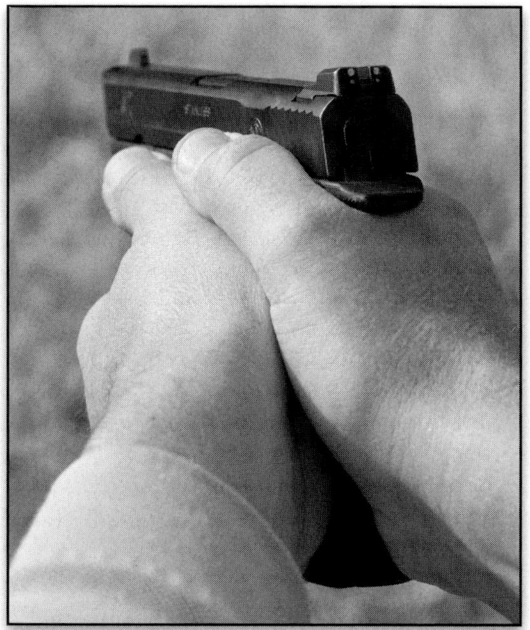

4.18 Fill gap with palm

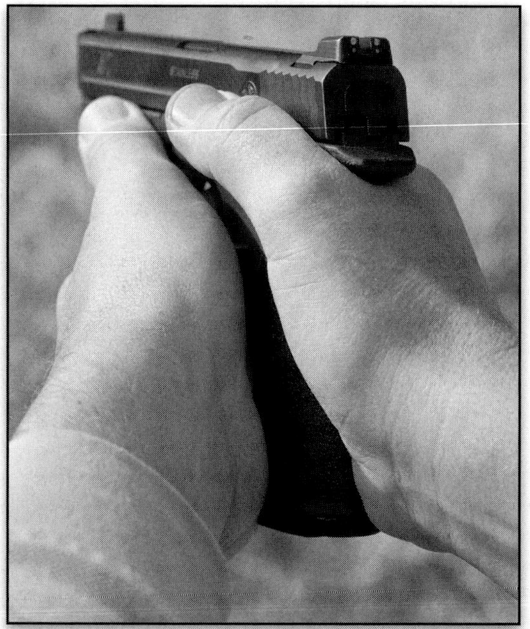

4.19 Gap creates a poor combat grip

4.20-28 The sights are quickly snapped back to the target using the 70/30 grip with the thumbs canted forward.

Grip Tape

You must be able to hang onto your weapon and if adding grip tape, or skateboard tape makes this possible, I am all for it. I will give you some ideas that may help when you decide to go crazy with the tape.

If the weapon you are adding grip tape to is a concealed carry weapon, only add grip tape to the support side of the weapon. This will help with two things. First, you won't have grip tape pulling on your clothing that covers the pistol; you will have it rubbing against your skin or your undershirt. This can be uncomfortable too so be easy on the tape at first. Second, if you only use grip

4.29 Grip tape only applied to the support side of the weapon.

4.30 Strong side of weapon left slick to allow rotation of weapon for reloads.

4.31 Skateboard tape is an easy enhancement to your weapon's grip.

4.32 Burner Grip on Beretta 92/M9

tape on the support side of the weapon, you will be able to quickly maneuver your weapon for reloads that require hand movement.

If you are shooting a 1911, SIG, or Beretta 92, the best recommendation I could pass on would be to use Burner Grips on the support side of the weapon. Jerry Barnhart designed these grips and they really work. They are grips with the sand paper built into them. They work great.

Grip Enhancement

Sending your pistols to the plastic surgeon sounds a little sketchy, but it is a way to make them feel better about themselves and more confident in public, and did I mention they are nice to look at too?

4.33 Smith & Wesson M&P with Boresight Solutions grip modification.

4.34 Grip modification.

4.35 Full size and compact M&P Pistols with grip enhancement.

4.36Grip modifications by Bore-Sight Solutions

4.37 Glock 21 with grip reduction and enhancement by Bowie Tactical Concepts.

All joking aside, if you are looking for a cleaner way to add grip rather than using sticky grip tape, a grip enhancement is in order. I prefer to have certain areas polished, to prevent bite, such as the bottom of the trigger guard. I also prefer the stippling on the strong or right side for right handed shooters to be a little less aggressive than that on the left side. As I stated above, you do want to be able to rotate the weapon efficiently in your hand during reloads as well as during the draw. The support side of the weapon can deal with a little more aggressive texture; this will keep the support hand from sliding forward during the firing cycle. When I have Ben at Boresight Solutions work on the grips of my pistols, I always specify exactly how I desire the grip. He can make suggestions, but you need to ultimately make the call. He can always grind the texture down if it is too aggressive. His texture jobs are not only grippier, if only that was a word, but they look great too.

Grippy Grip

If you like to use powder or grip gel, they work extremely well to help with your grip. I would try showing up to the range, on occasion, without the use of these products, to see how you will perform without. You don't want to use a crutch that won't be available during the actual gunfight that you have been training for.

4.38 Progrip, great for improving grip without being sticky.

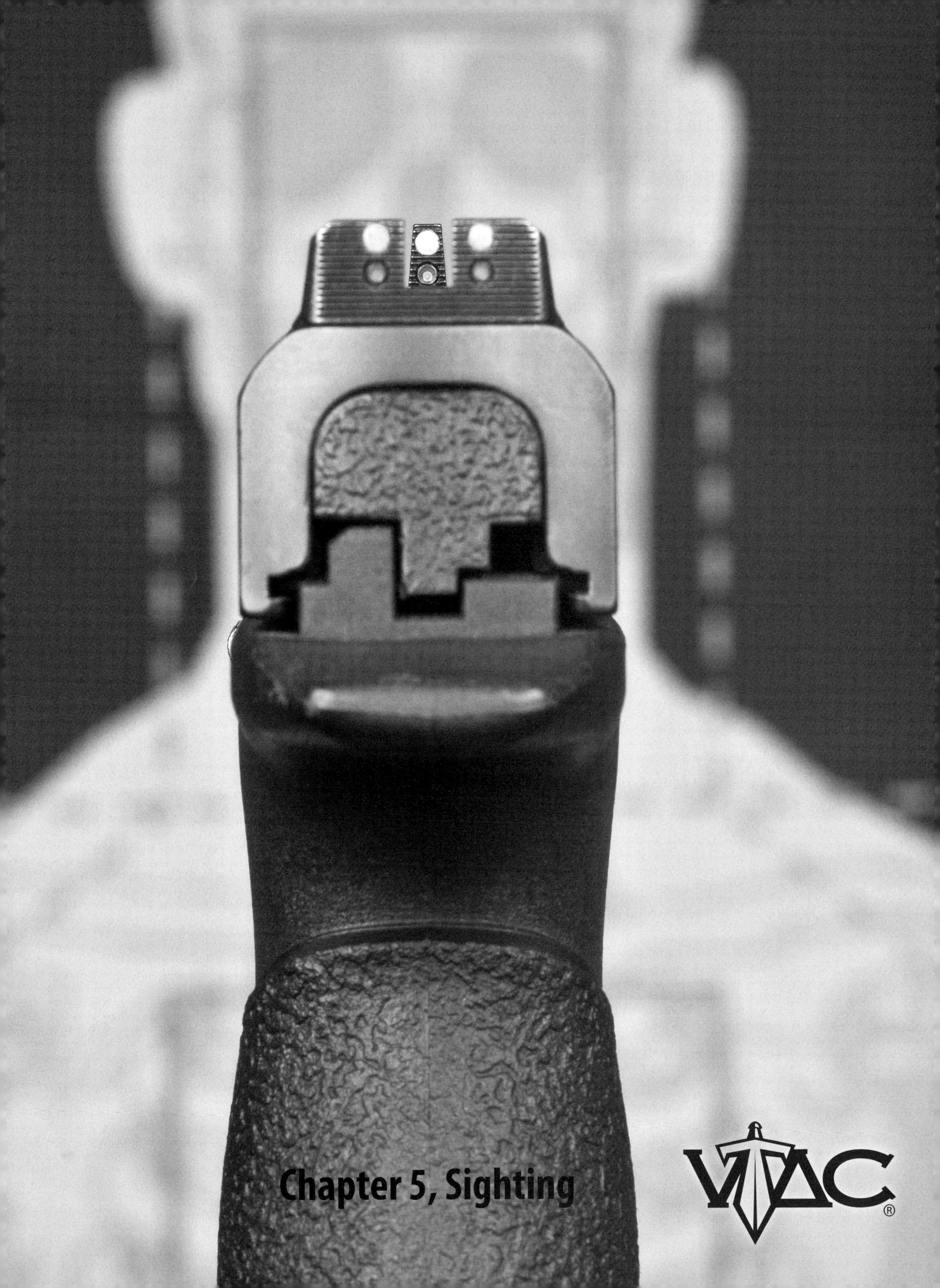

Chapter 5, Sighting

5. SIGHTING

Sight Selection

Discussion of sighting would not be complete without first discussing what sights are available and some of the recommended sights out there.

Sights are very much a personal preference, but I try to take a few different requirements into the equation when talking Combat Pistol Sights. First, when will you engage a threat? You don't know for sure, but more than likely it will be during hours of limited visibility, therefore you probably need sights that can be seen at night. So Tritium sights that glow would seem to be the obvious answer, not so fast. When do we normally train? Hours of daylight, right? LE and Military personnel don't seem to like to be out late on the range, however there are a few night owls, but by and large, daylight training is the norm. So what works well in the day? Either straight up, good ol' iron sights, or in the past few years, fiber optic sights. Fiber Optic sights are simply iron sights with a section of fiber optic tube mounted to gather light and give the effect of a powered, bright sight. These fiber optic sights have been thought to be fragile, and initially they were, however during my testing, quality fiber optic sights have held up well. Of course irons will be more durable, but which sight will allow for quicker target acquisition during daylight operations? Fiber Optic.

5.1 Viking Sight by Viking Tactics, Inc.

I have used every sight you can imagine, and finally decided to design our own, to fit what the gunfighter actually needs. The Viking Sight™ has everything that could possibly be needed during operations that take place day, night, or even with a light. The Viking Sight™ has the fiber optic for day, along with a serrated front and rear sight to eliminate glare. Below the fiber is a set of tritium vials from Trijicon, that are barely visible, that is until the light goes out. We also tapered the front sight to draw you in much quicker to the sight in a surprise situation. You will also notice that these sights are very slim, fine enough for precision shooting if need be. Lastly, we cut the notch of the rear sight a bit deeper than needed to allow the shooter to see where the front sight needs to be moved in order to achieve the proper sight alignment.

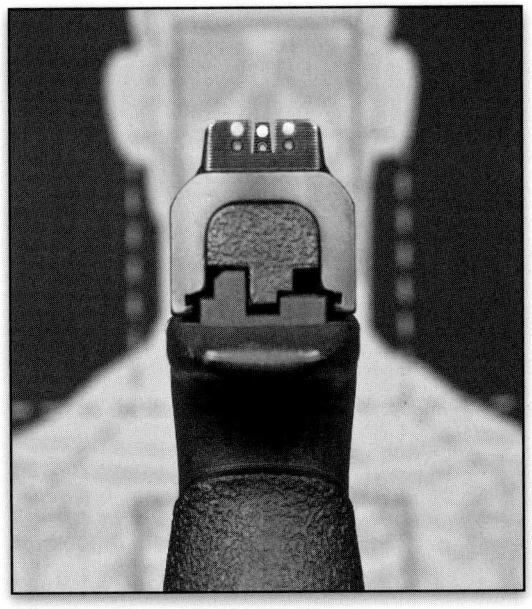

5.2 Note tapered front sight. Top of sight is .095" tapering to .145". Rear notch is .135" wide and .185" deep.

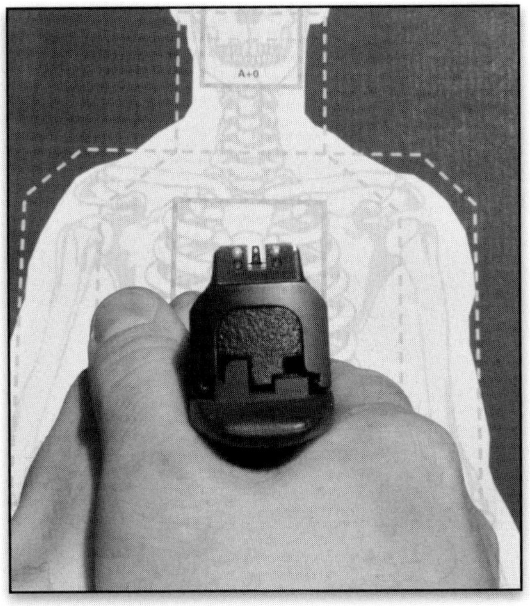

5.3 Actual view of VIking Sight on target.

Following are a broad selection of sights, you will need to decide what works for you.

5.4 Heinie Slant Pro Straight Eight Sights, Glock 21.

5.5 Novak Low Profile Ghost Right Sight, Browning Hi-Power

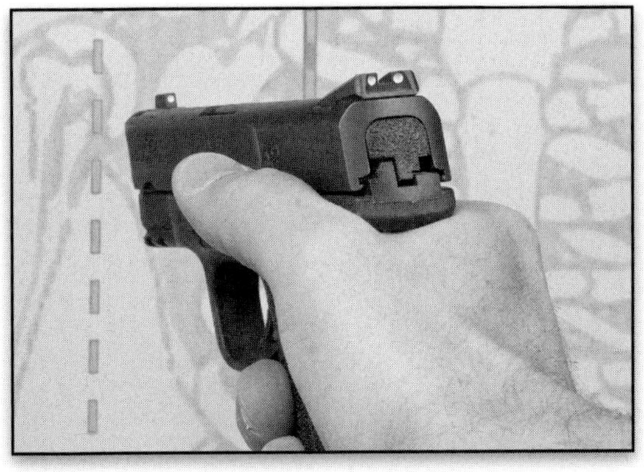

5.6 Novak Sights, S&W M&P compact

5.7 Millet Adjustable Sights, Glock 17

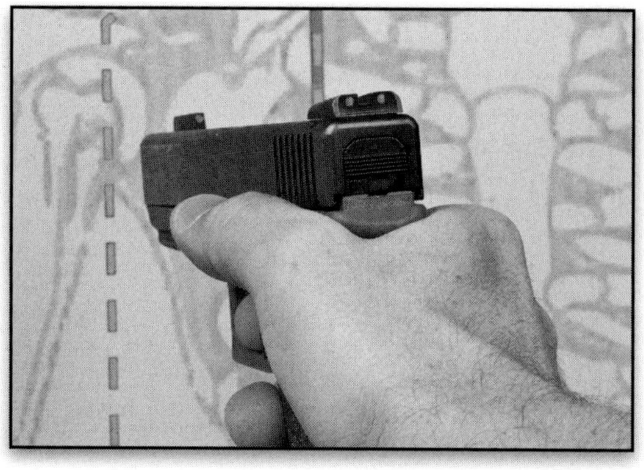

5.8 Tru-Glo Tritium Fiber Optic Sights, Glock 22

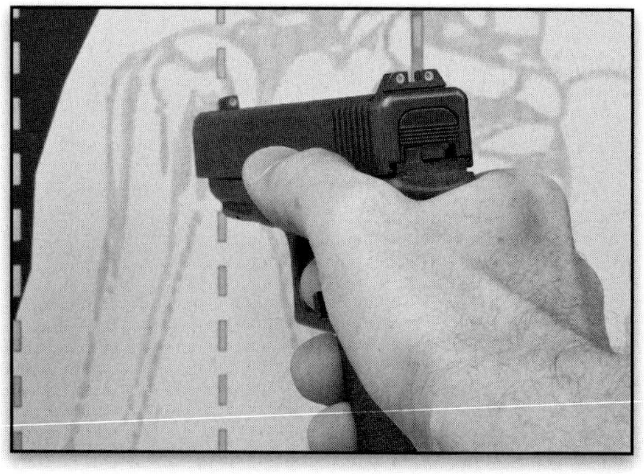

5.9 Stock Glock Tritium Sights, Glock 34

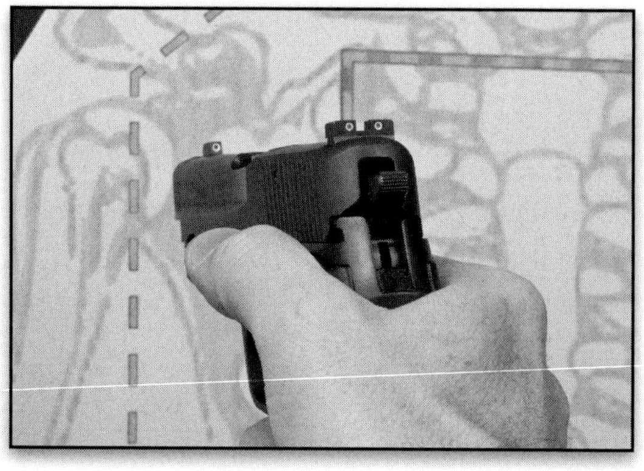

5.10 Trijicon Night Sights

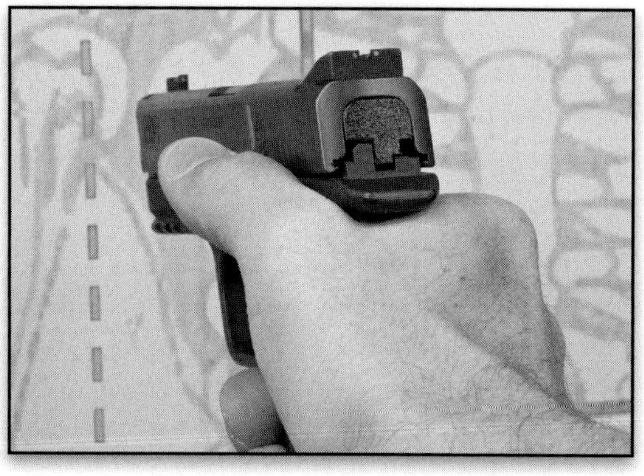

5.11 Dawson Precision Fiber Optic Sights, S&W M&P

5.12 Stock Sights, Beretta 92/M9

Proper Sight Picture

Proper sight picture for engagements with the pistol should be as follows. Front sight relatively clear. Top of the front sight aligned with the top of the rear sight, and of course, centered. Focusing on the front sight during your accuracy drills will help to drive home the point of front sight focus. As you start to engage more quickly at close range, the focus can change slightly. This is also where your sight selection will help determine how quickly you can actually shoot. If you use the fiber optic, you will be able to focus more on the target, target discriminate quickly, and engage immediately without losing your sights.

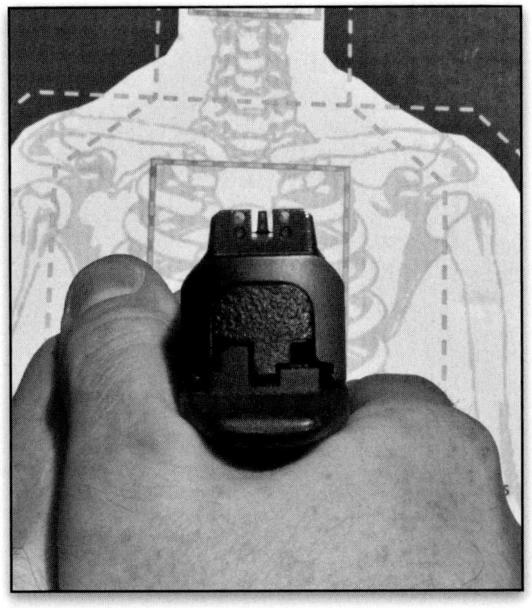

5.13 Proper sight picture

Acceptable Sight Picture

What should we expect or accept as we engage in Combat pistol shooting? The need for speed in a gunfight is crucial; you must beat the enemy to the punch. But this only counts if we can do it with the accuracy needed to eliminate the threat.

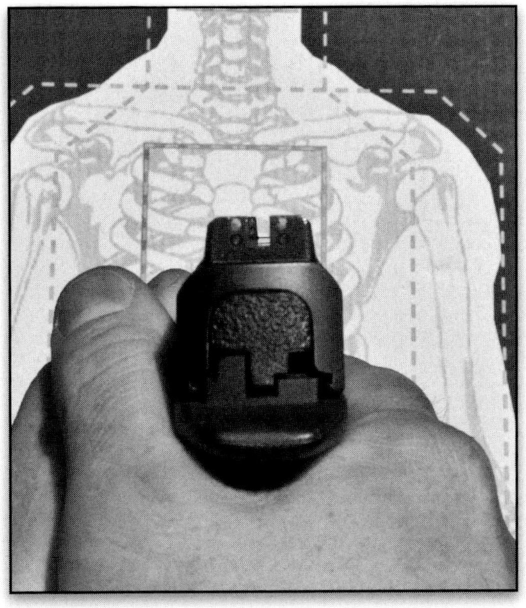

5.14 Improperly aligned sight, but is it acceptable?

5.15 Groups being shot from 5, 10, 15, 20 yards with front sight being held to the left of the notch.

Normally we would concentrate to make sure the front and the rear sight are absolutely aligned correctly. This is not as necessary at closer ranges. See the pictures below that show what happens at the different yard lines with the front sight aligned all the way to the side of the rear sight notch.

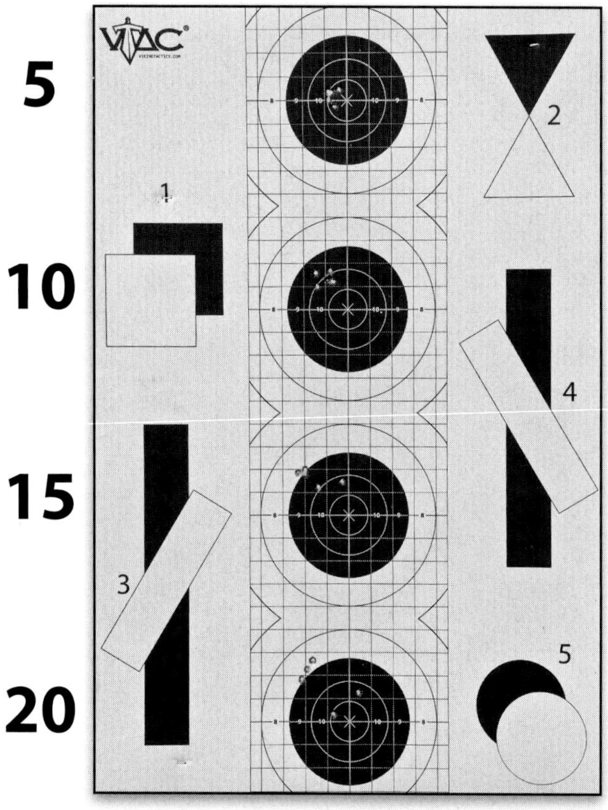

5.16 Target shows where groups will impact with sight held to the left of the notch. Don't laugh at the 20 yard group.

Squinting

It is common for shooters to squint as hard as they can with their non-firing eye during pistol training. This has both good and bad results. The good that comes from squinting is a tighter shot group. The bad is the loss of peripheral sight. It is extremely important that you are able to see what is going on near your flank; this may save your life, or your partner's life. Most shooters can achieve over 50 Degrees more arc of vision to their side, with both eyes open. This is 25-35% more vision by keeping both eyes open, a huge advantage in the tactical world.

Cross Dominance

If you are right handed, but you have a left dominant eye, we call this cross dominance. This happens every now and then, so what should you do? You could continue to fight the problem, or just slightly turn your head allowing the dominant eye to fall in alignment behind the rear sight. Attempt to look straight from the dominant eye, or as best you can. The more you twist the head, the more you lose vision to your support side.

5.17 Shooting with right hand, right eye.

5.18 Cross dominance, right hand, left eye.

5.19 Both eyes open.

5.20 Left eye closed, decreased peripheral vision.

Additional Sight Requirements

What other specifications are needed on a Combat Pistol Sight? Should you have adjustable sights? Adjustable sights are nice, especially on a competition pistol, but on a Combat weapon, they are really not needed. The additional moving parts can cause more breakage and headaches than is worth the advantage of easy adjustment.

Having the ability to clear malfunctions by using the rear sight as a handle, or hook on clothing, or your holster is also important. Some sights are so slick and snag free that you will never be able to get the slide to the rear with one hand. I prefer a sight that is slick, but has enough of a hook to allow easy manipulation of the slide using my holster, a pant seam, or a pocket.

5.21 VTAC Sight hooked in pants pocket.

5.22 VTAC Sight hooked on belt.

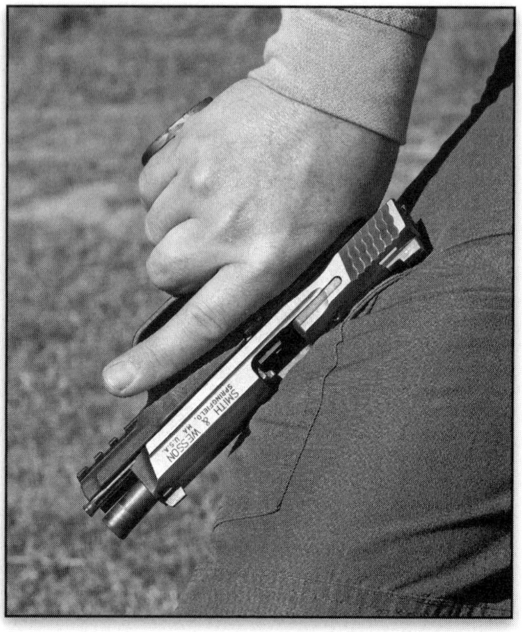

5.23 Using seam on pants to pull the slide to the rear.

Point Shooting

A chapter on sights would not be complete without a brief discussion on the subject of Point Shooting. Ah, the time honored, gunslinger's choice of technique, Unsighted fire. First of all this does not work. The time wasted trying to establish the perfect place to hold the weapon and still get hits on a close target would be much better used for structured firearms training while using the sights. Many point shooters sing the praises of their technique, but none will show up at the largest competitions in the world to put the money in their mouth. Is this a challenge, absolutely not; however the folks I train cannot use this technique. They are Law Enforcement professionals and Military members that must use sighted fire to quickly dominate a situation, save the good guy, and not injure an innocent bystander. As you discuss this technique, remember, we are not talking about contact shooting. Contact shooting is target engagement that is so close you can feel your opponent's breath, and smell the stench as well. This type of engagement does not require the use of your sights, simply because you are touching or almost touching your target.

As we practice we have to keep an open mind to allow speed and accuracy to come into alignment. As you get closer to the target, front sight focus is not as important as it will be at 25 yards. But if there is a hostage standing in the midst of the situation, you had better get dialed in.

What distance should you be zeroed?

This will be a bone of contention with some, but I prefer to zero my pistol at 25 yards, or meters for those of you that are metrically inclined. This zero allows you to not worry from 25 yards to up close and personal ranges.

When would you not zero at 25? If you are unable to group at 25 yards, you cannot reliably zero. A group must be able to be distinguished if you are to get a true zero. I will caveat this by saying; this is for a full size carry pistol. If you are shooting a small revolver or extremely compact weapon, you will need to adjust the distance that you check and refine your zero. Small pistols and revolvers should be able to be zeroed at 12-15 yards. When I zero I use point of aim, point of impact. This implies that exactly where the top of my front sight is placed on the target the bullet will impact. The differences are that some marksmanship competitors us a 6 o'clock hold, which is holding at the bottom of their bulls eye target, with bullets impacting in the middle of the bull. Not a good zero for the combat shooter. There are also other techniques called the flat tire, also a marksmanship competition technique. This simply means the bulls eye will look like a flat tire with the front sight held slightly in the black of the target. You should always reconfirm your zero when you head to the range. If you have to hold off the intended impact point to get a hit, this will not work efficiently in a life and death shooting situation.

Chapter 6, Presentation of the Pistol

6. PRESENTATION OF THE PISTOL

Presentation

This may seem backwards, but why not cover the Draw before firing the weapon? I prefer to have a strong understanding of the presentation process of the pistol and the mechanics that are needed to make the perfect shot. Once you have a handle on this procedure, it is relatively easy to add the draw.

In this chapter we will focus on the presentation of the pistol beginning when the shooter's two hands come in contact with the pistol.

Position 3

We will start with Position 3. Position 3 is the most important position before we actually fire the weapon. If you have a solid Position 3, everything else will fall into place, as far as the grip goes anyway. Position 3 is a retention position that you naturally progress through during the draw sequence. Positions 1-4 should always be the same. So when you head to the range or dry fire these Presentation techniques from Position 3, ensure that this is in fact the position you use during the draw as you pass through Position 3. This should not be a position that is for range use or presentation drills only; it must reflect your true applied Position 3. A common misconception is that both hands have to be in the perfect grip to push the weapon to the target; this is not true, and it is almost impossible to achieve. Position 3 should allow the shooter to have a straight strong side wrist; if your wrist is broke or bent at Position 3 you are not in a true retention position. Position SUL (see sidebar) is not Position 3, and definitely not a retention position.

6.1 Position 3.

Other examples of Position 3 are the muzzle up positions, which are obviously not part of the draw stroke. If they are part of the draw stroke, you need to re-examine your draw. During the draw, the muzzle should never go above your intended target. Depending on the distance, you may need to engage a threat at any time during the draw stroke.

Take a look at the bore axis of your pistol in this ready position. Will it allow you to start squeezing the trigger and actually hit the target? If not, you must lower the muzzle of the weapon. Sometimes this doesn't brief well to competition shooters, but remember, this is the ultimate competition, combat.

Here are a few examples of a poor Position 3 which do not allow you to successfully engage a target from the retention position:

6.2 Low ready or no ready.

6.3 High Sabrina - not ready for a gunfight. Also, not part of your drawstroke.

6.4 Believe it or not, I have seen this Charlie's Angels' position used by some shooters. Note loss of vision with weapon in front of face.

6.5 Weapon obstructs vision.

While in Position 3 you should have your hands prepared to assume the perfect grip as you push the weapon towards the target and not while in Position 3. In order to accomplish this, you should already have your firing hand in the perfect position on the pistol's grip. Your grip should be as high as possible. The non-firing hand should be in the receive mode, and not necessarily with a perfect grip. I use my knuckle of my index finger on the support hand as an indexing point. What this means is, as I draw the weapon, my left hand goes towards Position 3 to be prepared to receive. Once the weapon gets to this point, I reference or index the bottom of the trigger guard with the knuckle of my support side index finger. Once I feel this contact, it is just a matter of pushing the weapon towards the target as I cam or rotate my support hand up into the firing grip. If you work on this position without the draw it will help you immensely.

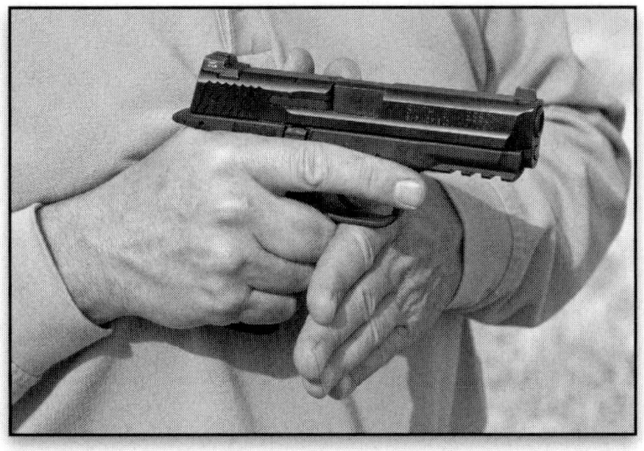

6.6 Support hand index finger indexed to bottom of trigger guard.

6.7 Support hand index finger indexed to bottom of trigger guard.

Always remember when presenting the pistol, do not let the sights go above the target. Do not be in a hurry, yet… we will get to that.

Trigger Prep

As I push the weapon towards the target, I start to prep the trigger. This does not mean we jerk the trigger, it means we take some of the slack out of the trigger as we push the weapon towards the target. The reasoning behind this is that we need to get the weapon to fire as soon as the sights stop on the desired aiming point. Remember this is a race. All gunfights require speed; the first shooter to hit a vital area on their enemy normally wins.

As you prep the trigger during the presentation, you will become more and more familiar with the amount of weight required to make the weapon go bang. As you dry fire, you should be able to get to the point of having the hammer drop (or striker if you are one of those guys) as soon as the weapon stops. Continue to practice until you are smooth from Position 3, through the presentation to Position 4, which is the position where

6.8-21 Once index point is reached at Position 3, push the weapon towards the target while rotating your support thumb to target.

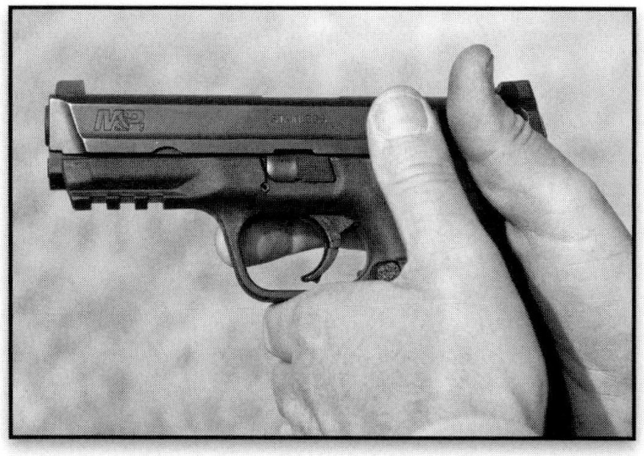

6.8-21 Continued

6.22-26 Prepping trigger as pistol is pushed towards the target

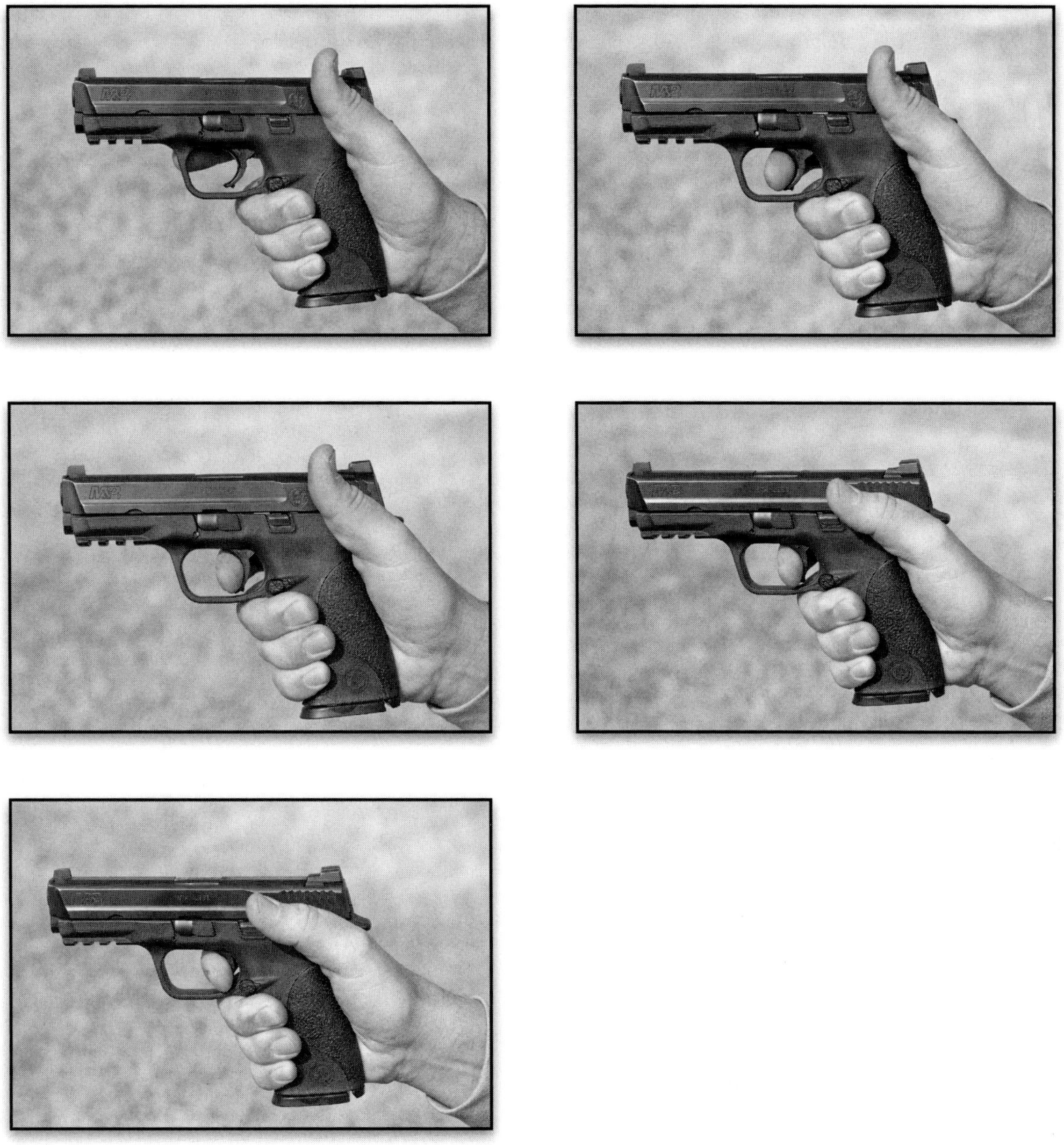

6.27-32 Quickly acquire and align your sights as you present the pistol

the weapon will actually fire. Some say there is a Position 5, but since this is my book, and the arena I was trained in only had 4 positions, that is how it will be taught.

Sight Alignment

As the weapon is pushed from Position 3 to Position 4, sight alignment is critical. The distance to the target will determine the appropriate sight picture. During training you should always work to achieve the perfect sight picture as you go through these basic presentation drills. Once you are tested during a speed drill, you will see that you can quickly acquire and align the sight as you present the pistol.

Trigger Control

When will it end? Well it isn't over until you have fired the shot, oh, and then there are other required tasks as well. Trigger control starts after you have moved to Position 3, pushed the weapon towards the target as you prepped the trigger, aligned your sights correctly, now it is time to squeeze the trigger. This task can drive all of us completely insane, but it is extremely important that this rule is followed: we must attempt to pull the trigger straight to the rear of the pistol, (see Sidebar: Pulling the Pencil) and not at an obscure angle, but straight to the rear. You should place your trigger finger in a comfortable position that allows for smooth trigger pull.

Do not slap the trigger; this is a huge mistake that will send your sights sailing off target, right along with the bullet that follows. Ensure that you maintain steady pressure throughout the entire trigger squeeze process, watch your mates shoot and see if they are squeezing or slapping. This is one of the easiest shooting issues to notice since the trigger slap requires a little more energy and animation to make the shot fire.

Once you have squeezed the trigger, it is now time to go onto the next step of the Pistol Presentation equation, the Follow Through.

Follow Through

Follow through, as defined for a shooter would read something like this: "Ensuring that you watch your sights throughout the firing sequence, which includes the hammer or striker igniting the primer, the burning powder launching the bullet, the bullet hitting the target, as the weapon comes out of battery, slide moves to the rear, another round is fed into the chamber, you release the trigger slowly until the disconnector clicks, and your sights have now come to rest back on the target." (Run-on sentence intentionally left intact.) Oh, I forgot to mention that you had to call your shot to tell us where you hit. All of this must be done before the bullet even has time to make it to the target.

Sounds difficult, and it is, but this will be key to your success as a Combat shooter.

Follow Through

6.33 Drive your sights to the target.

6.34 Slowly squeeze the trigger straight to the rear.

6.35 Weapon fires.

6.36 Eyes on sights throughout the firing sequence.

6.37 Good grip immediately drives front sight back to the target.

6.38 Slowly release the trigger until the disconnector clicks.

6.39 Repeat as necessary.

No Follow Through

6.40 Shooter may have a good trigger squeeze.

6.41 During recoil, shooter releases the trigger.

6.42 As weapon fires, shooter does not maintain an aggressive grip.

6.43 Pistol continues to rise, no follow through.

6.44 Pistol not pushed back to the threat.

6.45 Finally the target becomes visible over the pistol.

6.46 If the threat needed to be re-engaged, we are way behind the power curve.

We must drill this until it is second nature. If you are missing the follow through during a gunfight, you will end up losing the day. You must continually call your shots and drive the weapon back to the target to make the next shot. One shot one kill? That is only in the movies. In the real world, "one mag, one kill."

Forced follow through can also become the norm if you are not aggressive with your support hand grip. Forced follow through will look as though you fired the shot, the weapon recoils, but it does not come back down to your line of sight to the target, it must be forced back on target. If the weapon is recoiling, and you have to force the weapon back on target, change your support hand grip. This grip will get the pistol to have a mind of its own and immediately improve your follow through.

I get questioned a lot about follow through. Where do I look? You should be looking at your sights because there is no reason to look down range at the bullet holes. You just watched where your sights were when the weapon fired; you should know where the bullet hole is. Of course on a real target, you won't normally see holes through clothing, so there is no sense training to look for something that cannot be seen. If you are to look at anything, it should be the demeanor of the threat. If the threat is eliminated, there is not a need to continue to fire. But if you make what you perceive to be a perfect shot, do not stop. Follow through and continue to fire and adjust your point of aim for target movement or to engage another vital area. Remember "one mag, one kill" may appear to be a joke but at the same time is very true.

Don't drop your head

As you press the weapon towards the target you should not be dropping your head behind the sights. Your head should have already been in this position as you were drawing the weapon. It will slow you down if you have to press the weapon all the way to Position 4 and then drop your head. I try to keep my head upright to have better peripheral vision as well, but if you plan to drop your head slightly, do it before the weapon is in front of your face.

Correct

6.47 Start draw with head upright.

Correct, cont.

6.48 Drive weapon aggressively to target.

6.49 Build grip as you press the weapon.

6.50 Keep eyes to threat, sights appear in peripheral.

6.51 Sights align and trigger is prepped.

6.52 Heads up

Incorrect

6.53-55 Head starts to drop increasing tension in neck and shoulders. Arms tend to be too rigid and head positioning does not allow for relaxed quick gun handling.

Trigger Finger Placement

After conducting numerous classes it has become evident that it is necessary to dig deeper into the subject of trigger finger placement. Trigger finger placement is crucial to successfully engaging the target without disturbing your sights. The question always comes up: How much finger on the trigger? Most instructors have a pre-determined amount of trigger finger engagement required to make the shooter successful. This is simply wrong.

You must place YOUR finger on the trigger where it is comfortable and allows for a smooth trigger pull. The weapon is not designed with each shooter's hand size in mind; therefore it cannot be the same trigger finger placement for every shooter. Finger placement will always be dictated by the size of the shooter's hands, no matter the weapon system.

Too much finger on the trigger is not a bad thing if you are trying to shoot accurately or shoot with one hand. As I shoot faster and faster, I put less and less finger on the trigger. There is no magical trigger finger placement, however you need to work with your pistol and your hand and determine what works best.

6.56 Both shooters have their trigger fingers where they feel comfortable.

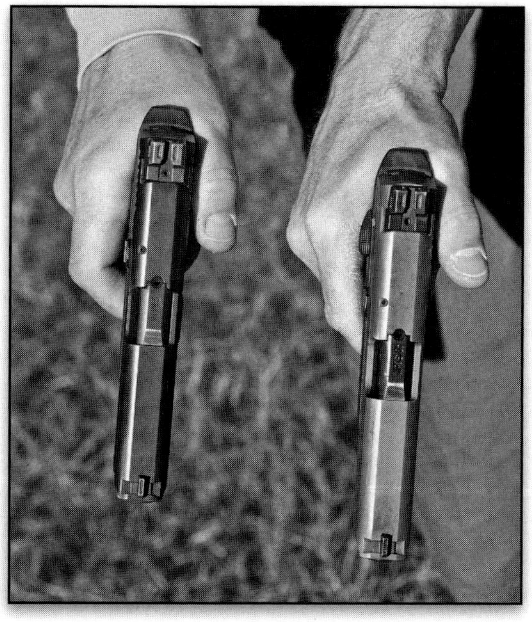

6.57 Incorrect trigger finger placement for both shooters. Don't force shooters to place their finger in the same spot as you. It may not work for their hand size.

Just be aware of what I said before, I move my finger on the trigger depending on what I am trying to accomplish. Speed, less trigger finger. Accuracy, more trigger finger. This is what works for me and may not work for you.

Rubbing your finger on the frame should be avoided if possible. If you are rubbing the trigger finger on the frame, this is an easy way to disrupt the sights as you shoot. Rubbing the finger on the bottom of the inside of the trigger guard should also be avoided.

Ball and Dummy

The Ball and Dummy drill is designed to assess a shooter's trigger squeeze and follow through. This drill is accomplished by having your partner load your weapon, and safely place it in your holster as you remain looking down range at the target. Once they tap you on the shoulder, signifying that the weapon is ready, you go through the slow fire process, ensuring you have a perfect draw and presentation. Bring the weapon out of the holster to Position 3, you should have a perfect grip with your strong hand before drawing the weapon, present the pistol to the target, tighten your support hand grip, align your sights, prep the trigger as you

6.58 Shooter locks slide to the rear and hands empty magazine to coach.

6.59 Shooter holsters.

6.60 Coach decides if he will load live round or give shooter an empty chamber.

6.61 Coach loads live round into magazine.

6.62 Coach safely takes weapon from holster.

6.63 With weapon pointed in a safe direction, coach loads weapon.

6.64 Slide is released.

6.65 If holster has a hood, rotate it into position.

6.66 Coach places weapon back in the holster, do not point weapon at shooter.

6.67 Coach taps shooter on the shoulder to start draw stroke.

6.68 Shooter initiates draw stroke.

6.69 Squeeze the trigger.

6.70 Weapon fires.

6.71 Shooter ensures slide is locked to the rear.

6.72 Coach chooses to not charge the weapon with a live round.

6.73 Keep weapon pointed in a safe direction.

6.74 Repeat as necessary.

6.75 Use dummy rounds in available.

push forward, then CLICK. Did you jerk the trigger, thinking the weapon was loaded when in fact your partner had placed an unloaded weapon in your holster? If so, do it again and repeat this drill as often as you can. This is a great drill for new and old shooters alike.

If you know what it sounds like to have a round feed into the chamber, please turn off your headphones or double plug your ears, as this will help you to get the full benefit of the drill. Another fix is to use dummy rounds, which will speed up the ball and dummy drill considerably.

Position SUL

Position SUL was actually developed as an administrative position. The position works well for that, but I prefer to place my weapon in the holster if I am going Admin. The issues I have seen with Position SUL on the flat range are not necessarily safety issues, that is until movement and shooting positions are put into play. Shooters who have been taught Position SUL cover themselves very frequently with the muzzle of their weapon. This becomes very evident when shooters assume a kneeling position or work inside a vehicle. With total disregard for their own well being, they drop the muzzle to the SUL position and cover both femurs as they get out of a vehicle. This is unbelievably dangerous, and slow. If you want to lower your muzzle for safety reasons, lift the firing elbow, keeping the wrist straight and strong. This will allow for great weapon's retention as well as it is a familiar part of your Draw Stoke.

6.76 Position SUL

6.77 Kneeling position SUL

6.78 Muzzle pointed at femur, unsafe position.

6.79 Strong retention position, weapon pointed in a safe direction.

6.80-83 This retention position still allows the shooter to use their natural draw stroke.

6.84 Alternate weapon retention position.

6.85 Firing wrist is straight and strong.

6.86 Support hand thumb over slide of pistol for additional strength.

6.87-90 Still natural to drive weapon towards threat aggressively.

6.87-90 cont.

6.91 Position SUL.

6.92 Weak wrists.

6.93 Not a strong retention position.

6.94 Suspect grabs for weapon.

6.95 Suspect has easy time of starting the gun grab.

6.96 Suspect has the mechanical advantage.

6.97 Weapon easily rotated from officer's grasp.

6.98 Not a good day.

6.99 Weapon already pointed at shooter's legs.

6.100 Weapon covers both femurs - this is a no-go.

6.101 Unsafe movement continues with position SUL.

6.102 Thigh still covered with weapon.

6.103 Knee is still covered with weapon.

6.104 Weapon almost clear to shoot.

6.105 Position SUL

6.106 Start position is the same.

6.107 Shooter uses support hand to pull body from vehicle.

6.108 Drive weapon muzzle over the steering wheel.

6.109 Hands come together at position 3 for a strong retention position.

6.110 Officer has a good Position 3.

6.111 Safely out of the vehicle without pointing weapon at your legs.

Safety Circle

While conducting courses across the country, I have come across a technique that is being taught called the Safety Circle. This is a technique by which the shooter engages a threat, then immediately drops their muzzle away from the target. This is extremely dangerous for the shooter, not because they will shoot themselves or their partner. However, you are breaking your own wrists, which will allow someone to take your weapon with little to no struggle, whatsoever. It is preferable to bring the weapon back to a safe retention position, which will allow you to quickly reengage if need be. You should always try to bring the weapon back to a position somewhere inside of the draw stroke if possible.

6.112 Shooter engages threat.

6.113 Now shooter breaks wrist to go to the safety circle. This is a very unsafe technique and not part of your drawstroke.

6.114 Be prepared at any time to re-engage the threat from Position 3.

6.115 Aggressively drive weapon to threat.

Pulling the Pencil

The mere fact that we would discuss pulling the pencil seems a bit odd; however it does quickly illustrate the need for a straight trigger pull. With the pencil eraser on your trigger finger, simply start to move the finger and see what the pencil does. Does the pencil track straight to the rear, or does it sway to the side of your hand? If the pencil is getting pulled to the side you will quickly understand why we place this importance on the straight trigger pull. If you do not pull the trigger straight to the rear it will be detrimental to your accuracy, period. When my friend Mike Voigt showed me his little pencil pulling trick several years ago, it really made sense and quickly shows students the point we are trying to make.

6.116 Use a pencil with eraser as your trigger.

6.117 Ensure pencil stays straight as you move trigger finger.

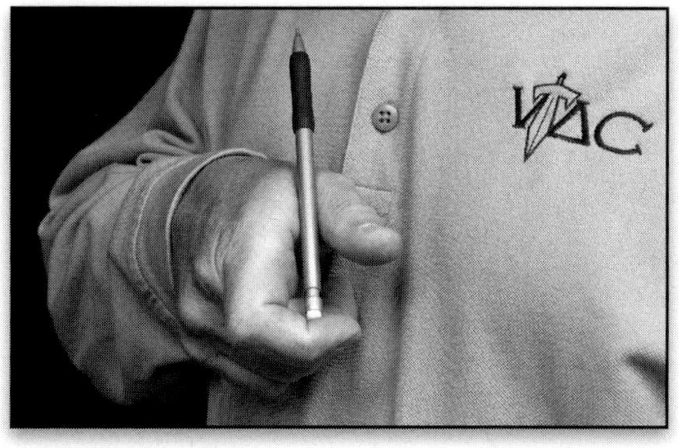

6.118 Straight to the rear.

6.119 Same start position.

6.120 Definitely not going to help your accuracy.

Chapter 7, The Draw

7. THE DRAW

Smooth is fast. Or is it?

I constantly hear shooters and instructors talk about "slow is smooth," and it is true, if you are smooth and fast, great. If you are just slow and smooth, it won't make you fast. I prefer to say, "smooth is fast, but slow is just frickin' slow." The reason I bring this up and try to get under slow shooter's skin is this: Gunfighters need to be fast, you must beat the bad guy to the punch. There absolutely must be a sense of urgency when you draw your pistol. I am not telling you to be sloppy, or careless, I am telling you to have a sense of urgency. Most shooters, even very seasoned professionals, do not move with a sense of urgency when drawing the pistol. Once they clear leather, kydex, or whatever space age resin is holding your pistol, they shoot extremely fast. That is not my goal.

My goal is to do everything else as quickly as possible so I can slow down and squeeze the trigger.

Why would we want to move like pond water right up until the point that defines success or failure, hitting or missing the target? Quickly get the weapon to bear on the target and then slow down and make it count; your life depends on it. If this doesn't make sense, hang in there. By the end of the book it should be crystal clear.

"Slow down and go as fast as you can……" Kyle Lamb

Numbered Positions of the Draw

As I discuss the draw, I would like to further break it down to make you aware of the key positions and what should be happening at each point.

Position 1

I consider Position 1 the point when your hand first comes to rest on the pistol. It will be the point at which you establish your strong hand grip. This position should include or start to include the breaking of thumb breaks or any other retention device that allows removal of the pistol from the holster. I cannot stress enough how important it is to have a holster that will allow the firing grip while at Position 1.

Position 2

Position 2 will be the position at which your pistol has cleared the holster and the muzzle begins to cam up toward your intended target/threat. You must be in a position to shoot the threat from this position, at least in the pelvic region.

Position 3

The retention position or Position 3 is the point at which the hands come together on the pistol. This position does not have to be your perfect shooting grip. At this point you should think retention.

7.2 Interview position.

Position 4

As you press the weapon from Position 3 to Position 4 there will be several things taking place, but ultimately we want to end up with the safety disengaged, the sights on the threat, and our finger on the trigger. The trigger is prepped, taking the slack out but not firing until you have attained the acceptable sight picture. Last but not least, we fire the weapon. Upon firing the weapon, you will follow through, let the trigger reset, and follow up with as many rounds as needed to eliminate the threat.

Position 5

Due to cutbacks and the lack of Stimulus from the Stimulus Package, Position 5 has been terminated.

7.3 Shooter moves towards Position 1

7.1 Ready to fight.

7.4 Ensure you drive hand down on the pistol. Support hand moves to your chest ready to receive pistol.

7.5 Position 1 - the perfect grip is attained before drawing.

7.6 Ensure you drive hand down on the pistol. Support hand moves to your chest ready to receive pistol.

7.7 Once perfect grip is attained, simultaneously deactivate thumb break or retention devices.

7.8 Position 2, weapon out of holster ready to shoot if need be.

7.9 Position 3, hands come together high in the chest, ready to shoot or drive the pistol to the target.

7.10 Position 2, weapon out of holster ready to shoot if need be.

7.11 Position 3, hands come together high in the chest, ready to shoot or drive the pistol to the target.

7.12 Continue to press, building a better grip.

7.13 Finger starting to move to the trigger.

7.14 Continue to press, building a better grip.

7.15 Finger starting to move to the trigger.

7.16 Trigger prepared.

7.17 Continue aligning sights and squeezing the trigger.

7.18 Trigger prepared.

7.19 Continue aligning sights and squeezing the trigger.

7.20 Confirm acceptable sight picture and squeeze the trigger.

7.21 Confirm acceptable sight picture and squeeze the trigger.

7.22 Weapon fires, Position 4.

Position 1

Position 1 is where the sense of urgency I talked of earlier comes into play. What will happen if you quickly move your hand to the pistol? Nothing, the only bad that can happen is if you continue that quick movement, trying to snatch the pistol from the holster. We do not want to snatch or grab, we want to move the hand to the pistol quickly, and at that point we stop for a split second to attain the perfect grip. If you don't get the grip right now, you will be fighting the poor grip throughout the entire draw stroke. It may not look like it, but this is what great shooters do every time they draw their weapon. You must also be moving your thumb or index finger to the correct point to deactivate any holster retention devices. If I am using a thumb break type holster, I normally move the thumb break as I move from position 1 to position 2. This will help you to maintain the perfect grip throughout the draw sequence. You should not sweep the thumb break out of the way, and then grasp the pistol. You should grasp the pistol, and then as you deactivate the thumb break, you remove the weapon from the holster. Ensure that your thumb is not kept in a down position blocking the grip from the support hand. This sequence is unbelievably important, and you will see this as you continue to strive to improve your speed.

The support hand should also start moving into the correct position during the initial movement of the strong hand for the pistol. The support hand can move to receive near Position 3, which will be covered shortly. I actually tell most students to touch their chest with the support hand; this naturally puts the hand where it is needed to quickly, safely, and most importantly, consistently, receive the pistol.

7.23 Be prepared to move as quickly as possible to Position 1.

7.24 Hand snaps to the weapon, attain the perfect grip.

7.25 Deactivate the holster's retention device(s) while maintaining the perfect grip.

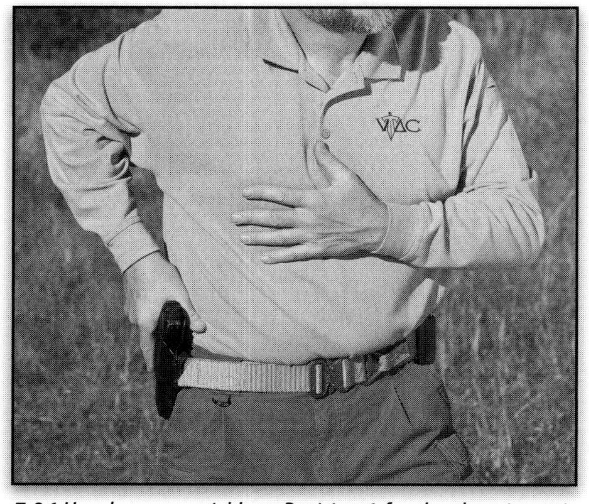

7.26 Hand moves quickly to Position 1 for the shooting grip.

7.27 Keep your thumb up in the desired location to allow the support hand room to build your grip.

Position 2

Position 2 is not a position that requires a lot of focus. It is a position that you should quickly maneuver through to get to Position 3. There are a few key points that we do need to make sure you understand. Position 2 is not executed until you have attained the perfect firing grip during the execution of Position 1. Once you have this grip, and you are capable of releasing any retention devices on the holster, you should snap the pistol from the holster into Position 2. Position 2 is also the first point in the draw when, if needed, you can actually fire the weapon. This is why it is important to rotate or cam the weapon's muzzle up to come in line with the threat. If at any point you are in an extremely close quarters situation, which will not allow you to raise your pistol to align with your eyes, this will be the position that you may have to shoot from. The only difference will be the trigger, sights and safety. Normally the trigger finger does not enter the trigger guard until past Position 3. In a contact shooting type scenario, you may have to violate this rule due to the close proximity of the threat.

7.28 Weapon clears holster and is ready to point at threat.

7.29 Position 2

7.30 Position 2

7.31 Weapon clears holster and is ready to point at threat.

7.32 Weapon at Position 2, ready to fire.

7.33 One round to the pelvis.

7.34 Two rounds to the pelvis.

Position 3

As you moved to Position 1, your support hand moved to touch your chest. At this time, the support hand should be open and waiting for the arrival of the firing hand with the pistol. If you were successful in grasping the pistol with the preferred strong hand grip, the pistol should be ready to quickly join up with the support hand and drive towards the target. The key to a smooth and successful Position 3 is to have a reference point/index point that lets you know all is well. I try to index on the bottom of the trigger guard with the index finger of the support hand, between the second and third knuckles. If this finger hits the bottom of the trigger guard, two things will happen. First, I will feel it and know I am in the right position. Second, I will be able to quickly drive the weapon past Position 3 to Position 4. As I press the weapon past Position 3, I will also ensure I rotate my support hand forward. Remember to point your support thumb forward towards the target to help with recoil control when you finally fire the weapon.

At Position 3, your muzzle should not be above the target. During the draw stroke the muzzle must never go above the threat. The Muzzle High technique will work for competition, but for tactical shooting, there is no place for it. If the muzzle goes above the target, we can't fire from Position 3 if the need arises. The same can be said for the movement from Position 2 towards Position 3, always ensuring the weapon is pointed at the intended target and never above it.

7.35 *Support hand touching chest.*

7.36 *Position 3, both hands on the weapon.*

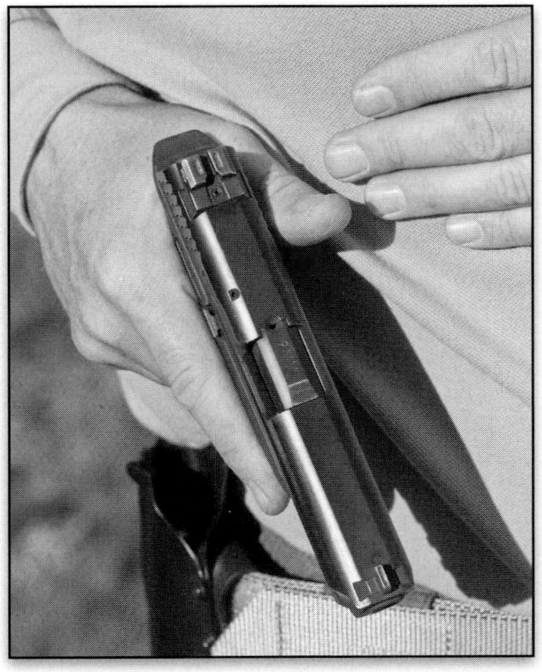

7.37 *Support hand and firing hands close to your body.*

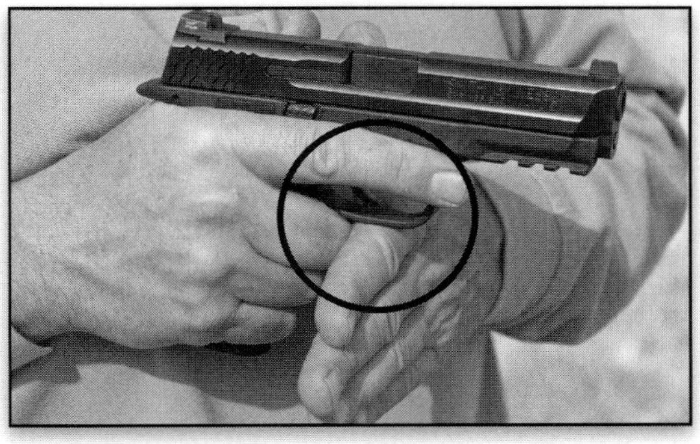

7.38 *Support hand index finger touching bottom of the trigger guard.*

7.39 *Support hand index finger touching bottom of the trigger guard.*

7.40 Hands start to press toward Position 4.

7.41 Support hand rotates into position for recoil control.

7.42 Trigger finger preps trigger.

Position 4

Position 4 is ultimately where the weapon should be fired. With that being said, there are a few things to keep in mind as we move from Position 3 to Position 4. At Position 3, your support hand is in a position to receive the pistol and drive the weapon to Position 4. You will also need to deactivate your safety if you have that type of pistol. You will also begin prepping the trigger as we discussed in the chapter on Presentation of the Pistol. Don't get excited about prepping perfectly to fire as the weapon stops at Position 4, this will take lots of practice. Press the weapon forward, prep the trigger, align the sights, continue the trigger squeeze, fire the shot, call your shot, and follow through to be prepared to fire again.

7.43 Position 4.

7.44 Muzzle at threat.

7.45 Muzzle high, decent grip but no chance of engaging the target.

7.46 Position 4, weapon fires.

Draw recap

Once again, remember the following. Quickly move to Position 1, get the perfect grip on the pistol, slowing down in order to make this happen. Your support hand should also be moving to its Position 3 receive posture. Once you have the perfect grip, in one motion, deactivate any retention devices and quickly snap the weapon out of the holster to Position 2. Ensure that the muzzle has rotated into position, and has aligned with the threat. Do not pause at Position 2, move the weapon to quickly meet with your support hand at Position 3. Once the index finger of the support hand feels the bottom of the trigger guard, drive the hands toward Position 4. As you drive the pistol forward, rotate the support hand so the thumb on the support hand is pointing towards the target. Start the trigger prep, sight alignment, trigger control, call the shot, and follow through.

This process can seem easy, but don't be fooled. If you want to have a quick draw, which leads to a quick shot, you must practice. Practice over and over. If you miss a draw, do not stop; continue to fight through until the task is completed.

7.47-55 The proper draw stroke (Left to right, top to bottom)

Draw Problems

Here are a few issues we see when shooters are drawing their weapons.

Don't Look Down

When it is time to draw your weapon, don't look down. You should know where your weapon is and be able to quickly put a hand in the correct position to draw. If this isn't the case, practice, practice, practice. If you start to look down for the weapon, an experienced threat will seize the opportunity and move quickly to close the distance. Once you look back up, it may be too late. This is also true during reloads; you should be able to quickly gain control of a weapon or magazine without visually looking for it. How will you do this at night?...practice, practice, practice.

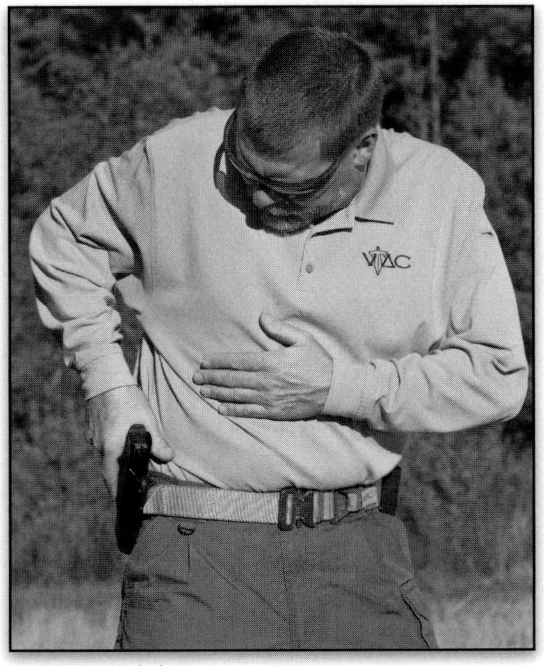

7.56 Don't look down.

Porpoising the Weapon

As the name implies, the shooter Porpoises the weapon. Maybe not to the extent that good Ol' Flipper would be proud, but porpoising nonetheless. This issue is caused by not driving the weapon straight to the target from Position 3. It can also be caused by not getting the support hand in a high enough position to receive the weapon. Porpoising will cause the shooter to be much slower in getting rounds on target, accurately. Ideally you should see the sights in your peripheral vision and drive them as though they were on a string, directly attached to the center of your target.

7.57 Still correct.

7.58 Muzzle above threat.

7.59 No way to shoot.

7.60 Still unable to fire.

7.61 Weapon dropping into Position 4.

7.62 Finally able to engage.

Sweeping Up to the Target/Stiff Arm Technique

A technique that we also see on a regular basis is the Stiff Arm technique. This is a technique that has been perpetuated by Law Enforcement trainers around the country. What is being taught is to come from below the target in a stiff arm position. Both arms locked out or even from the Weaver stance with the weapon lowered. The problem that occurs is that this position is not a quick target acquisition technique. Worse yet, retention of the pistol is minimized due to the weapon being presented (as in a gift) to the threat without the sights on the target. A fast draw should never end up in the stiff-arm position; the weapon should be driven in a straight line from Position 3 to Position 4. If there is no threat, stay in Position 3 until you feel it is necessary to drive the gun at a perceived threat.

From the Stiff Arm position you are also not able to shoot immediately. From Position 3 you can immediately engage a threat that you encounter at an extreme close range.

7.63 Good Position 2.

7.64 Very low Position 3

7.65 Inefficient draw stroke.

7.66 Stiff arms driven to align sights.

7.67 Finally on target.

Hands not together at Position 3

Not having your hands together at Position 3 can cause issues. The difference being that the hands meet the pistol somewhere between position 3 and 4. Of course you won't always have this luxury, but train to keep the hands together on the weapon, and close to the body. If you touch your chest with the support hand during the draw, it will almost completely eliminate this problem. The closer to the body the hands come together, the quicker and more consistent the draw and presentation will be on the threat. This poor technique will also defeat your retention position. If you have both hands on the weapon at Position 3, it will be almost impossible for someone to take your weapon… without one heck of a fight, that is.

7.68 Support hand not in a receive position.

7.69 May cause the shooter to flag own hand with muzzle.

7.70 Still not together.

7.71 Very good chance to miss your grip.

7.72 Shooter can now fire.

Starting the Draw

When you practice your draws, what position do you start from? I witness a lot of shooters starting in a surrender position, which is hands above your shoulders, fingers pointed up as though you were surrendering. When would you get in this position in the real world? More than likely, not at all. If you end up in this position, you may have done something a little wrong earlier in the day.

It is best to practice from the positions you will most likely be in when things go wrong. For Law Enforcement officers, this will more than likely be the interview position. If you are a SWAT member, Soldier, or Marine whose primary weapon is a carbine, then practice as though you were transitioning from primary to secondary. Assume the correct position for firing the rifle, then step into the draw if need be.

If you deal with a vehicle most of the day, practice the draw from the seat of your vehicle. Do you wear a seatbelt? If you do, always practice with the seatbelt fastened. Train as realistically as possible and remember to dry fire these techniques before going Hot.

7.73 Interview position.

7.74 Fighting position.

7.75 Now this is realistic.

7.76 Transitions from rifle to pistol.

7.76 Surrender position.

Chapter 8, Don't Double Tap

8. DON'T DOUBLE TAP

You bring your weapon's sights to bear on the threat, you quickly double tap to eliminate the threat, but to your surprise, the target is not as impressed with your two rounds as you thought he would be. Now you must bring the weapon back to the target and continue to fire. Hopefully the lesson is learned; shoot until the threat is eliminated.

Why no double taps?

Constantly we are faced with slaying the Double Tap Dragon. He rears his ugly head when shooters are trying to push their speed and feel this may be the way to increase the pace, but there are pitfalls. The largest hurdle to overcome when you choose to use the Double Tap, is simply not knowing where the second round will impact.

In order to conduct a double tap, you must jerk the trigger twice, as fast as you can. A common analogy is that you must start a double tap at your toes, moving through your body, eventually making it to your trigger finger. I have never seen any shooter who can double tap with consistent accuracy. I am not going out on a limb here, this is a fact. Double taps may appear to work when you are at certain close ranges, but as you push no shoot/hostage targets tighter to the threat targets, or simply add a couple tough shots, the walls come crashing down.

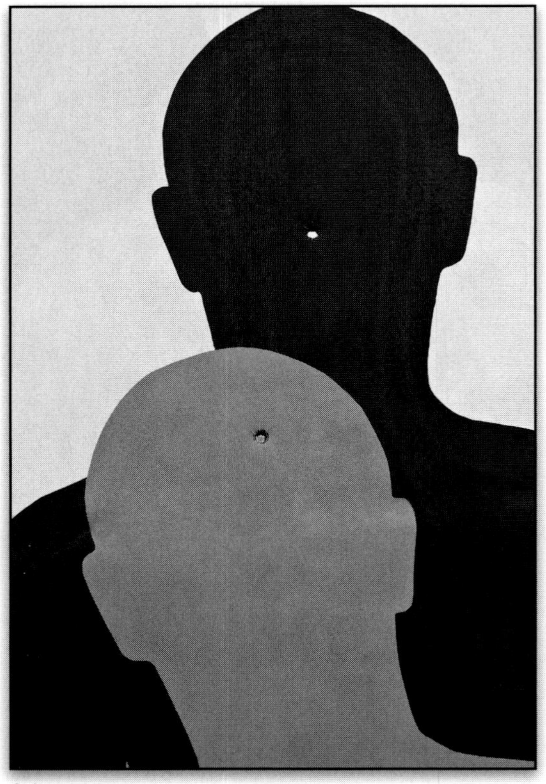

8.1

8.2 Draw and fire six shots into three targets from seven yards.

8.3 Total time 2.90 using double taps.

8.4 Splits .19 shot to shot on the 1st target, split .45 from 1st to 2nd, splits .19 on 2nd target shot to shot.

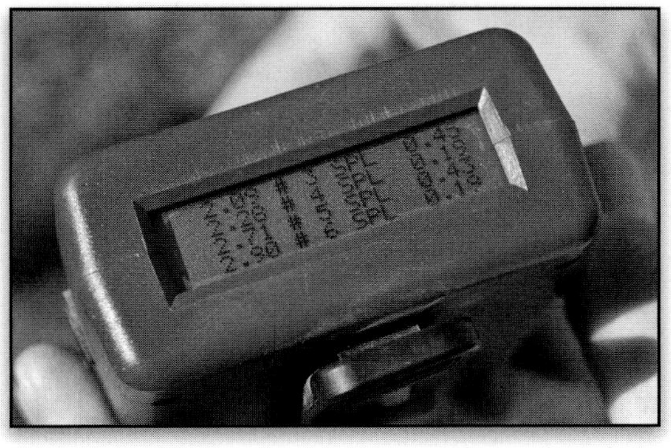

8.5 Split from 2nd to 3rd target .43 and shot to shot of .19.

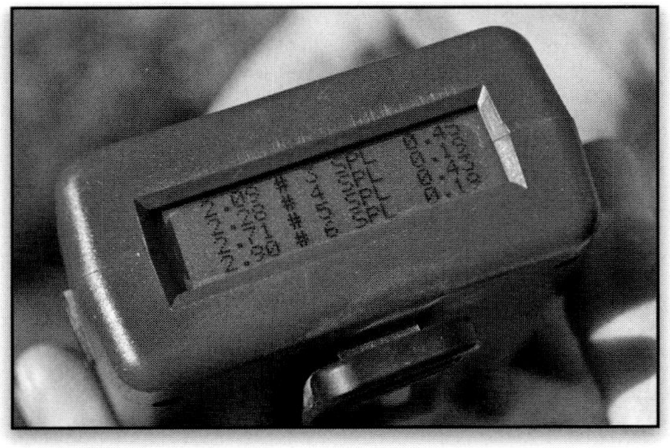

8.6 Split from 2nd to 3rd target .43 and shot to shot of .19.

If contact shots are required, you should still focus on making shots that will eliminate the threat and the standard two rounds may not be what the Doctor ordered.

See your sights

As a tactical shooter, you must see your sights on every shot. You must account for the impact of all rounds fired. Contact shots are a different story, but the same is true in these instances regarding accountability.

Once you are able to master the idea of seeing your sights as they move around on the target and follow through awaiting the realignment before starting the next trigger squeeze, you will be a much better shooter.

The most important goal of tactical shooting must be hitting the target. We need speed, but quickly putting the round inside the kill zone is the primary mission.

Controlled Pairs

Controlled pairs may be the answer you are looking for. The intent with controlled pairs is to get two shots, and three sight pictures. The process begins with the first sight picture, followed by the first shot, followed by follow through. Next comes the second sight picture, second shot fired, follow through, third sight picture, and finished. May sound simple, but it does take practice. If you feel you have mastered the basic controlled pair, start adding more shots. Ideally you should be able to conduct this drill with six to ten rounds without issue. It will instill the correct mentality for making good shots into your muscle memory. If you want to practice with three shots per target on multiple targets, you will see the difference when compared to a shooter who only uses double taps. You should use multiple shots in most of your drills to instill the point of shooting until the threat is eliminated.

To test your abilities at driving the weapon as well as using controlled pairs, try setting up three to five targets, 2-3 feet apart. Engage each target with two or three rounds. Your shot to shot splits and your target to target splits should be about the same time if you are using the correct technique. If the shots are .15-.17 splits and the target to target splits are .40-.50, you are shooting too fast and moving too slow. Step on the gas between targets, aim each shot.

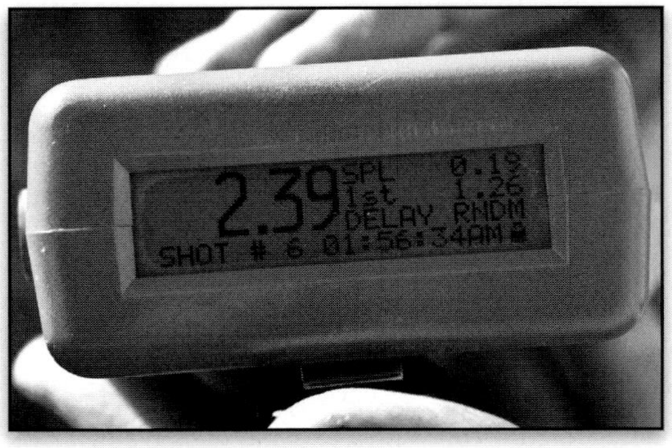

8.7 Total time 2.39 using controlled pairs. 1st shot draw 1.26, .19 faster than the other run.

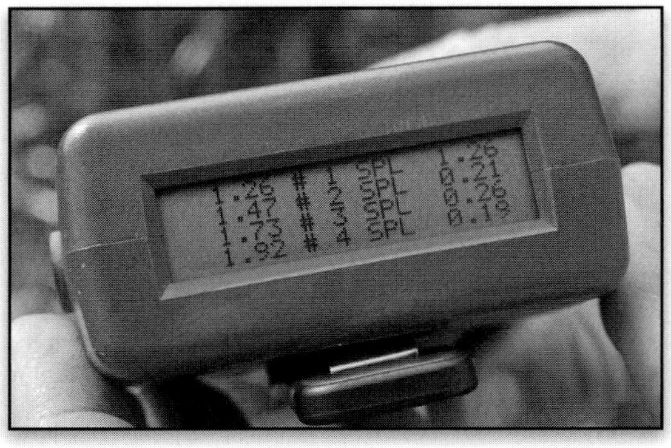

8.8 1st target shot to shot of .21, split between targets .26.

8.9 Split between targets 2 and 3 of .28 and between 5th and 6th of .19. Overall better run pushing the weapon from target to target.

Chapter 9, Loading and Unloading

9. LOADING AND UNLOADING

Loading the Weapon

Why would you want to read the Loading section if you are an advanced shooter? Well, please see what we have to offer, I think you will see a different mindset with our loading procedure. The most important difference is that we always try to load as though it were a speed reload, but without the speed.

Locking the slide to the rear

I normally do not lock my slide to the rear when I load my weapon. This is an extra step that I don't feel is necessary to ensure the weapon is properly loaded. Naysayers will tell me that they want to see the round feed into the chamber, and I would agree, but how can this be performed at night? You will not see the round feed, so lets use a technique that will work day or night. Normally, shooters that use the slide lock technique will also load by locking the slide to the rear when they have just fixed a malfunction and are still in the fight. Not a time to lock the slide, it is a time to load and shoot, immediately.

9.1 Starting loading process with slide forward.

9.2 Or start loading process with slide locked to rear.

Seating the Magazine

When you prepare to seat the magazine, ensure that you start with the magazine in the support hand, index finger aligned with the front spine of the magazine. This will help your hand to guide the magazine into the magazine well. Remember, we are always trying to train with the goal of making our overall shooting better; a completely administrative loading procedure is not going to help with your combat shooting.

Once the magazine starts to slide into the weapon, seat it with the same vigor you would during a speed reload. Make sure you don't double tap the magazine during your initial load. If you start seating the magazine and tapping it once more to make sure it is seated, you will also do this during your speed reloads as

9.3 No matter the pouch type.

9.4 Grab magazine as though you are performing a reload.

9.5 Index finger aligned with front spine of magazine.

9.6 Index finger almost touching bullet of first cartridge in the magazine.

9.7 Start driving the magazine into the weapon.

9.8 Seat the magazine aggressively with one motion.

9.9 Seat the magazine agressively with one motion.

9.10 Seat the magazine agressively with one motion.

9.11 Pull down to ensure the magazine is seated.

well as during slide lock reloads, both of which require speed to get back in the fight.

After you have seated the magazine, pull down to ensure the magazine is held in by the magazine catch. Obviously if it isn't, you will get a heck of a surprise when you try to fire the weapon.

Racking the Slide

When you rack the slide to put a round in the chamber, pull the slide all the way to the rear, then let it slam forward, do not ride the slide forward. Once the slide has slammed into battery, conduct a check to make sure there is actually a round in the chamber.

9.12 Pull the slide all the way to the rear.

9.13 Let the slide slam into battery.

Press Check

Always conduct a press check with your pistol, you must be 100% sure that your weapon is loaded. There are several ways to conduct a press check, make sure your technique will work day or night. I try to anchor the weapon with both hands working together, if you don't do this you will end up pulling the slide too far to the rear and causing a double feed or eject an unfired round. Once I have anchored the hands together, pull the slide just enough to allow a visual check or a digital check with your finger. As I said, there are several acceptable ways to conduct this check, just make sure it always happens.

A bad habit that I formed while shooting a 1911 was to grab the front of the slide to pull it to the rear. Although this works, there are better, safer techniques to accomplish the same task. We even milled front cocking serrations into the slide to aid in the grip for this maneuver. In the Prehistoric times, we actually conducted a press check with the thumb inside the trigger guard and fingers at the muzzle, pushing back on the recoil spring plug. Obviously, not a smart move.

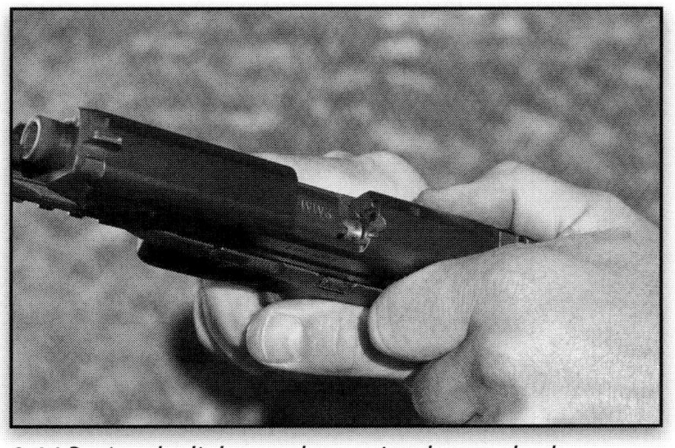

9.14 During daylight, conduct a visual press check.

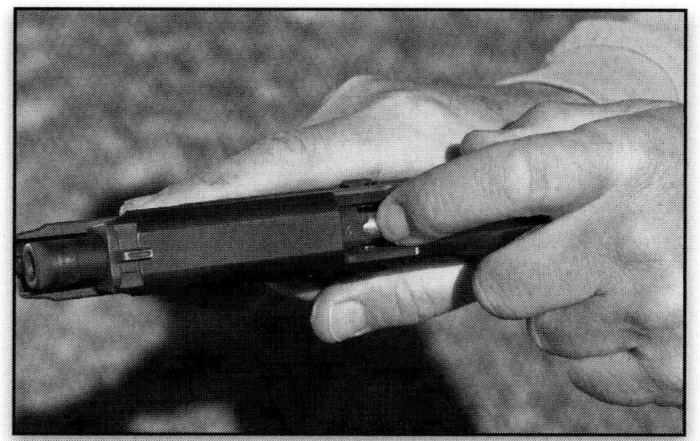

9.15 At night, conduct a digital check to ensure the weapon is loaded.

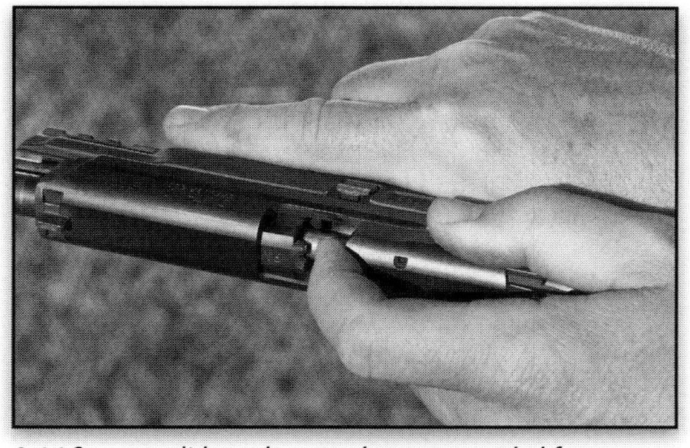

9.16 Squeeze slide and create the space needed for your fingertip to feel the round.

9.17 Load as though it were a speed or slide lock reload.

9.18 Weapon held in same area as during speed relaod.

9.19 Cycle slide.

9.20 Grab magazine correctly.

9.21 Index finger touching or near first bullet.

9.22 Seat magazine with a purpose.

9.23 One push, don't double tap magazine.

9.24 Pull down to ensure magazine is seated.

9.25 Pull slide completely to the rear

9.26 Let slide slam forward.

9.27 Ready for the fight.

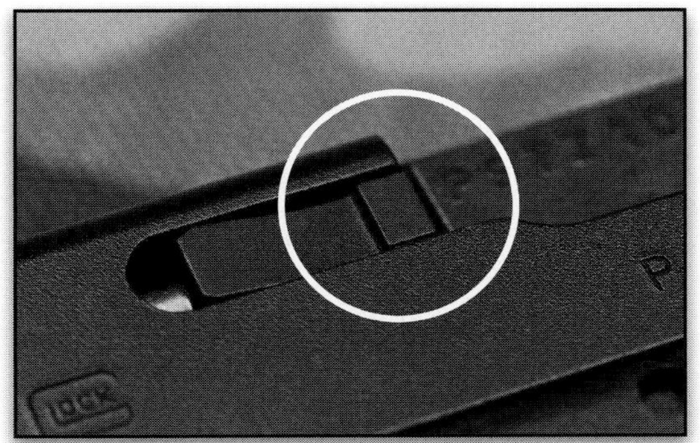

9.28 Glock unloaded.

Loaded Chamber Indicators

If you have a weapon with a loaded chamber indicator, do not rely on the indicator to tell you 100% that the weapon is loaded. Always check visually or with your finger tip.

Loaded chamber indicators can give a false reading or may not work well with gloves in the dark. Some loaded chamber indicators, such as the Glock, will actually feel as though you have a round in the chamber when the weapon is very dirty or you have debris under the extractor. Never trust these indicators.

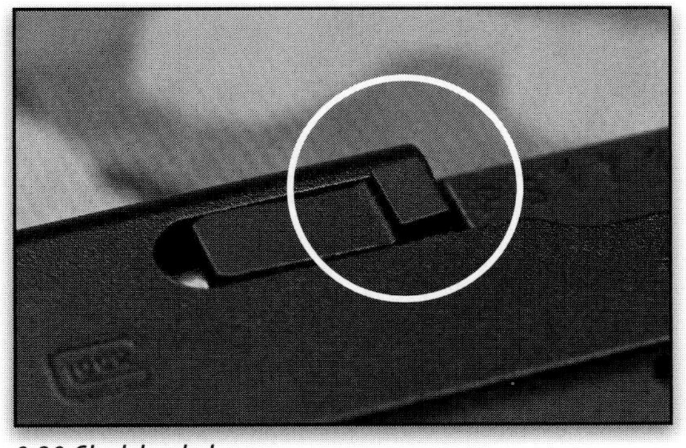

9.29 Glock loaded.

9.30 Smith & Wesson M&P unloaded.

9.31 Smith & Wesson M&P loaded.

9.32 Springfield XD unloaded.

9.33 Springfield XD loaded.

9.34 Grab the bottom of the magazine.

9.35 Release magazine into hand.

Unloading/Clearing the Weapon

I believe that unloading or clearing the weapon is an administrative function. The reason for this statement is so that you will understand that there is no need to clear the weapon quickly, specifically not during the unloading process. Once again, the process that you use should work day and night as well though.

Once you have finished shooting, remove the magazine; place it in a pocket or pouch that will not be used for fully loaded magazines. This is important, don't just throw that magazine into your normal pouches, this will come back to haunt you. Once you ensure that this

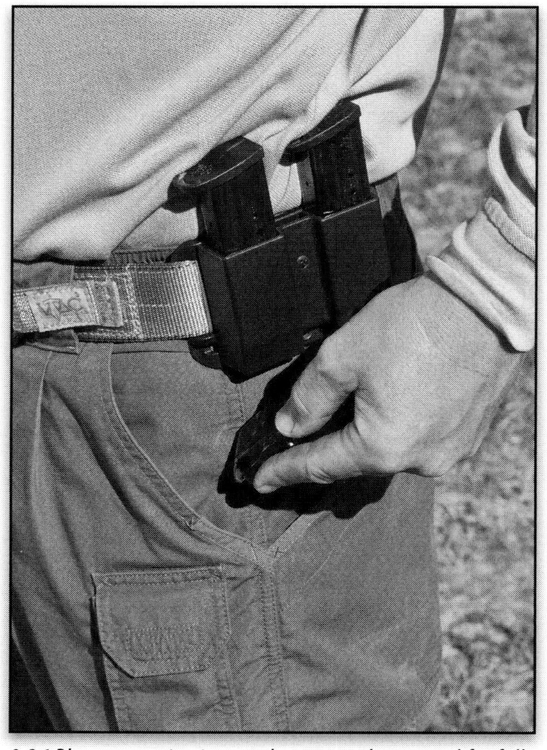

9.36 Place magazine in a pocket or pouch not used for full magazines.

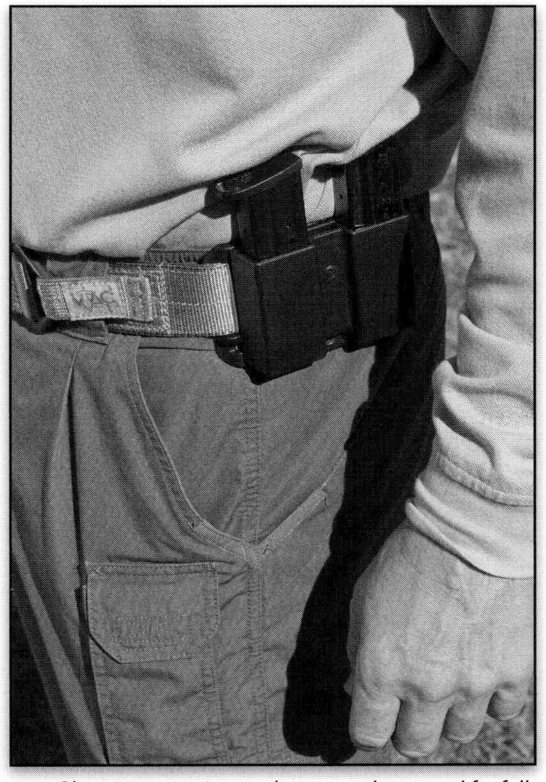

9.37 Place magazine in a pocket or pouch not used for full magazines.

9.38 Grab rear of slide.

9.39 Pull slide to the rear.

9.40 Let round hit the ground.

9.41 Do not try to catch the round.

magazine is secure, pull the slide to the rear, do not cover the ejection port with your hand and do not attempt to catch the round in your hand. The reason for the clearance of the ejection port is for two reasons. First, we don't want the round to hit your hand and fall back into the chamber. Secondly, there is a chance with certain weapons that the round will drop out of the chamber, allowing the ejector to hit the primer, and actually cause the round to go off. This is a rare occurrence, but I have personally witnessed it four times. Once it was with the pistol I was shooting. I was lucky; I had my hands clear of the ejection port, it was a surprise, but there was no bleeding involved. Two other times it happened, the round exploded injuring the shooters; shrapnel

went into their hand. This can easily be avoided by rotating the weapon slightly away from your face and keeping hands clear of the ejection port.

Next we need to conduct a three point safety check. Check the chamber and make sure there isn't a round in the chamber. Check the face of the slide, just in case a cartridge has stuck under the extractor. Lastly, double check that you have in fact removed the magazine.

After confirming that the weapon is clear, allow the slide to go forward, point the weapon in a safe direction and squeeze the trigger. Remember, a safe direction may not be downrange, a safe direction is the spot you don't mind firing a round. The only AD (Accidental Discharge) or ND (Negligent Discharges), I have seen, all happened with what the shooters swore were unloaded weapons.

If you spend enough time on the range, you will have an accident. Please make sure when you have your accident, no one is injured.

9.42 Check the chamber.

9.43 Check the face of the slide.

9.44 Check for magazine.

9.45 Slide forward.

9.46 Drop the hammer or striker on an empty chamber.

Chapter 10, Reloads

10. RELOADS

No matter the capacity of your weapon system, there comes a time in every man's life when he has to reload. Some experts have said that after studying hundreds of gunfights, they see a very small chance that you will need to reload during a confrontation. So you're saying there's a chance... then we must train for it.

As tactical wizardry seems to abound in the firearms training community, some of you may disagree with certain styles of reloads that we will discuss. If you are close-minded and don't want to think outside the box, please skip these controversial reloads. If you are ready to enhance your skills for whatever may happen to occur outside of the norm, I think you will see the applicability of these non-standard reloads.

10.1 So you're saying there's a chance.

Placement of your magazines

Placement of magazines is key if you plan to be efficient during your reload, no matter what type of reload you plan to execute. Even if you plan to use magazine pouches with Velcro or snap closures, you must have the magazines placed so you can not only access them quickly when needed, but can get to the same magazines with your strong hand if need be. Never say never when it comes to using your strong hand or support hand for everything. Strange things happen in gunfights.

When placing your magazines for normal duty wear, you can place them where they will be quickly accessible as well as comfortable when driving, riding, or conducting specialized operations. You should think of the best possible position for smooth reloads in a timely manner. You should also think through scenarios that are out of the norm to see if the magazines will still be accessible. Will the magazines be lost if you inadvertently open the pouch?

If you are setting your gear up for concealed carry/undercover operations, you will have to think differently than the normal patrolman. You will have to be concerned with placement for access and placement for concealment.

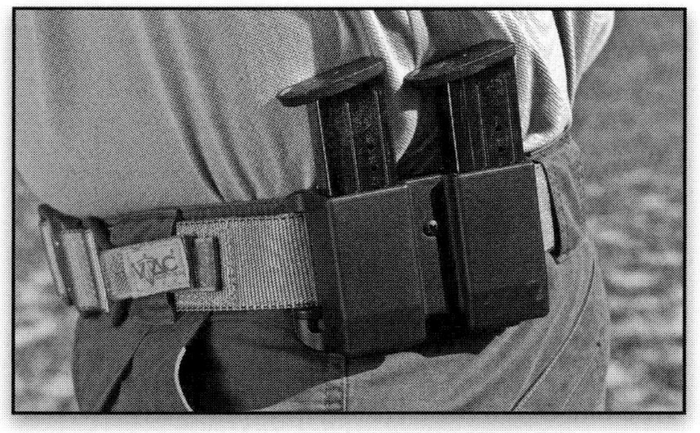

10.2 Standard open-top Blade-Tech® magazine pouches.

10.3 Open top duty pouches by Safariland®.

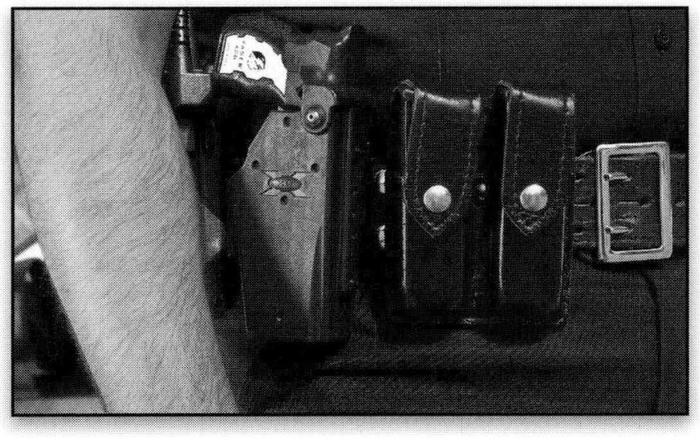

10.4 Snap closure duty pouches.

10.5 Open top used during concealed carry.

Bullets Forward

In order to be efficient, it is best to place magazines so the bullets are facing forward. The less movement required once you get the magazine out of the pouch the better. As you place your hand over the magazine, the pinky finger should help you to grasp the magazine. The key is to ensure that once the magazine comes out of the pouch, you have your index finger on the first round of ammo in the magazine. This will help you to guide the magazine into the magazine well much quicker than a poor magazine grip. You must also be able to reload the weapon during hours of limited visibility and this technique definitely helps then as well.

10.6 Perfect grasp on the magazine.

10.7 Index finger near the first round in the magazine.

10.9 Poor magazine grip.

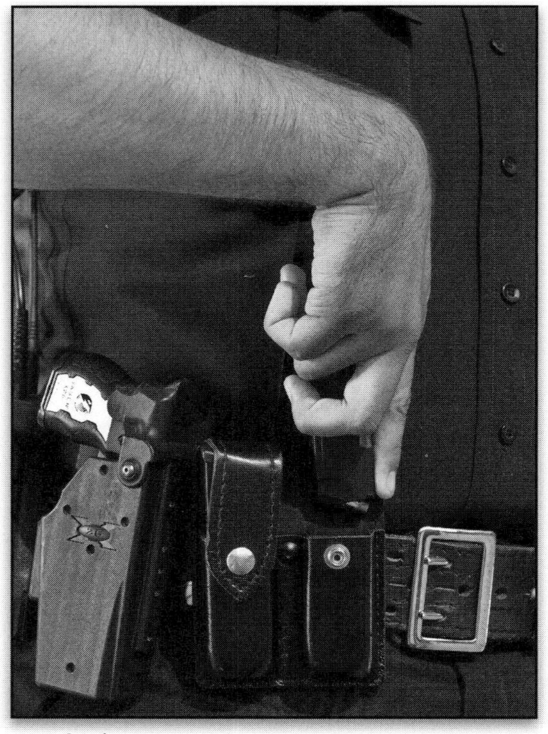

10.8 Good magazine grip.

Don't look down

Before we get into the mechanics of the reload, I want to address one of the problems we see even with the most seasoned shooter. Looking down! Why would you need to look for your magazine? You really shouldn't, the techniques we teach allow you to keep your focus forward. You should be able to index your hand into the correct position to access the magazine without having to glance down. No matter the situation, concealed or not, you do not need to look down.

10.10 Do not look down for your magazine.

Key Points for Successful Reloads

No matter the type of reload, there are rules to live by when getting a fresh magazine into the weapon.

Rotate the weapon in your hand

In order to have quick access to the magazine release, you may need to rotate the weapon slightly in your hand, do not confuse this with laying the weapon to the side at an angle. Allowing your hand to quickly rotate to a position that allows your thumb access to the magazine release seems like a minor detail but will quickly help you get the magazine out without the addition of oversize magazine releases, which are discussed in the Pistol Selection Chapter. I hear shooters with small hands complaining that they have to rotate the weapon. I have pretty large hands and I still rotate the weapon for quick access to the magazine release as well as to gain a mechanical advantage on magazine releases that have stiff springs. It is common for competition shooters to trim the length of the magazine release spring to give them a slight advantage when conducting speed reloads. This should be absolutely restricted to competition weapons, not to be used in self-defense weaponry.

10.11 Rotate the weapon ensuring it is still vertical to allow the magazine to drop free.

10.12 Aggressively press the magazine release, ejecting the magazine.

10.13 Magazine sticking because weapon was not vertical during release.

10.14 Grip changed to allow release of magazine.

10.15 Correct grip re-established before seating magazine.

Keep the weapon Vertical when dropping the magazine

As you make the rotation that I mentioned above, absolutely do not rotate the weapon from vertical. We want the magazine to be able to quickly fall from the weapon, allowing it to be replaced with a fresh magazine. If you rotate the weapon, so that the magazine has to come out at an angle, you will impede the magazine from falling free. This is especially true of weapons with polymer magazines, such as the Glock. If you do have a problem with the magazines not dropping completely free, see the Side Bar: Raking Out Stuck Magazines. It is also common for some shooters to flip the pistol to get the magazine to fall free. If your magazines do not fall free without the flip, get them fixed. You may need to polish your magazines whether they are plastic or metal, or you may need to replace them.

Re-grip the weapon before seating the magazine

Once you have dropped the magazine from the weapon, and before you start to insert the new magazine, re-grip the pistol with your strong hand. If you do not re-grip the pistol, as you would during the firing sequence, you will be much slower to acquire sights and engage a threat. This is a hard habit to instill in shooters, but once you get it, you will be more efficient with your movement. Rotate the weapon while keeping it vertical, depress the magazine release with your thumb, and re-grip the weapon with the strong hand as though you are going to fire. Practice this over and over until it is grounded into your muscle memory.

Don't over rotate when inserting the fresh magazine in the weapon

Now that you have dropped the magazine and re-gripped, it is time to rotate the weapon at a slight angle to allow easy access to the magazine well. You want to attain easy access so you won't have to contort your support arm and shoulder to get the magazine in the weapon. When you rotate the weapon, do not over rotate. Over rotation does not help with speed. One trick that will help is to keep the weapon higher, in front of your face. My rule of thumb is to never

10.16 Weapon held in front of face to allow eyes on threat and quick re-engagement if necessary.

put my front sight above or below the threat during a reload. The bore axis will not align with the target, but the height of your front sight will be roughly the same height as the target. In the old days, some instructors taught shooters to place both elbows against their rib cage while reloading. This does not make you faster or help with any indexing issues. It also changes drastically when you are wearing kit. If you simply rotate the weapon so you are able to see the opposite side of your magazine well, you will be in the perfect position. This also allows your wrists to stay in a straight and strong position. Try to conduct reloads and malfunction clearances in the vicinity of where you would clap your hands. Unless you are a golfer, then get with one of your buddies to show you the correct position.

Weapons with a Thumb Safety

If you are firing a weapon that has a thumb safety, which will give you additional leverage, use it. Be sure to place your thumb back on this type of safety before seating the magazine. This

10.17 Thumb not on safety.

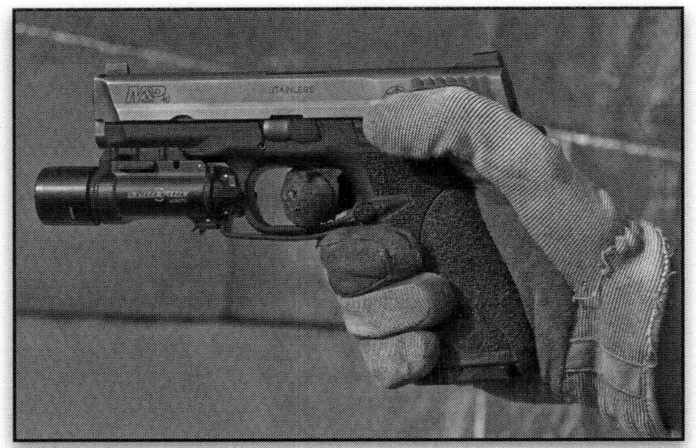

10.18 Thumb on safety.

should happen during the normal re-gripping procedure that I just referenced above.

Seat the magazine with a purpose

If you have done everything correctly up until this point, don't screw it up now with a half hearted magazine seat. You should have been going for a magazine while all of the above procedures were taking place. You should now have the magazine, with the bullet of the first cartridge in the magazine, touching your index finger. Your index finger should be running down the spine of the front of the magazine. Some teach to insert the magazine so that the rear of the magazine makes contact first. This may help you slightly if you are using a single stack pistol, such as the 1911. But if you are using any weapon with a tapered magazine, simply place the tapered portion of the magazine in the well and seat it with a purpose. Seating the magazine with a purpose does not mean you are trying to break anything, just get used to placing the magazine where it needs to be with some force. Don't double tap during this process, seat the magazine once and get back in the fight. It is also very important that you follow this guidance during the loading sequence at the beginning of the day. If

10.19 Index finger guides first round into magazine well.

10.20 Ensure the magazine is starting to guide into the well.

10.21 Seat the magazine with one forceful tap, do not double tap.

you fail to follow the same or very similar procedure at all times, you will build bad habits that tend to migrate from the first load of the day, to every speed and slide lock reload.

Practice, practice, practice

If you are working on a new technique, or just practicing your old technique, this can be done with an unloaded pistol and one empty magazine. Overall it is best to practice the complete sequence, but if I have a chance, and don't want to strap on magazines or a holster, I will practice with what I have available.

Ensure the pistol is clear, seat the empty magazine, point the weapon at a target, and when ready, go through the sequence to practice the load. The only difference is that I catch the empty magazine in my hand, get it rotated so that I have the preferred grip, rotate the weapon back to my firing grip but leave it slightly angled so I can just see the bottom edge of the magazine well, and then seat the empty magazine. I also practice touching the slide release, even though the slide is already forward. If you normally grab the slide to release it from the slide lock, practice that technique. Once the magazine is seated, I rotate the weapon back up to my target and start the sequence again.

Step By Step:
How to Practice Reloads

- **Clear Pistol**
- **Seat Empty Magazine**
- **Point the weapon at a target**
- **Start reload practice**
- **Rotate the weapon without canting to release the magazine**
- **Catch magazine in non-firing hand**
- **Rotate the magazine so you have the proper grip for reload with index finger touching where first cartridges bullet would be**
- **Rotate weapon back into the firing grip**
- **Slightly cant the weapon to receive magazine, just enough to see the bottom edge of the magazine well**
- **Start the insertion of the magazine**
- **Seat the magazine with one snappy motion**
- **Rotate the weapon back towards the target**
- **Always practice hitting the slide stop to release the slide during the dry fire process**
- **Repeat as necessary**

Slide not locking to the rear.

If you have a weapon that routinely does not lock to the rear on the last round, be careful how you train with this weapon. The correct procedure for getting a click, which is what you will get if the slide goes forward on an empty chamber, is to conduct a tap, rack, bang. A common mistake is to just drop the magazine when you get that click. This is setting yourself up for failure. If your slide will not lock to the rear, what is causing this malfunction? Common problems are thumbs resting on slide stops during the firing sequence. Other issues may be a broken slide stop or a bad magazine. Either way, you should train for the worst. The worst case scenario is that you have had a malfunction. If you have and you simply drop the magazine and replace it with another, you may still have a pistol that will not work. The most common malfunction that I see that fools shooters that use this technique, is the next round in the magazine going straight up in the pistol. Sometimes this is not visible, and the slide may be almost forward. So the shooter drops the magazine, replaces it with a fresh magazine, and exacerbates the problem.

10.22 Glock 34 with extended slide stop.

10.23 Thumb on slide stop will result in slide not locking to rear.

Types of Reloads

Tactical Reload with Retention

There are probably tens of ways to conduct a tactical reload with the pistol. Most of them will work. My intention is to show you a slightly more efficient way to conduct the same task. When I use a technique, I try to make all of these techniques work together. Why would you want to have different techniques for day and night, inside a vehicle or out? Therefore the Tactical reload should tightly mirror all of the other reloads that we will use in a tactical environment.

What does a Tactical reload with retention imply to you? It should make you think that you are in a situation where the pistol has been used, you are not sure how many rounds remain in the magazine, or you simply want to top the weapon off to its utmost capacity before continuing the task at hand. It also implies that you will retain the magazine that you take out of the weapon. Do not confuse this type of Tactical Reload with retention that an IDPA (International Defensive Pistol Association) competitor might conduct during a shooting match with what we will do in the real world. IDPA is a game. We want a reload that will work when we are talking real deal, life or death. In competition, shooters drop a partial magazine into their hand, place it in their pocket or a dump pouch, and then retrieve another fully loaded magazine to top off the pistol. What is wrong with this picture if you are truly expecting trouble? What happens if you are surprised after you drop the magazine in your pocket? Now you have one round in your pistol and no magazine in your hand. Not a good situation in the Dark world of reality.

The Real world procedure for completing a Tactical Reload with retention is as follows.

Seek cover if available. If there is no cover, try to at least use concealment. By the way, cover is something that will stop bullets. Concealment is self explanatory.

Using the proper magazine grasping technique, the same technique we would us for all of our normal reloads, secure a fully loaded magazine. Once you have the new magazine in hand, create space to allow the partial magazine to fall on top of the loaded magazine. This technique will allow you to always maintain a secure grip on full and partial magazines. Once the partial is free from the weapon, rotate the full magazine up into the magazine well and seat it with a purpose. As you seat the magazine, slightly rotate the hand which is holding the partial magazine so that you have power behind the seating process. Notice, with this technique we are not pinching magazines between pinky fingers, or allowing the weapon to be unloaded any longer than we have to.

Once you have the new magazine in the weapon, and feel confident that you are ready for whatever comes your way, place the partial magazine in a pocket or a pouch that will not be the place you grab if you have to conduct a slide lock or speed reload.

What happens if you are startled while conducting this reload? If you have not dropped the partial, you can engage the threat. If you have dropped the partial, we are minimizing the amount of time until you have a fully loaded pistol back in the fight.

Bottom line is this: don't confuse efficiency during a game with true efficiency on the battlefield.

10.24 Keep weapon loaded as long as possible.

10.25 Secure fresh magazine with your index finger pointed at first round in magazine.

10.26 Prepare to catch partial magazine with index finger and thumb.

10.27 Maintain good grip on fresh magazine

10.28 Drop partial when ready.

10.29 Quickly place full magazine in weapon. Note index finger still used to guide fresh magazine into place.

10.30 Once magazine starts, seat with purpose.

10.31 As magazine is seated, partial magazine is still maintained with thumb and index finger.

10.32 Place partial magazine in a pocket or pouch that will not be used for a speed or slide lock reload.

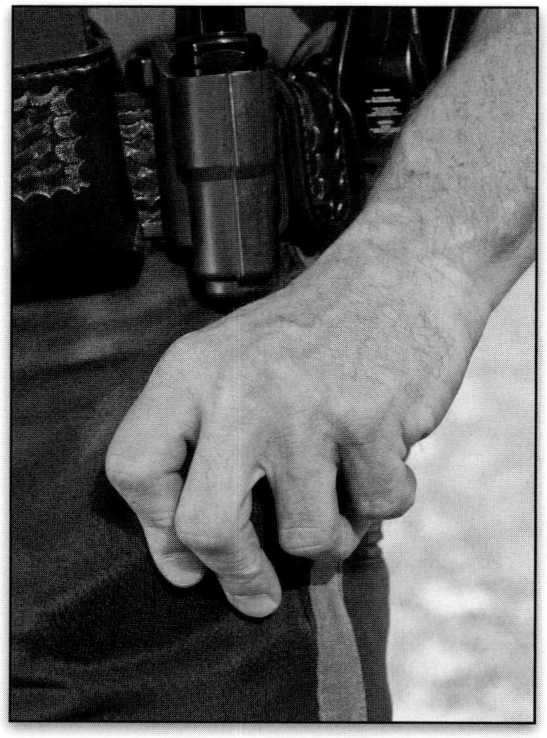

10.33

Tactical Reload without Retention

I might get sent to jail for violating another of the Tactical Ten Commandments here, but I am feeling a bit lucky, so here we go.

A tactical reload without retention is basically a speed reload with a pause to drop the magazine. What we are attempting to do is limit the time we have an unloaded or partially loaded weapon. To accomplish this reload, follow the procedures above, but don't attempt to retain the partial magazine. Bring the new magazine to the weapon before dropping the partial magazine on the ground. Once you drop the partial magazine, replace it with the full magazine. After completing the reload, if time and situation allow, retrieve the partial and stow it as we stated above. If you had to drop the magazine in the sand, it would be a good idea to knock the dirt out now, before you need it.

Well, lightning didn't strike, so I guess I will continue.

Our primary reasoning for this rendition of the tactical reload is the fact that you may not be as steady after a real world shooting as you are during your normal range time. This reload also works well for those that have small paws and struggle with the retention of the magazine. Don't be afraid to drop magazines, you can pick them up. If you add the additional movement of taking a knee, the magazines will normally be a little easier to find after the drop.

10.34 Bring full magazine to the weapon before releasing partial magazine.

10.35 Once ready, release the partial magazine.

10.36 Be prepared to get the fresh magazine into the weapon.

10.37 Quickly top off the pistol.

10.38 This technique gets you prepared to get back in the fight.

10.39 Ready for action.

10.40 Retrieve the partial magazine if time and situation allow.

Slide Lock Reload

The Slide Lock Reload is used, obviously, when the slide has locked to the rear. Ensure that the slide is only locking to the rear when the weapon is out of ammunition. If you continuously have issues with the premature slide lock, check hand placement. You may be hitting the slide stop up with the support hand causing the slide to lock back prematurely. You should also check weapon function. So, let's get on with the program.

As you are firing the weapon the slide locks to the rear, no matter the situation, you now must quickly get a fresh magazine in the weapon, allow the slide to slam into battery, and get ready for the next fight.

As soon as you realize the slide has locked to the rear, it is time to start the reloading sequence. Immediately! This may sound like a very obvious statement, but some shooters prefer to look at the weapon for awhile before they start the process.

First things first, immediately release the empty magazine. Do not attempt to catch the magazine or flip the magazine. Just let it hit the ground. This sounds simple, but what can we do to make this process more efficient? First of all, the magazine will fall more quickly if the weapon is still straight up and down and not canted to the side, which causes more drag on the side of the magazines. This is especially true of plastic or polymer magazines. Most folks want to lay the weapon to the side to aid in reaching the magazine release. I have pretty good size hands, but I still rotate the weapon to allow for a little more positive contact with the magazine release. This also works with every weapon you pick up that has the magazine release close to the same location. Notice I say rotate, not cant. This is key, with the weapon rotated slightly; you can still access the magazine release but not impede the ejection of the magazine.

As the magazine is being released, the support hand should be accomplishing its own objective which is the finding and grasping of the loaded magazine. Note that the proper movement of the hand to the magazine pouch is a crucial ingredient for a quick magazine change. The support hand should sweep from the front of the body with the index finger pointed down, thumb tucked to the rear, but feeling for the next magazine. We need to sweep from the front of our body, back towards the support side. This is important since magazines may shift position slightly or you may use different gear for different scenarios, e.g. duty, undercover, or concealed carry.

Once the magazine is found, it is important to grasp with the index finger touching the first round of ammunition in the magazine. This will allow the magazine to quickly find its mark, day or night. It is also imperative that the toe of the magazine have a slight purchase on the palm of your hand. This will be the area that forces the magazine into the weapon. The pinky finger is key to having a good grasp on the magazine; it will stabilize the magazine in your hand throughout the magazine seating process.

As the magazine is brought to the weapon's magazine well, you should have already slightly laid the weapon to the side, allowing you to see the bottom of the edge of the well.

There are several trains of thought as to where you should index the weapon, or elbows. What I would say is put the weapon about where you would clap,

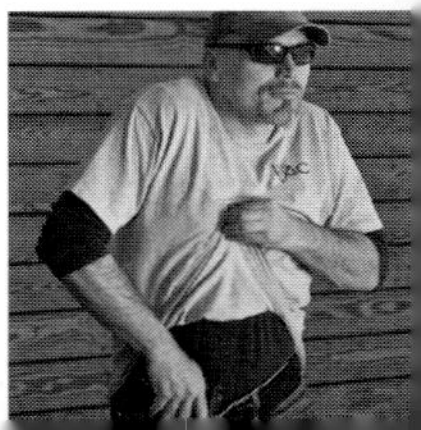

don't drop the weapon down to your belly. If you drop your head you are unable to see the threat as you make the reload. Keep your focus up, move the weapon back to a comfortable position, keep the focus on the target until the moment your magazine begins closing the gap with the magazine well. At that point, drop your focus to the opposite edge of the magazine well and start the insertion of the magazine.

As the magazine starts to slide into the magazine well, it is now time to change your focus back to the threat. This process requires practice, over and over.

Once the magazine is on its way, using your palm, slam the magazine into the weapon. If you shoot a pistol that releases the slide with the force of seating the magazine, you must fight the urge to over-slam the magazine. This will not work on all weapons, so try to use the same technique, regardless of the weapon type.

After seating the magazine, you have a few choices with regard to how you will release the slide.

10.41 Support hand hitting slide stop.

10.42 Slide locked to the rear prematurely.

10.43 Immediately release the magazine.

10.44 Support hand securing fresh magazine.

10.45 Briefly glance at the mazine well if needed.

10.46 Guide the magazine with your index finger.

10.47 Once magazine starts, drive the magazine with the palm of your hand.

10.48 Rotate the pistol back to the target.

10.49 Release the slide with your support thumb for right-handed shooters.

Using the Slide Release

If you choose to release the slide with the slide stop, this should be accomplished with the support side thumb, not the shooting hand thumb. If you use the firing hand thumb you will not be as quick and you will have to slightly break your grip. Even if you have large enough hands to do this with the firing hand on your pistol, it will not work on all weapon systems. This is why I use the support side thumb all the time.

Use of the support side thumb to release the slide is accomplished as the weapon is being pushed back towards the target. This technique should be completed in one fluid motion.

10.50 Seat the magazine.

10.51 Support thumb to slide stop.

10.52 Press the slide stop as you present the pistol.

10.53 Slide forward.

10.54 Ready to fire.

Sling Shot Method

The Sling Shot Method is used when the shooter does not want to use the slide stop to allow the slide to go forward. After making the load, grab the rear of the slide, pull it slightly to the rear, release and let it slam into battery. This technique works well. It is important that you allow the slide to slam forward, and don't ride the slide forward; let it slam so that you do not induce a stoppage. This technique is widely taught in the Law Enforcement community. It is not as fast as the Slide Release technique, but it works well.

10.55 Sling shot slide release technique.

10.56 Pull slide to the rear.

10.57 Let slam into battery.

Hand Over Technique

The Hand Over Technique is also used to release the slide. This technique is sometimes used when shooters don't feel they have the needed power with the Sling Shot Method. This technique works well, just ensure you do not cover the ejection port if you use this technique when clearing malfunctions. To use this technique, reach across the top of your weapon with the support hand. Your thumb should be pointed back towards your chest. If you feel you need more power with this position, push both hands toward each other with one quick motion. I use this technique when clearing stuck cases due to the power you can generate with your hands and elbows in this position.

If you are using a weapon such as the Beretta Model 92F, or any other weapon with a non-spring loaded decocker/safety on the slide, you should be cautious about using this technique. I have seen Soldiers place their weapons on safe hundreds of times, accidentally, while using this technique. Be very careful, or use the slide release technique.

If at all possible, try to keep your wrists from breaking while reloading. Your reloads will be better if the wrist does not break, with either hand.

10.58 Hand over slide release technique.

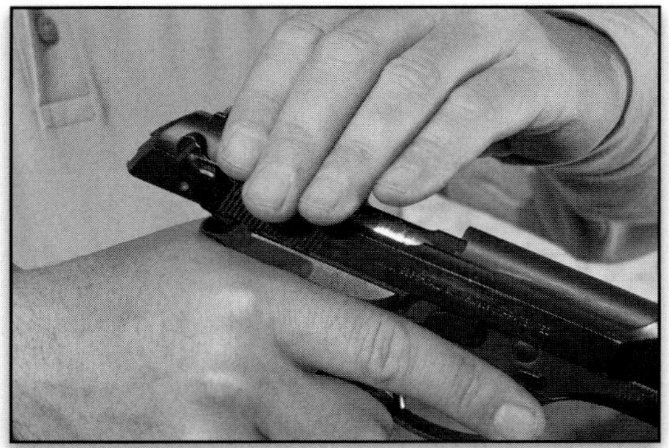

10.59 Hand over technique with Beretta 92/M9.

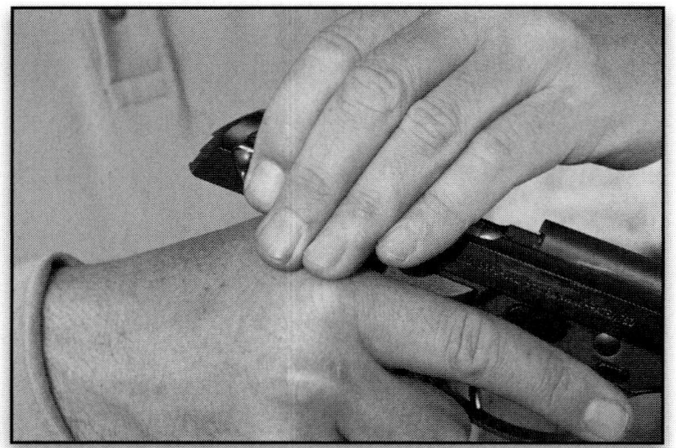

10.60 As you grab the slide to release, safety is rotated to safe.

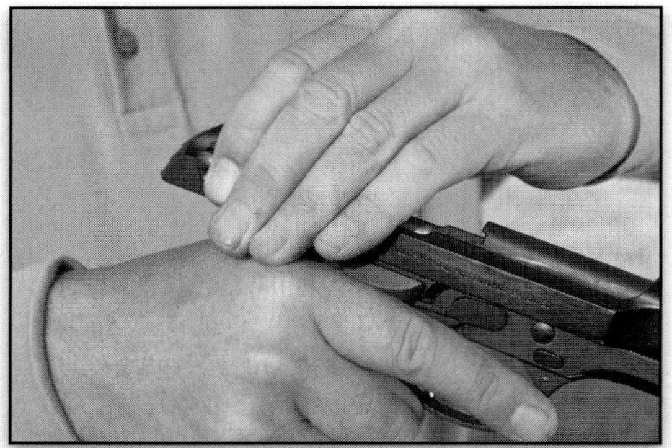

10.61 Slide pulled to the rear

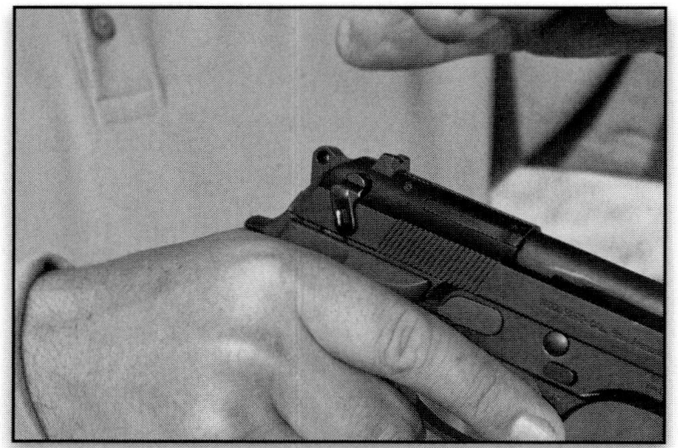

10.62 Slide released, safety on, weapon will not fire.

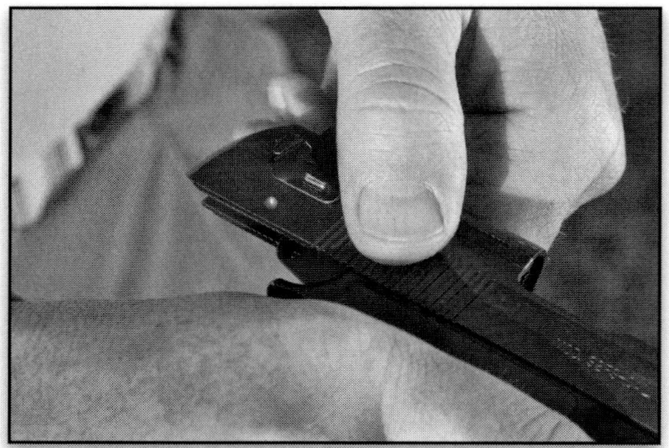

10.63 Sling shot technique with Beretta 92/M9.

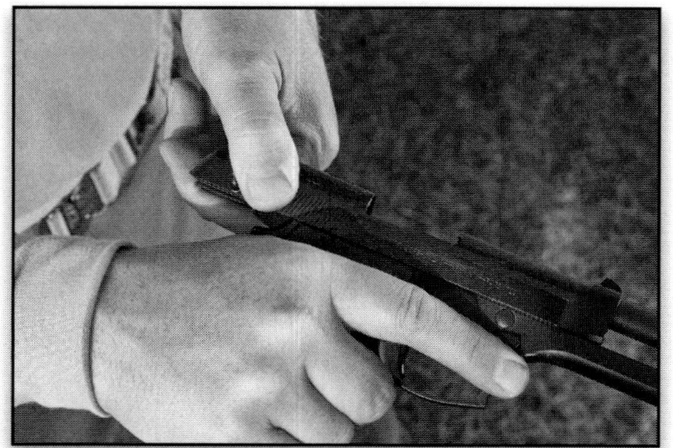

10.64 Weapon on safe.

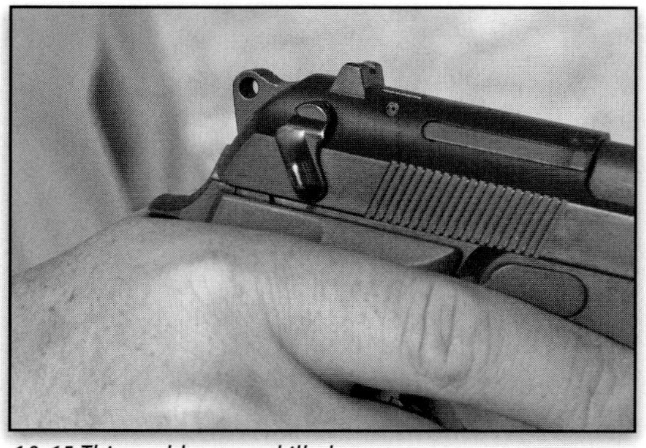

10.65 This could get you killed.

Speed Reload

10.66 When you feel the need for speed.

Speed reloads are often times taboo in the Military and Law Enforcement circles. Not really sure why you wouldn't want your soldiers or officers to have every tool available to use during a gunfight? I have seen many soldiers conduct speed reloads during real life contact with the enemy.

A speed reload is the same as the slide lock reload with the exception of not having to release the slide to go forward. This reload is used when speed is of the essence and you have the ability to go back and pick up the magazine you dropped, after the confrontation.

10.67 Release magazine as support hand moves to fresh mag.

I have also talked with Police Officers who have used this technique after engaging a suspect and moving to pursue. They don't want to take the time to stop and conduct a Tactical Reload, so they conduct a Speed Reload.

Speed Reload or Tactical Reload without retention, please call it what you want. The important thing is that you are happy and we have not upset any of the Gods of Tactical Pistol Craft.

On a serious note, your students are smarter than you give them credit for. Conduct drills that test all types of reloads. You are capable of setting up all kinds of realistic scenarios that will force the shooters to pick the type of reload to conduct. Stop dictating and start encouraging them to think outside of the flat range box.

10.68 As magazine is released, support hand is on fresh mag.

10.69 Partial magazine dropping, fresh mag on the way.

10.70 Weapon rotated just enough to see bottom edge of magazine well.

10.71 Start insertion of magazine.

10.72 Seat magazine aggressively.

10.73 Rotate weapon back to threat.

10.74 Quickly ready for action with a fully loaded pistol.

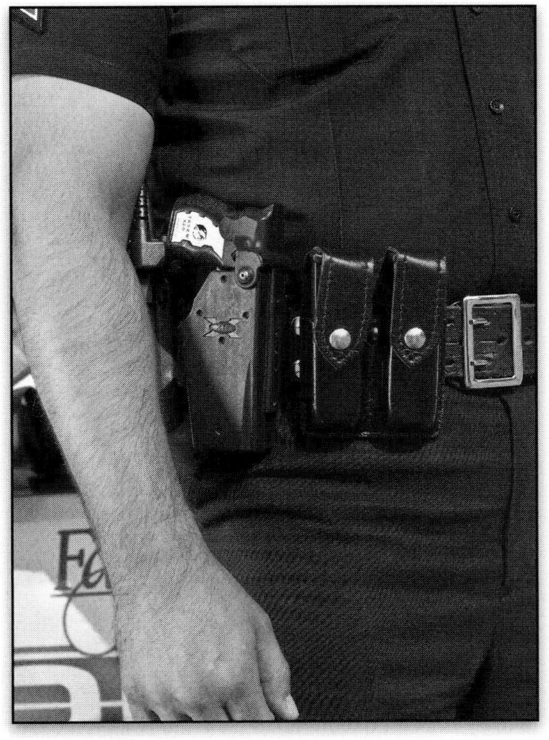

10.75 If using snap-top magazine pouches.

10.76 Use fingers to release snap.

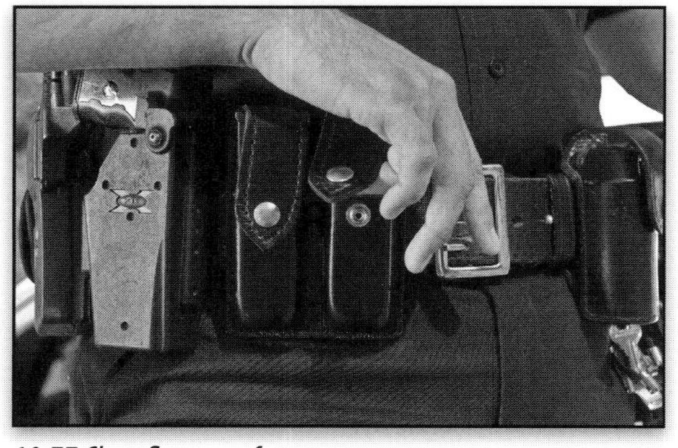

10.77 Clear flap out of your way.

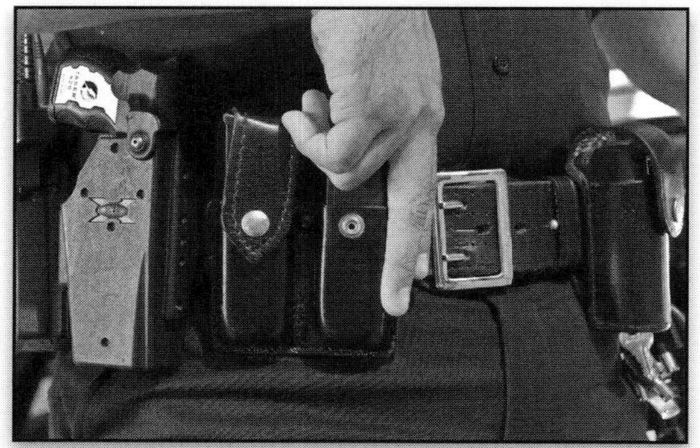

10.78 Get a positive, correct grip on magazine.

10.79 Pull magazine from pouch, ready to load.

Accessing magazines from under a jacket.

If you are attempting to access magazines from under a shirt or jacket, it is still critical that you get the same required grip on the magazine to conduct the load. If I am accessing a magazine while wearing a jacket or open front shirt, I use a knife cutting edge with the support hand. I start at my sternum and work straight to the rear, along my rib cage, until the hand is directly above the magazine location. I then go straight down to the magazines and use the same techniques that we have discussed in this chapter. The knife cutting edge works well to quickly get your hand where it needs to be. Not as fast as open and accessible magazine pouches, but still pretty quick.

10.80 Time to conduct a slide lock reload.

10.81 Start all movement simultaneously.

10.82 Knife cutting edge to sternum.

10.83 Transition to thumb/ribs.

10.84 Magazine released, correct grip on fresh magazine.

10.85 Quickly get the magazine from concealed pouch.

10.86 Drive the magazine to your pistol.

10.87 Look the magazine into the weapon.

10.88 Seat aggressively.

10.89 Once seated, start moving thumb to slide stop.

10.90 Release slide, eyes on target.

10.91 Ready to deliver lead on target. Repeat as necessary.

Raking out a stuck magazine

While reloading, you may run into magazines that don't quite fall all the way out, or remain stuck when the magazine release is pressed. If this happens to you, don't stop mid stroke and rip the magazine out. Continue with the reload to the point of bringing your fresh magazine to the weapon. At that point, use the edge of the magazine to rake the empty or partial magazine from the weapon. This is another reason magazine wells need to allow access to the front edge of the magazine. You should also have magazine base pads that allow you to get a purchase on the front edge. This can also be useful if you need to pull the magazine out but don't have the use of your support hand (getting shot, does happen). The extra protrusion on the front of the magazine will allow it to be hooked on the edge of a car door, door frame, or a piece of furniture.

10.92 Magazine release depressed but magazine stuck in the weapon.

10.93 Continue with normal sequence.

10.94 Hook baseplate of stuck magazine with edge of fresh mag.

10.95 Rake the magazine from the weapon and continue with reload.

Practicing your Reloads

After you have reviewed and truly understand the loading process, practice every type of reload to be ready for the day you are lucky enough to use your weapon for the elimination of an adversary. There won't be any time to think about what you are doing once the shooting starts.

Chapter 11, Malfunctions

11. MALFUNCTIONS

Training to fight through malfunctions is extremely important. If you have not only thought through but also conducted practical exercises with malfunctions and the clearances thereof, you will be way ahead of the game when a problem occurs in a gunfight.

Weapons are normally more prone to malfunction in a fight, so be prepared. These malfunctions may occur for several reasons. The weapon could become more exposed to dirt in a confrontation. You may not attain the perfect grip due to shooting one handed or having blood or rain on the grip of the weapon. Over gripping in a stressful situation may cause more malfunctions than normal. And the most likely culprit will simply be "Murphy," who is always there to jump in and screw something up.

As I discuss each malfunction, I will also describe how to fix the weapon in a timely manner.

Immediate Action

Immediate Action is what we will use to describe the immediate movement that you will take to rectify the malfunction. Immediate Action for a pistol will be Tap, Rack, Bang.

Tap Rack Bang

I have heard several descriptions of how to clear malfunctions, but for Immediate Action, Tap, Rack, Bang is the most simple and effective technique.

If you squeeze the trigger and nothing happens, or the hammer falls, striker drops, but nothing happens, we will immediately go into the Immediate Action of Tap, Rack, Bang.

Tap

First step is to tap the bottom of the magazine; it must be tapped with a purpose, not just touched. The reason for this first movement is to ensure the magazine is seated in the weapon. Not having the magazine properly seated is very common with pistols as well as carbines. Another reason we tap the magazine is to break loose any debris or ammunition that has jammed inside of the magazine. You may have dirt that causes rounds to stick, and the simple aggressive tap may break the rounds free from their obstruction. If a round is stuck on the feed ramp, the tapping may break the round loose allowing the weapon to go all the way into battery.

Rack

Second is the act of racking the slide. Racking is accomplished by quickly pulling the slide to the rear on the pistol. Once the slide is to the rear, it is unbelievably important to just let the slide slam forward. A common mistake during this step is to ride the slide forward with your hand, which retards the slide movement and can cause rounds to not fully chamber. In addition it can also cause other minute disruptions that will not allow the weapon to fire when you move to the last step, that being, the "bang."

Where you grab the pistol is important in the racking process as well. You have a better chance of quickly clearing the malfunction if you grab the slide from the rear and not near the front. Many custom weapons have front cocking serrations, they look great but you will be more efficient and safer if you use the rear serrations.

Bang

Now it is time to engage the target. The weapon's malfunction is cleared; you reassess the threat as you drive the weapon back to the target, you are absolutely sure it needs to be engaged.... Squeeze the trigger, Bang.

In order to properly practice the malfunctions that can be corrected with Immediate Action you will have to improvise. I prefer to start practicing these malfunction clearances with an unloaded weapon. You do not need a magazine in the weapon to practice Tap, Rack, Bang. Dummy rounds or training rounds work extremely well when mixed in with live ammunition to train yourself to instinctively correct these malfunctions. Always ensure that you remove all training ammunition before you head back out onto the street.

Which Malfunctions can be cleared with Immediate Action?

Poor Quality Ammunition

If you have ammunition that is questionable, such as poor primers or slightly mis-sized cartridges, these stoppages usually can be remedied with Immediate Action. Bad primers are not common, but they do exist, and Immediate Action will allow you to quickly get your weapon back into operation. If you get a click or a soft trigger, Immediate Action is the answer. Some poor quality ammo will also be slightly out of spec and will not run flawlessly in your weapon. Once again Immediate Action should work.

11.1 Weapon fails to fire.

11.2 This may look like an exaggeration, but I want you to tap as though your life depended on it.

11.3 Tap.

11.4 Rack using sling shot technique.

11.5 As you rack, roll the weapon towards the ejection port side.

11.6 This should help debris fall from the weapon.

11.7 Ensure slide is pulled all the way to the rear.

11.8 Let the slide slam forward.

11.9 Regrip.

11.10 Bang if necessary.

11.11 If you use the hand-over technique to rack the slide.

11.12 Ensure you keep the ejection port clear.

11.13 Let the slide slam into battery.

Magazine not seated

If the magazine is not seated correctly during the loading process or if you have taken a fall where inadvertent magazine release takes place, Immediate Action will fix this problem. Some shooters get ahead of themselves and skip the tap portion of Immediate Action. The tap is crucial in getting you and your weapon system back in the fight.

11.14 Magazine not seated.

Failure to Load Correctly

This may seem like a silly malfunction to have, however, I see this malfunction almost as much as I see any other. I must add this is usually with new or un-trained shooters. Once shooters understand the proper loading sequence, this malfunction can almost completely be eliminated.

Remedial Action

Remedial Action is the process that is required to fix a malfunction that Immediate Action won't fix. There are several trains of thought on Remedial Action. I may do things slightly different than others, but the end result is the same. The technique I use just happens to be a little faster, and we are in a gunfight.

Remedial Action usually entails the following. First you will conduct Immediate Action, and if this does not work or causes you to exacerbate the problem, we will move on to Remedial Action. My first step is to remove the magazine which may not be an easy task. Most teach the shooter to lock the slide to the rear before removing the magazine. I feel this is usually an unnecessary step, it is also time consuming and dangerous when attempting to do with one hand. Once the magazine is removed, you will be able to cycle the slide to the rear which should help to dislodge any ammunition or debris. I prefer to cycle the slide a minimum of two times. This will ensure that if you do lock the slide to the rear and have a spent or bad cartridge in the chamber, once you release the slide, you will cycle it again at least one additional time to remove the cartridge from the chamber. I teach the same principle for the Carbine, trying to streamline the process.

Remedial Action with a 1911

If you happen to be using a 1911 type pistol, you will be better off locking the slide to the rear before removing the magazine. Most high capacity weapons will not require this. Just be aware of the sequence if the 1911 is your pistol of choice.

Alternate Remedial Action

Another method that works well is simply holding the magazine button in and cycling the slide. If you attempt this with modern weapon systems you will have great success. Push the magazine button in, start cycling the weapon, the magazine and its contents should all hit the ground. Once the weapon is clear reload and get back to rocking and rolling.

11.15 Weapon malfunctions.

11.16 Initiate Immediate Action.

11.17 Tap.

11.18 Rack.

11.19 If this does not rectify the malfunction...

11.20 Rip the magazine from the weapon.

11.21 Let it drop.

11.22 Recover it later.

11.23 Cycle the weapon at least twice.

11.24 Be quick and use snappy movements.

11.25 This should allow any problem cartridge to fall free.

11.26 Reload the weapon.

11.27 Do not use the bad magazine.

11.28 Seat firmly.

11.29 Get a round in the chamber, get back in the fight.

Stovepipe

A Stovepipe malfunction occurs when a spent cartridge does not completely eject from the weapon. It is usually caused by a slightly weak extractor and possibly a poor performing ejector. This malfunction can also be caused by limp wristing (and yes, that is a technical term), or having a weak wrist when shooting with one hand. You may also experience a Stovepipe if you hold your weapon too close to a barricade or obstacle. Normally, the spent case will be stuck in the ejection port, not allowing the weapon to go completely into battery. More often than not, you will have a live round already beginning to feed into the chamber.

The Stovepipe malfunction doesn't really fit into Immediate or Remedial Action. If you conduct Immediate Action with a Stovepipe you will induce a double feed. As we stated earlier, a spent cartridge is blocking the forward movement of the slide which has already, more than likely, started to feed another live round into the chamber. If you conduct Remedial Action, you are wasting much needed time.

11.30 Stovepipe.

The first and most popular way to clear most stovepipes is to create a knife cutting edge with your non-firing hand, then sweep across the top of the weapon, dislodging the brass. There are two ways to sweep. If you sweep from the rear to the front it will work. But if you sweep from the front to the rear of the weapon you are moving your hand in the direction that allows for movement of the slide to aid in dislodging the brass. You also seem to have more power when sweeping from front to rear. You may need to slightly tap the rear of the slide to ensure it goes into battery. As you practice this process, be careful not to slice your hand on the sharp edge of the case mouth.

11.31 No matter how you look at it, you have a stovepipe.

The second way to clear a stovepipe is to grab the rear of the slide, pinching and pulling the slide slightly to the rear while rotating the weapon towards the ejection port side. This creates the space needed to let the brass fall from the weapon. Once the cartridge falls, simply let the slide slam forward into battery. You may need to slightly tap the rear of the slide with the heel of your hand to ensure it is in fact in battery.

11.32 Knife cutting edge of hand against stovepipe.

11.33 Be careful not to cut your hand.

11.34 Stovepipe should fall away, allowing you to fire the weapon.

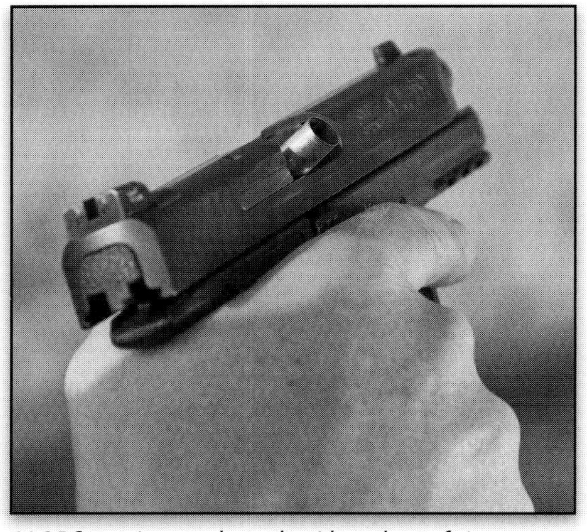

11.35 Stovepipe may be to the side and out of view.

11.36 Use same procedure.

11.37 Sweep quickly to the rear.

11.38 Ready to go.

Double Feed

The Double Feed usually causes more heartache than any other malfunction. That is, unless you have a completely inoperable weapon. The Double Feed can be caused by the magazine, or shooter error. As discussed previously, if you have a stovepipe and attempt to clear it with Immediate Action, you will induce a Double Feed. If your weapon's magazines are questionable, they will also induce a Double Feed. This occurs as the pistol's slide is pushed to the rear of the weapon during the firing cycle. As the slide goes to the rear, it pushes the rounds in the magazine down slightly. Once the slide is all the way to the rear of its travel, the top round of ammunition in the magazine may pop out, floating in the chamber/ ejection port area. As the slide moves forward it then also picks up the next round that is still held in the magazine, thus creating a Double Feed.

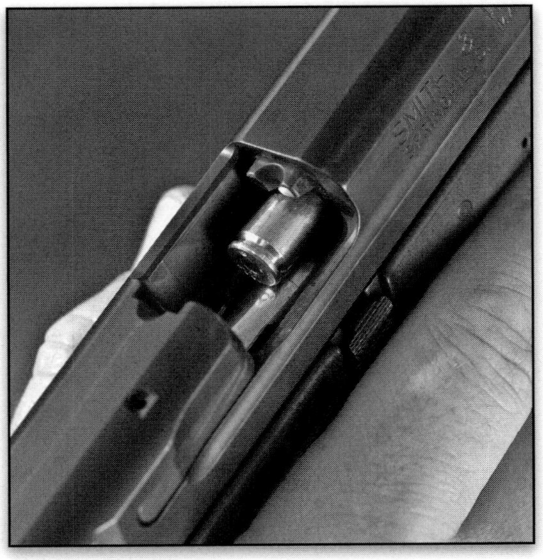

11.39 Double feed.

To clear the Double Feed you will first start with Immediate Action. Immediate Action may work if you are able to slightly roll the weapon towards the ejection port side. If this does not remedy the situation, move to Remedial Action. Remedial Action for a Double Feed is to remove the magazine, cycle the slide until you have no ammunition in the weapon, then reload the weapon with a fresh magazine and get back in the fight. Notice, I also did not lock the slide to the rear before removing the magazine. If you prefer to lock the slide to the rear first or you are shooting a 1911, by all means do so. There is nothing wrong with this technique other than it is more time consuming. I prefer to let the magazine hit the ground when clearing a Double Feed. I do not retain the magazine until I have loaded the weapon and am ready to react to any threat and then I will pick up the dropped/bad magazine.

If you have Double Feeds, mark that magazine to let yourself know that it is in fact bad. Also, in case you skip the Chapter on Gear, make sure you have all your magazines numbered so you know which magazines are working and which ones are suspect.

11.40 Another technique for clearing a double feed.

11.41 Press magazine release.

11.42 Cycle slide while holding magazine release.

11.43 Magazine will drop, rounds will fall out.

11.44 Continue to cycle until clear.

11.45 Once clear, reload.

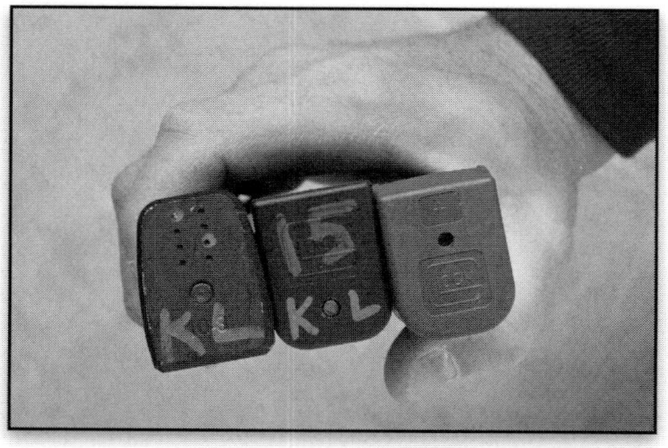

11.46 Number your magazines for easy identification.

Stuck Case

Once you feel you have mastered the malfunctions listed above, along comes the Stuck Case. Most Stuck Cases can be cleared without tools, that is, if the extractor is able to hold the cartridge. Most Stuck Cartridges I have seen are live rounds, not fired and empty casings. This sometimes stumps students when it is actually a very easy malfunction to clear. As you conduct Immediate Action you will notice that the slide is stuck forward, and not easily jerked out of battery. At this point I take the support hand and grab the top of the slide with my thumb towards my chest, in an overhand grip. Once I have a firm grasp, and I am not covering the ejection port with my support hand, I use the firing hand to aggressively drive the frame forward. This motion has to be quick and snappy, you do not want to lose control of the weapon and become unsafe. You are trying to break the round loose with this quick pop. Once it is released, transfer the weapon back into the firing hand and clear the round from the weapon with your normal slide manipulation.

Most Stuck Cartridges are just not sized correctly; it is rare that you will see a stuck case with a fired round. Most weapons have extremely reliable extractors.

11.47 Over-handed grab on rear of slide.

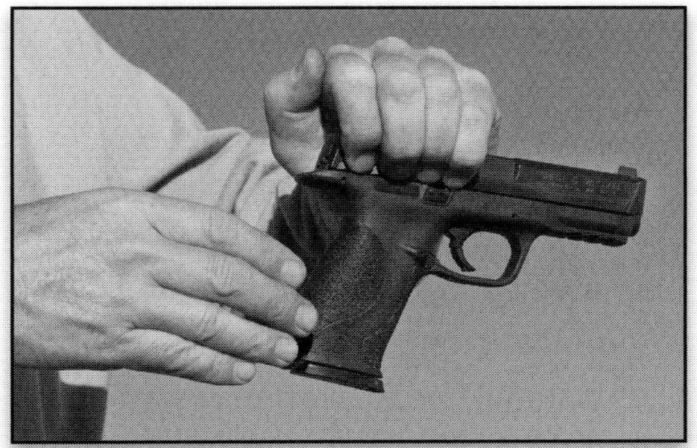

11.48 Maintain a good grip with support hand.

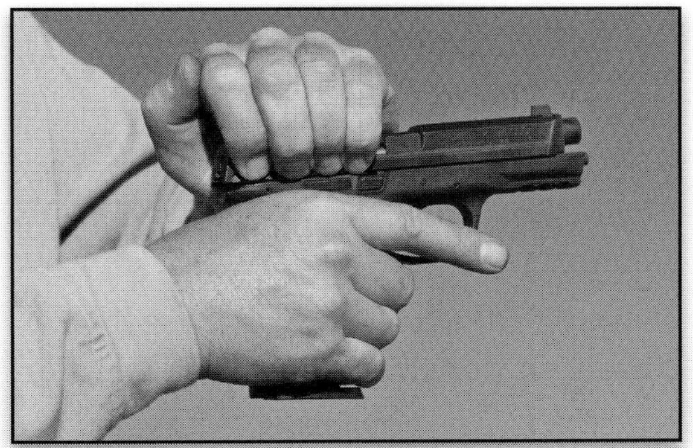

11.49 Slam firing hand forward to dislodge stuck case.

11.50 Continue pulling to the rear to clear the case. Slightly rolling the weapon towards the ejection port can help clear the cartridge.

Failure to Extract

A Failure to Extract is similar to a stuck case; however the weapon may cause it more than the ammo. If you have a Failure to Extract, you will routinely need to clear the weapon as though it were a Double Feed. In fact you may have a malfunction that looks a lot like a Double Feed, with the exception being that the cartridge in the chamber has been fired. This is also the difference between the Stuck Cartridge and the Failure to Extract. A Stuck Cartridge usually happens with a live round that did not go all the way into battery.

A Failure to Extract may involve removing your pocket tool to help with the extraction of the spent case. The causes of a Failure to Extract may vary, most I have seen involve a broken or poorly adjusted extractor. Other Failures to Extract that I have seen are caused by weak case rims that are torn through by the extractor.

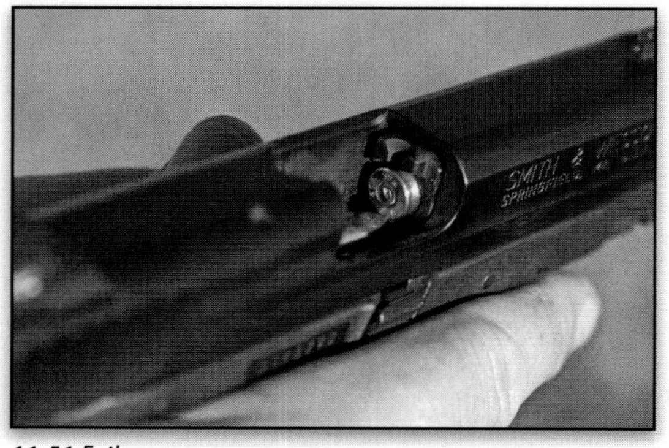

11.51 Failure to extract.

Malfunction Summary

The malfunctions discussed here are the most common that we see on a daily basis during pistol courses and the most likely for you to encounter.

If you have a proper functioning weapon, the above malfunctions will still occur. Always work to analyze these malfunctions and remedy the situation.

You may experience several other types of malfunctions that are related to the weapon's operation. If you have a weapon that is not working correctly, there are several other issues you may encounter. Each weapon type has problems that may come about if there are broken parts or parts that are not fitted correctly; you may also encounter issues if the weapon is dirty.

During your practice sessions pay attention to what malfunctions you have. As we stated earlier, number your magazines and sort out the culprits if it happens to be a magazine related malfunction. If it is not a magazine issue, try to determine the cause, e.g. poor ammo, or a broken or worn part. Do not enter the real world with a weapon that is questionable. Get the weapon fixed and always have a backup plan. As we say in the Army, "Two is one, and one is none."

Get back in the FIGHT

Malfunctions are often an afterthought to our day-to-day tactical training. You must practice these malfunction clearance techniques until they become second nature. Too often shooters have a tendency to stop, analyze, and then attempt to fix their weapon rather than reacting and automatically going into Immediate and Remedial Action. You are creating bad habits by not practicing and drilling these techniques. You must work with a sense of urgency to get the weapon back in the fight; you may not have much time.

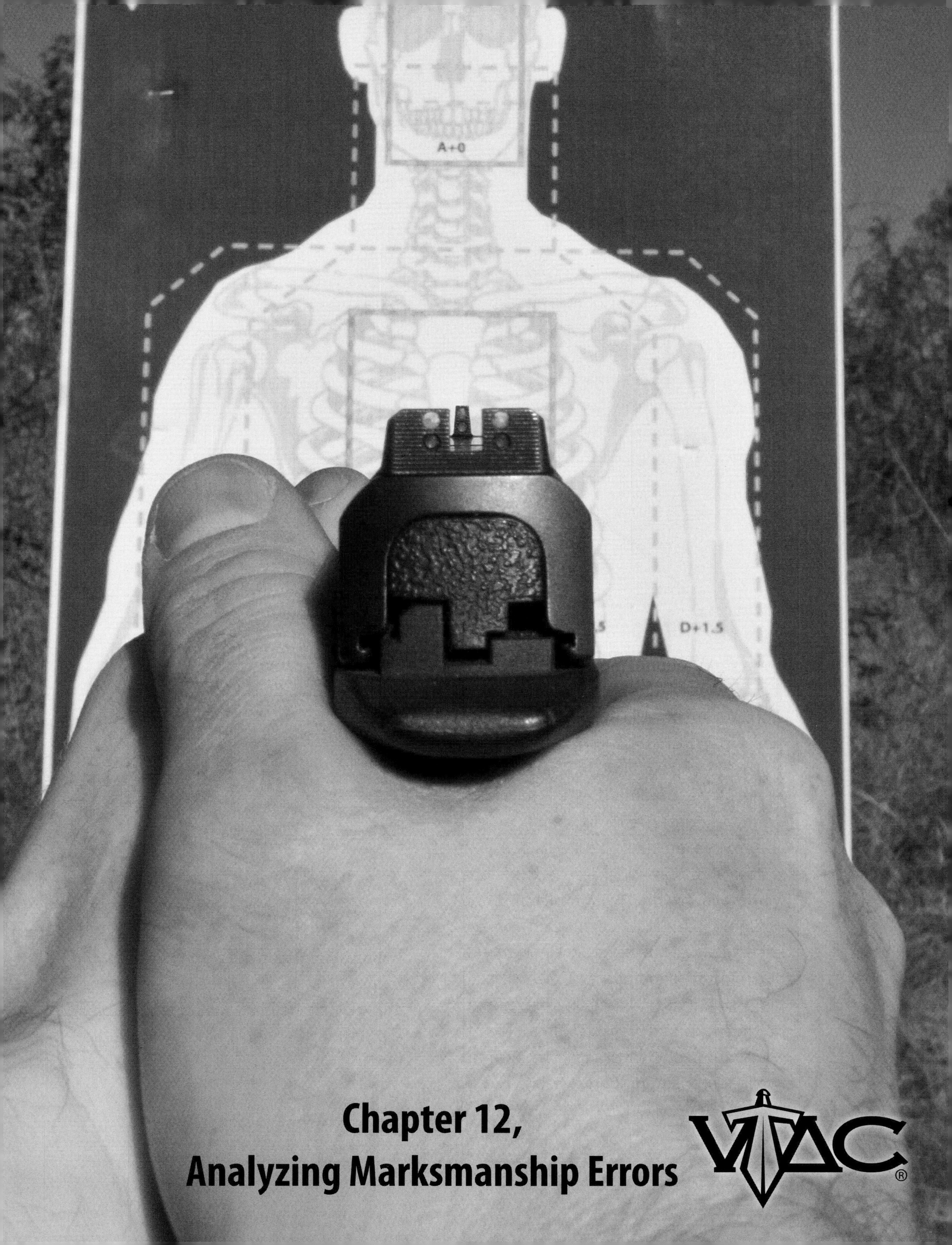

Chapter 12, Analyzing Marksmanship Errors

12. ANALYZING MARKSMANSHIP ERRORS

Basic analytical tools

Common Marksmanship errors are constantly occurring no matter your level of expertise. If you do not hit exactly where you wanted to, there was an error. The chart below outlines some causes, but we need to reference these mistakes and discuss them in depth so you will absolutely understand the issue that may be affecting your marksmanship.

The diagram below is referenced for a Right Handed shooter, for Left handed shooters, reverse the image. This diagram was built with the Pistol Marksmanship shooter in mind, not the tactical shooter. Some say it is the same, I would agree up to a certain point, right up to the point where we put two hands on the weapon. Therefore the tactical shooter must break off and take a slightly different path if you want to make gains in speed, coupled with accuracy.

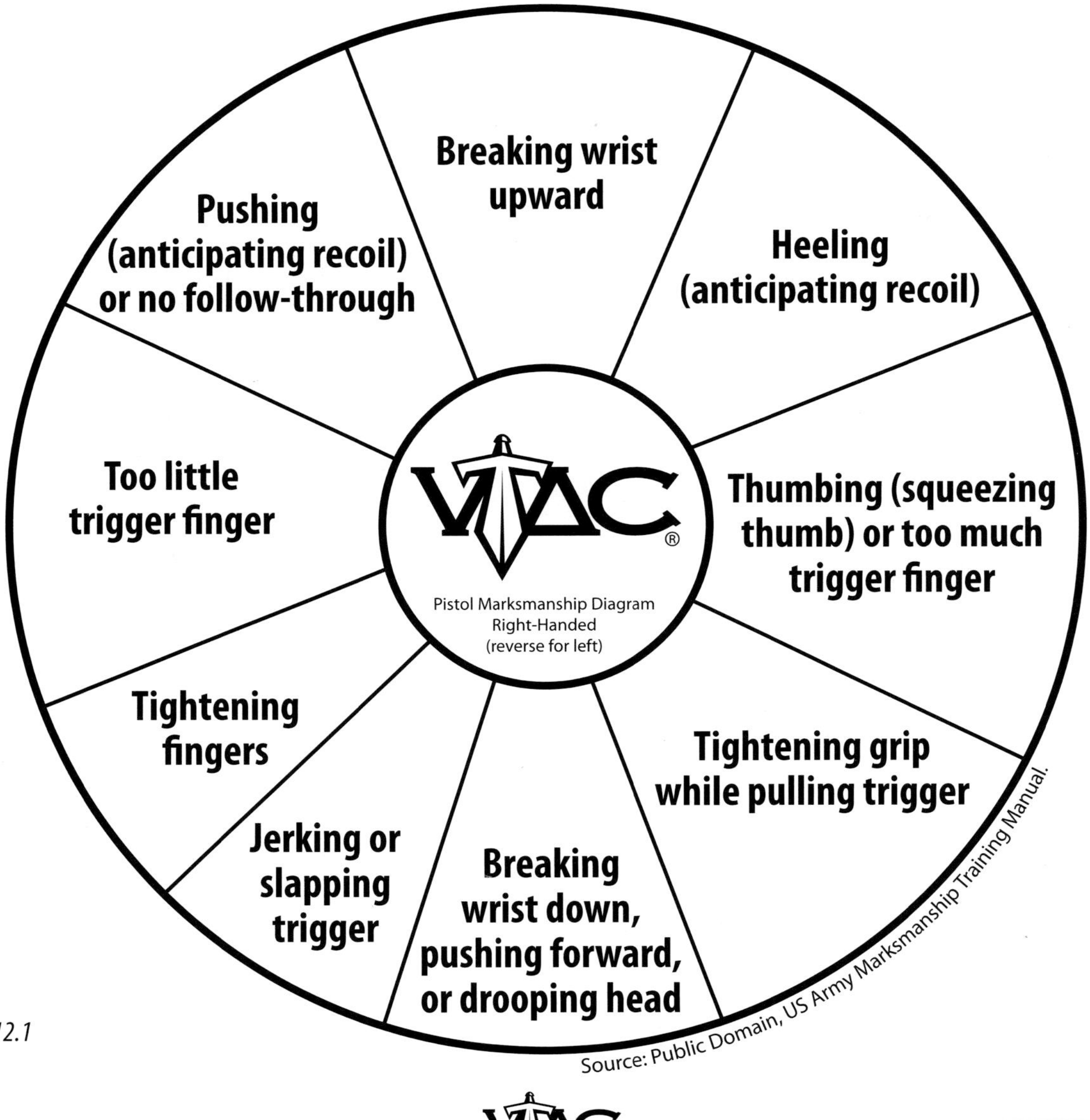

12.1

Natural Point of Aim

In order to have a good Natural Point of Aim you must first clearly understand what this term means. Natural Point of Aim is where you naturally point your weapon. Eyes closed, where does your weapon point? Where does the weapon want to go after recoil? I would classify this as your Natural Point of Aim. Some shooters do not believe that Natural Point of Aim applies to Tactical Shooting. I would disagree with this statement. If you can somewhat set your stance to shoot close to where your Natural Point of Aim would lie, then why not do it? I do feel this is more relative to the Carbine and Rifle, however you should try to attain a perfect Natural Point of Aim when working on your pistol accuracy as well. Get into a comfortable Fighting Stance; bring the weapon to bear on your target. Close your eyes and move the weapon slightly back and forth until you feel completely comfortable. Now open your eyes, where are you pointed? If you are not pointed at the target, readjust your feet to align with the Natural Point of Aim. This will take some practice, but before you know it you will naturally rotate your body into the correct position without needing to close your eyes. This skill will help to improve your accuracy as well as aid in quickly getting back on target after recoil.

Common Errors

Jerking the trigger

Probably the most prevalent problem that we see is the trigger jerk. There are several factors that come into play when jerking the trigger. Anticipation of recoil is one, trying to make the weapon fire is another. The weapon should surprise you with each shot, not to the point it is making you jump, but you shouldn't be making the weapon go off. Hard to explain, but if you are not seeing the sights recoil from the point that you are aiming at, you may be anticipating the recoil and jerking the trigger.

Another cause is having an extremely heavy trigger pull. This is common with Law Enforcement who through frivolous lawsuits and poor training have decided that a heavy trigger will answer all of their problems. You don't want a light trigger (2-3 lbs) but you also don't want a heavy trigger (8-12 lbs). A happy medium is about a 4.5 lb trigger weight. This is a safe trigger, won't surprise you accidentally, but also doesn't require a weight belt to pull.

Over gripping the weapon will also cause a trigger jerk. The firing grip should remain at about 30-40% of your grip; the support hand should be doing 60-70% of the work. If you over grip you will lose your fine motor skill that is needed to efficiently and smoothly pull the trigger straight to the rear. This over gripping

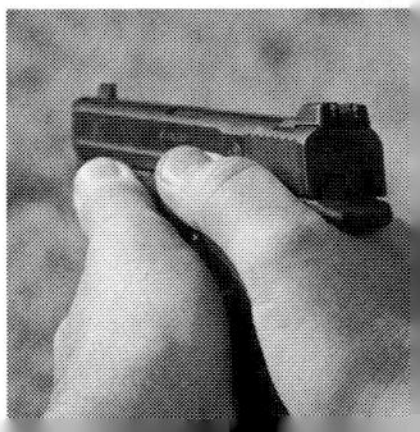

will also degrade your ability to make multiple shots quickly without jerking not only the trigger finger but the whole hand. I see this all the time when we push shooters' limits as they gyrate their entire hand due to the excessive pressure.

Jerking the trigger will cause your rounds to impact low left for a right-handed shooter, and low right for a left handed shooter.

Anticipating Recoil

I cannot stress enough how anticipating recoil can destroy your accuracy. Obviously we all are aware of the recoil pulse that hits us when we fire the weapon, however we cannot let this influence our sight alignment until the bullet has left the barrel. Relax and let the weapon surprise you with every shot.

Looking over the weapon

It isn't highlighted in the chart; however, shooting low is often caused by looking over the weapon with all of your focus on the target rather than your sights. Some shooters decide they can shoot faster by looking at the target, and in most cases they are correct, they can shoot really fast. Problem with this is they can't hit anything. You must continue to look through your sights, even if you slightly change your focus down range, you must see the sights in alignment with the target. Point shooters push the point that they look at the target, not at their sights. If you are going to be successful, you absolutely must see your sights. Dull sights are still sights, at closer ranges the crystal clear, sharp image is sacrificed for speed. Do not try to construe this as point shooting, it is absolutely not. If the target is farther away we have crisp or clear sights and a somewhat fuzzy, out of focus target. As we get closer the focus will shift from crisp sights to slightly fuzzy but still properly aligned and a more focused target. Using sights that are highly visible will aid in shooting extremely fast and accurate at the closer ranges. The Fiber Optic sights will definitely help in this type of daylight scenario, and at night the iron sight outline or the tritium will help to force the sights into alignment.

Drive with your legs

A key indicator of incorrect stance and use of the legs is this: your plate hits get progressively higher or lower as you swing across a rack of steel targets or across a bank of several paper targets.

Not hitting steel plates on a plate rack should indicate that you might want to check your stance and what parts of the leg are being used to drive the weapon. If your stance is not driven by the quads you may have issues with the sights driving up or down as you twist across the targets. In order to check for this problem, drive the weapon's sights to the first target, once you are comfortable that you are where you want to be, close your eyes and drive the weapon to the last target. Open your eyes and see where your sights are aligned. Are you high or low? If so, it is more likely your stance and the drive of your legs than anything else. Keep working your stance until you figure out the issue. If you don't get this corrected you will be making adjustments as you shoot that are not necessary. With a little practice you will have this issue dealt with.

For those of you who are disciplined Marksman, this is the equivalent of natural point of aim for the tactical marksman. You want to naturally look at the target and be able to naturally push your weapon in that direction.

12.2 Aggressive fighting stance.

12.3 Shooter has driven the weapon using his legs and hips.

12.4 Shooter not driving with legs, just twisting upper body resulting in a less-than-desireable stance.

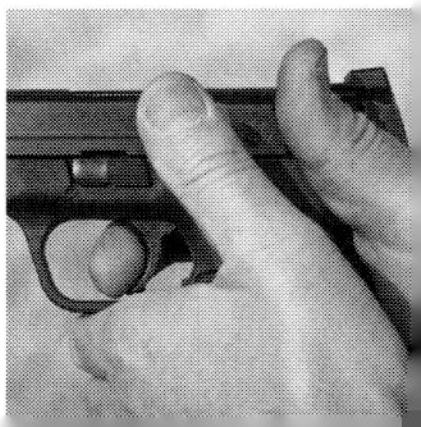

Not enough finger on the trigger

Many instructors preach less finger on the trigger. It has been my experience that most shooters could use a little more trigger finger. This is very true of the M-4 type platform, but it is also true with the Tactical Pistol. Pulling the trigger finger out of the trigger guard to get less finger on the trigger can cause the shooter to be in an un-natural position. This doesn't just affect the finger; this will have an impact on your grip as well. If you let the hand lay naturally, think a little more rather than a little less finger and it will probably make a difference with your speed and accuracy at normal engagement ranges.

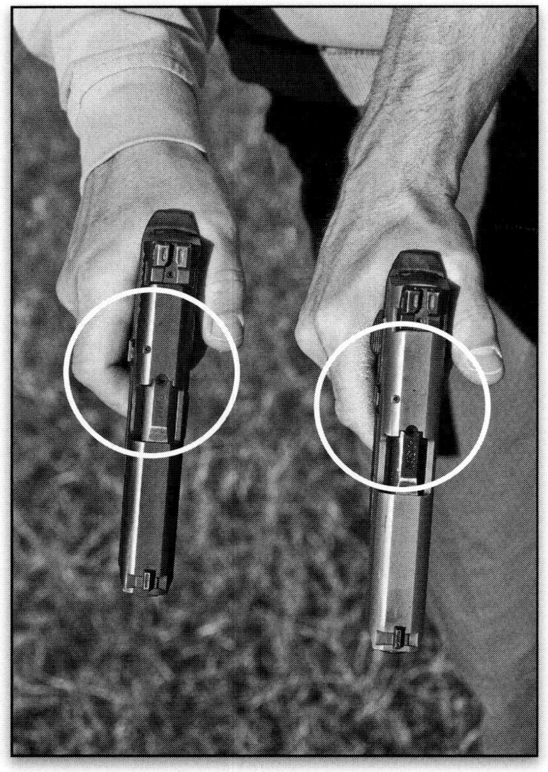

12.5 Unnatural finger placement.

12.6 Shooters should find what works for them.

Shots going high and low, no consistency

This is usually caused by the support hand grip. If you do not have the correct grip with the support hand, there will be no definitive stopping point for the weapon during recoil. If you have the support hand in a position creating the forward cant towards the target, the weapon should automatically come to rest in this position after the recoil sequence has been completed. Once again, this is part of follow through. If you continually have to press the weapon back down to be correctly aligned with the target, this is the support hand. If the support hand is not working more than the strong hand, you need to switch the percentages to 60/40, or 70/30 support hand pressing harder than the strong hand.

Over-swinging Targets

This will be discussed several times, which should drive home the point of how critical this can be. If you are over-swinging targets, you are not leading with your eyes. Get those eyes out in front of the weapon every time you move your pistol. This is unbelievably important. Where your eyes go, the weapon will follow. Just like pointing a finger.

Check for a complete grip

In the chart you will see many problems caused by parts of the hand, other than the trigger finger. To complete the grip, you must ensure that you have your strong thumb up allowing the support hand to gain as much grip as possible. Also, make sure the support hand is not gripping the trigger guard; this won't be possible with a weapon mounted light, so don't do it without the light. You will also have a tendency to pull the weapon from side to side if you grab the trigger guard with your support hand.

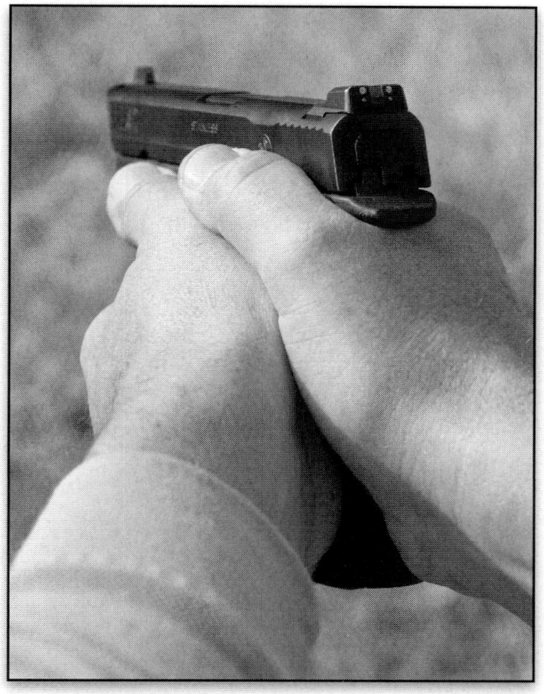

12.7 Complete grip.

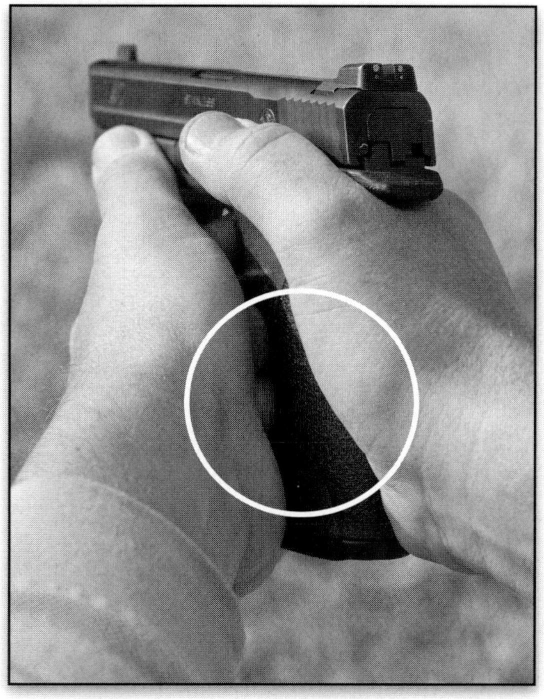

12.8 Poor grip, not making use of complete pistol grip.

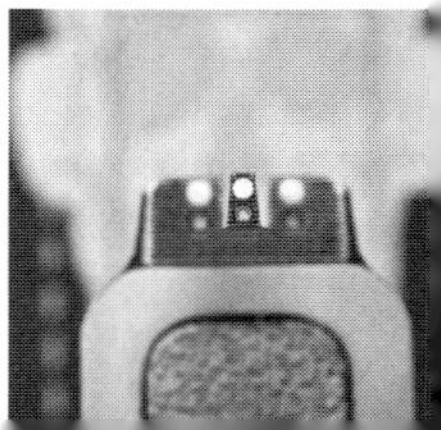

Hands coming apart during recoil

This issue is normally easy to fix with a positive grip, ensuring that the strong and support hands are together towards the heels of the hands. If the hands snap apart, you should also check to see that your support hand is using the ledge formed by your strong hand's fingertips. If you are an Officer or Military shooter, you should be shooting with gloves anyway. That of course is if they are part of your daily deployment uniform.

12.9-10 Note during this sequence, poor recoil control, including hands coming apart during recoil.

Pushing with the Support Side thumb on the frame

Your support hand thumb should not put pressure on the frame or the slide of the weapon. Over gripping with the thumb will cause you to push the weapon towards your strong side. You may also induce a stoppage if you have the thumb on the slide of the pistol.

The importance cannot be emphasized enough, you must know what causes your shooting errors. Find a credible instructor to help you quickly figure this out. If you are planning to instruct you must be able to quickly help your students. They may head out the door directly into a gunfight. If you are training yourself, slow down and work through all of the issues you come upon. You too will be in a gunfight sooner than you may think.

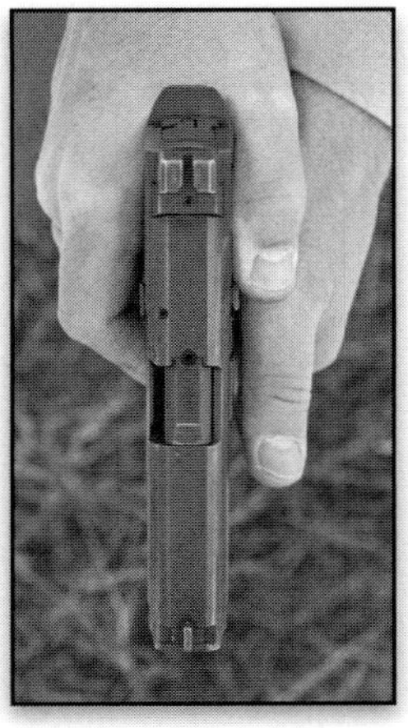

12.11 Correct grip - thumb not pushing on frame.

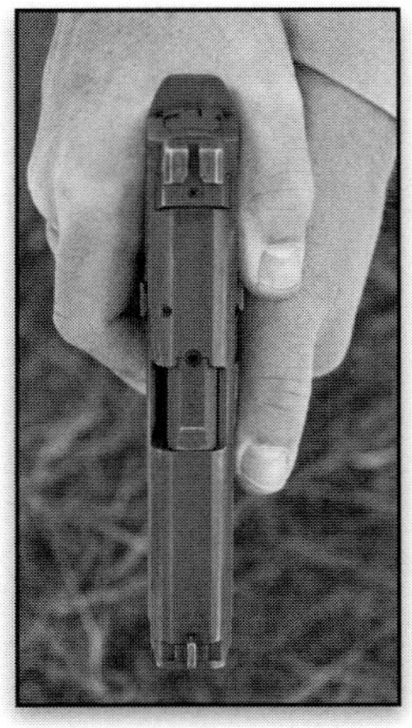

12.12 Pressure on frame from thumb will cause accuracy issues.

Chapter 13, Pistol Selection

13. PISTOL SELECTION

When it is time to select your pistol and accessories, simple rules should apply. If your pistol is an issued weapon, then you may or may not have much say in the situation. Most pistols on the market today are extremely high quality and have great reliability. There can be significant differences in shootability, but reliability must rate high on a Combat Shooter's pistol scale.

No matter what type of pistol you have in your holster, there are certain rules that should apply to most. We will also cover specifics pertaining to some pistols on the market.

Caliber Selection

The age-old question that keeps most gun magazines in business is "Which caliber is the best?" Over and over, every month of every year we continue to see articles citing some supposed, real world engagement that caused a shooter to come to some great conclusion with regard to ammunition performance. The bottom line is this: Shoot good quality ammo in a package that is well suited for you.

I carried a .45 ACP pistol for years, it was an issued pistol. I was happy to have .45 ACP, but not especially happy with the limited capacity of the pistol or with its pathetic performance in austere conditions.

If you have small hands or are unable to control the recoil of larger calibers, you will be much better off getting a pistol that will fit your hands and is relatively controllable. The other benefit of a smaller handgun caliber is the larger capacity. 9mm ammunition will perform well against the human target, especially in this modern day and age with an abundance of quality ammunition on the market. 40 S&W may perform slightly better than the 9mm, but will start to degrade magazine capacity and is significantly harder to handle during recoil. Lastly, if you have to compensate for some shortcoming in your life and need to carry a 45 ACP pistol, (just kidding guys, wanted to make sure I had your attention) you will more than likely have 10 or less rounds and may experience more malfunctions than those shooting pistols in 9mm or 40 S&W from the same manufacturer.

I will purposely skip the discussion of any other calibers that are on the market due to the fact that this book is intended to be about shooting, not the arms race. There are plenty of other calibers that will satisfy your needs, just ensure that the caliber you chose allows you to successfully eliminate a threat if necessary.

Pistol Selection

As I stated earlier, you may be issued a pistol. If this is the case you may still want to read this section to better understand what is available and why others may or may not have selected certain pistols on the market.

13.1 Top-bottom: .45 ACP, .40 S&W, 9mm

Pistol Action Types

Just to clarify descriptions later in this chapter and the rest of the book, I would like to explain differences in action types.

Single Action Automatic

Single Action pistols are pistols that have a thumb safety that must be disengaged before firing. The weapon is in a cocked position at all times. This means that the firing mechanism is ready to fire the weapon as soon as the sear releases the hammer. The most popular Single Action pistol is the 1911 type weapon system. The benefit of the Single Action pistol is that the weapon has a decent trigger pull with very little **take up** (the amount of movement required to make the weapon fire) or **over travel** (the amount of rearward movement of the trigger after the weapon fires). The **reset** (amount of distance the trigger must be released, in order to reset the disconnector so the sear is prepared to fire again) is normally minimal as well. The downfalls of this particular weapon are that it can be somewhat dangerous for those that have not trained extensively on it. Some organizations also feel that the weapon is unsafe since the safety may come off accidentally during normal carry. With respect to the 1911, there are additional safeties that are also built into the weapon. 1911's have a grip safety that is located where the web of your hand rests and must be pushed forward to allow the trigger to be pushed to the rear. This was

13.2 Single action, automatic 1911.

13.3 Single action, automatic 1911.

always difficult for me, so in order to allow a positive disengagement, I actually had the grip safety deactivated. If you decide to deactivate this safety, you must be absolutely sure the thumb safety is used since it will be the only remaining safety. The 1911 also has an exposed hammer, which can become caught on clothing as well as is exposed to dirt and debris.

During the battle in Mogadishu, one operator attempted to fire his 1911 pistol at an enemy that was sneaking up to his position. When he pulled the trigger the hammer did not go forward, it seems a large amount of sand had been blown into the hammer mechanism during the Helicopter insertion. Luckily he had a hand grenade that he employed on that particular threat.

13.4 Grip safety on an 1911.

13.5 Browning Hi-Power 9mm and 1911 .45 ACP.

Double Action Automatic

Double Action pistols are pistols that generally have a first trigger pull that is similar to that of a revolver. Typically with these pistols, the trigger squeezes of the first and second rounds are completely different. This is good and bad; it is good because the pistol is relatively safe when carried. It is bad because you have a painfully long, heavy, trigger squeeze for the first shot, followed up by a much lighter, single action type trigger squeeze on the second shot. The M9 (Beretta 92) that was adopted by the US Army is such a pistol. If you decide that you are finished shooting, you also have to depress a de-cocking lever to get the hammer to move safely to the forward position. Many shooters have mastered this type of pistol, but for some they are difficult and border on unsafe if you don't have a good habit of de-cocking. Another version of the double action automatic would be the Sig 226; these pistols are very popular with certain military units as well as LE personnel. There are slight differences in the operation of the de-cocking levers for these two pistols. The Sig's lever is spring-loaded and will return to the fire position; the Beretta 92, on the other hand uses the de-cocking lever as a safety as well. If the weapon is de-cocked and the lever is not put back into the fire position manually, the weapon will not fire. Since the Military adopted this version, Beretta has improved on the design, adding a spring-loaded de-cocking lever in the same position. Now there is no worry

13.6 Double action autos, top: Beretta 92, bottom: Sig Sauer P228, both 9mm.

13.7 Kahr P9 9mm DAO (Double Action Only)

with regard to accidentally leaving the lever in the wrong position, or putting it in the safe position during reloads or any time the hand comes in contact to pull the slide to the rear.

DAO: Double Action Only

Double Action Only pistols are those that not only have the Double Action first shot, but every shot after that as well. These pistols are not easy to shoot, but they do make sense for some organizations. The best part of this design is that you don't have to de-cock the pistol once you are finished shooting. Once you release the trigger, the system goes back to its original configuration. I feel like I am shooting a revolver every time I handle a DAO pistol, the consistency does help some shooters though. Accuracy can sometimes suffer with this type of pistol, as DAO is a large hurdle to jump, over and over again.

Striker Fired

Striker Fired pistols are some of the most popular pistols in the Law Enforcement world. Glock has the most commonly used Striker Fired pistol on the market. In the last few years others have started to follow suit. Smith and Wesson with their M&P series pistols, as well as Springfield Armory with the XD pistol. All of these have slight differences, but overall they are quite similar. The Safe Action pistol does not require extensive training since the trigger is the same on every squeeze; but these pistols can be viewed as dangerous when you realize that all you have to do is squeeze the trigger, no manual safety is involved. Smith and Wesson has designed a version of their M&P pistol with an external thumb safety, this should be very popular in years to come. Other departments have increased the trigger pull weight to incredibly insane levels. The New York trigger for a Glock tips the scales at 11-12 lbs. Not a lot

13.8 Striker fired, top: Glock 19 9mm, bottom S&W M&P 9mm

of accurate shooting going on with that trigger, but the good thing is we have taken care of those poor creatures who infest the higher ranks of some Police Departments and worry more about liability than their own Officer's safety.

Reliability

Reliability is the absolute, number one, most important feature I seek in any pistol I use. This is what has driven me for years to figure out what needed to be done to improve reliability. I have heard shooters say, "My pistol is very reliable, the magazines just don't work." Well the magazines are part of the system. If they don't work, you are really not getting the reliability you are looking for. Ammunition is part of this equation as well, but your pistol should be reliable with a large variety of ammunition types, bullet weight differences should not shut your pistol down.

Maintenance

Maintenance is a fact of life if you want your weapon to function flawlessly. There isn't a modern firearm on the planet that

13.9 Reliability: The #1 need in a combat pistol.

will continue to work without proper cleaning, lube, and parts replacement. Even for the shooter who does not fire an excessive amount of ammunition through their weapon, the need to clean is still relevant. More importantly, the need for lubrication is huge. I am known for a lack of maintenance to my weapon systems. I do joke about this; however, if you look at my weapons, they are all lubed above and beyond the normal amount. I keep the barrels extremely clean, and the rest of the weapon well lubed. If the weapon is to be carried daily, I still apply generous amounts of lubrication, not excessive, but very generous. This results in a few

13.10 Toothbrush, gun oil, bore snake and multi-tool.

clothes ending up with oil stains. This is just the price of doing business with a weapon.

Parts Breakage

Another important part of the reliability equation is parts breakage. I want a pistol that has extreme reliability, and I will not stand for constant parts replacement and parts breakage. The parts I have seen break most are the following.

1911 Pistols

Normally in the 1911, extractors are the most frequently broken part. Whatever the reason, the 1911 type extractor continuously breaks hooks. If this part breaks, the weapon will not work. A properly tuned extractor will limit but not totally eliminate this parts breakage.

13.11 1911 extractor.

Beretta 92F/M9

The Beretta has a locking block mechanism that has been the number one part I have seen break in classes throughout the years, both in and outside of the military. If the locking block breaks, the weapon will cease to fire. Ensure you have the latest versions of the M9 locking block; this will make a huge difference in the life span of this part.

Sig P220

The SIG P220 has a reputation for breaking the take down lever, which is surprising to the shooter when their slide flies forward of the firing line. Of course if the slide isn't on the weapon, your shooting is over.

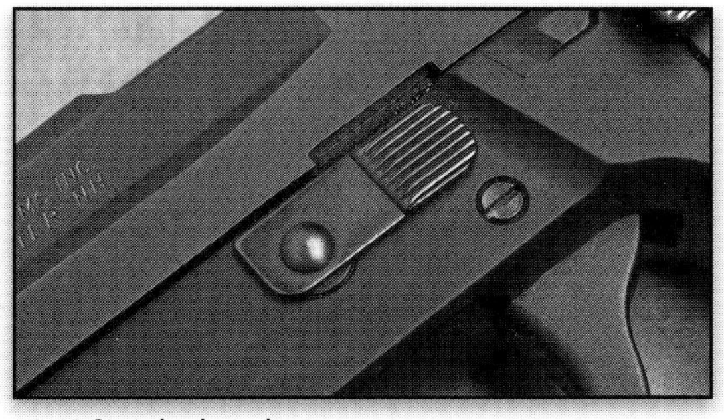

13.12 Sig take down lever

Glock

I have seen several slide stop springs break in the Glock. However, even with this spring broken, the weapon would continue to fire, as long as you held the slide stop in the down position. I have

13.13 Glock slide stop with spring.

also seen a few trigger pins break in the Glock pistols, and once again the weapons continued to fire.

When the Marine Corps tested the Glock 21, several trigger pins broke, the weapons never stopped firing, and the broken parts were only detected during routine cleaning and maintenance. This story is often told, but those opposing modern weapons that contain polymer parts, routinely leave out the part about the weapon continuing to function. It seems the pistol did extremely well, passed the test with flying colors, but the Commandant of the Marine Corps at the time decided he knew better and didn't want his Marines to have a plastic pistol. This has been the case in many arenas, hard line, and anti anything new and improved. The old way is not always the best way.

After Market Parts

When I have students wondering what the biggest contributing factor to malfunctions might be, I would have to say that it is normally after market parts. A good example of this would be magazine base pads. Magazines that normally work can become unreliable, almost immediately, with the addition of a capacity enhancing, magazine base pad.

Trigger parts that have been added to improve trigger weight are also culprits for disrupting the normal function of the weapon system. With all of this being said, the worst functioning guns are those that have been plumbed on, by an unqualified gunsmith. Don't think I am throwing stones, I fall into that category. I am better off on the shooting end, not on the gunsmithing end. I have a good pit crew that keeps my racecar on the road, and lets me focus on driving. The money spent on a gunsmith will easily offset the cost of migraine medication if you decide to do it yourself.

Shootability

It may sound absurd, but some shooters don't consider shootability when they purchase a pistol. All things being equal with regard to weight and reliability, why wouldn't you want the most shootable weapon? Here are a few things to keep in mind. How does the pistol fit your hands? Do you have enough room if you have huge hands, or if your hands are small, can you actually reach the controls? I have seen several smaller handed shooters who had difficulty even reaching the trigger on their Double Action Pistols.

If the weapon hurts to fire, you need to fix the issue. An example of this is the bump on the bottom of the Glock trigger guard. I make sure to grind this bump down and polish it, to eliminate pain when I shoot a heavy recoil Glock such as the Glock 22/40 S&W. You may not notice this when firing 50 rounds, but try 500 and see what needs to be smoothed and polished. You will also need to realize that toughening your hands is part of the game. But if there are sharp edges, no amount of toughening will eliminate sore hands, or worse yet, bloody hands.

Smith and Wesson developed the beavertail on their M&P pistols simply for the shootability aspect of this equation. They looked at what was wrong with other pistols and fixed the problem. I have not seen a shooter get slide bit on their hand yet, when shooting the M&P. This also adds to the shootability of this weapon system, by getting the shooter's hand as high as possible.

The ability to easily change the grip inserts on the M&P is another great feature. This has allowed the shooter to use the medium insert on their 9MM and 40S&W size frame and the small insert on the .45ACP frame, now the difference in frame size is truly negligible.

Extended Controls on Combat Weapons

Extended controls are absolutely needed on some weapons used in Combat and home defense situations. On the other hand, some extended controls are nothing but a solution to a problem that didn't exist. The first weapon on the list to discuss is the 1911.

1911 Extended Controls:

Beavertail Grip Safety

The original 1911 design had a less than desirable grip safety, after limited firing the shooter normally had a bruised or bloody hand. Adding a Beavertail grip safety does not degrade the functioning and reliability of the 1911, unless installed incorrectly. If you ask me, this is a must on this type of weapon.

Extended/Ambidextrous Thumb Safety

I am a firm believer in being able to shoot your weapon with either hand at any time with little to no problem with safety disengagement. The only way this is possible with the 1911 is by the addition of the ambidextrous thumb safety lever. I also prefer a slightly extended version that allows my thumb to sit securely during firing of the weapon, which will actually help with recoil control and muzzle rise. It is important that a gunsmith fits these parts because they are not drop in parts. If used properly, this part will be used to help eliminate muzzle rise. The additional torque put on this part will easily break the part if it isn't extremely rugged. It is common for some versions of the ambidextrous safety to come lose during firing and not allow

13.14 Smith and Wesson M&P sits low in hand and has nice beavertail, very shootable.

13.15 1911 sits low in hand, has great beavertail when modified, thumb safety for leverage against recoil, very shootable.

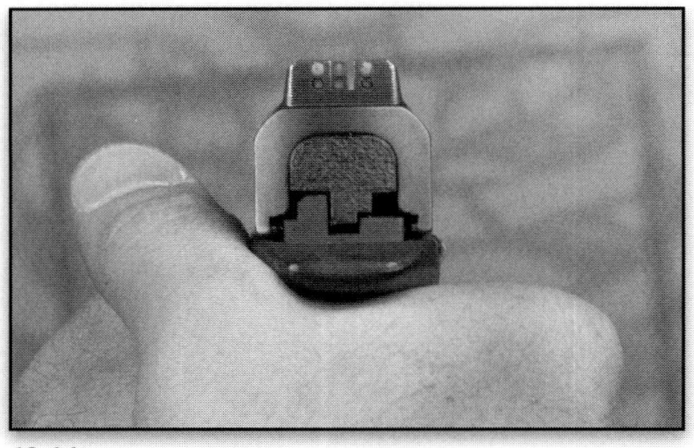

13.16

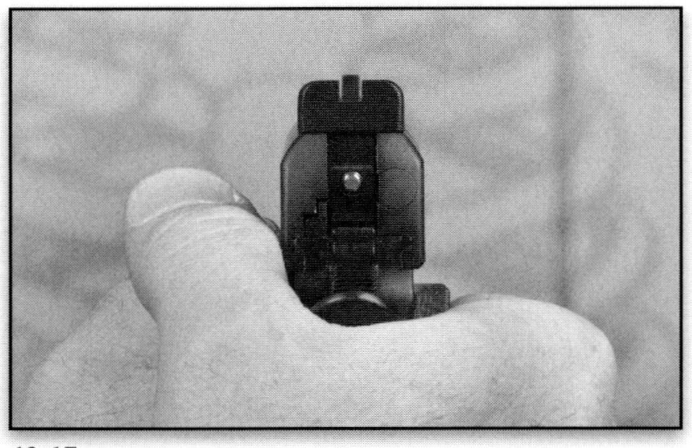

13.17

13.18 Glock sits low in hand, but has no beavertail, very shootable.

13.19 Sig P228 very high bore axis above shooter's hand, thumb easily reaches slide stop causing failures to lock to the rear, long reach to trigger

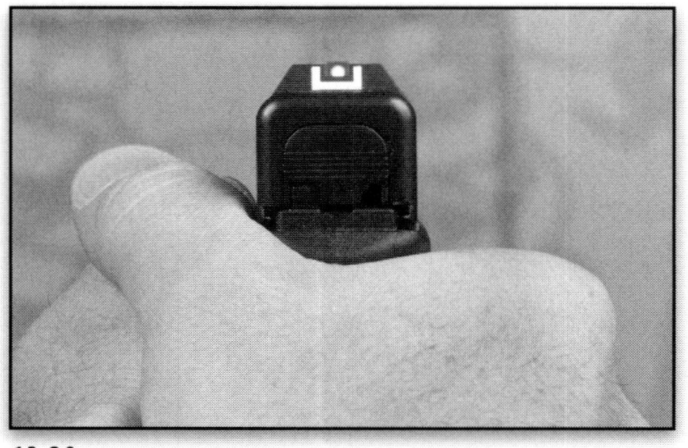

13.20

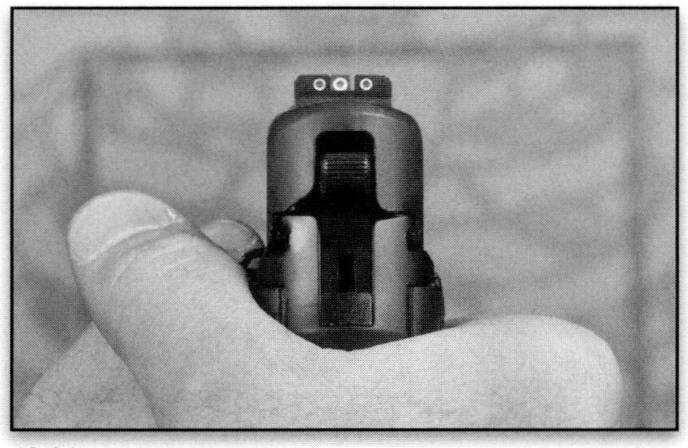

13.21

13.22 Smith and Wesson M&P has grip panels that are easily changed to accomodate different hand sizes.

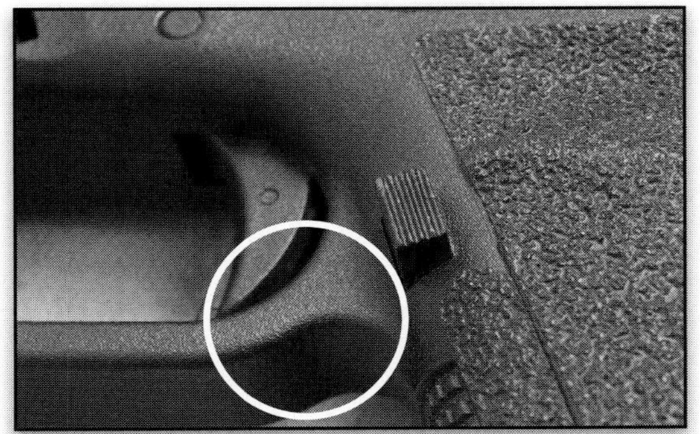

13.23 Glock trigger guard bump.

13.24 Smith and Wesson M&P beavertail vs. Glock

the shooter to disengage the safety when firing left handed. This is unsat, get one that works.

Extended Slide Stop

On the 1911 there is absolutely no need for an extended slide stop. I have only seen this type of accessory degrade the functioning of the weapon. Why is this part needed? If the shooter uses the sling shot method to release the slide after a slide lock reload, the extension is not needed. If the right-handed shooter releases the slide with the thumb of the left hand after the reload it is also not needed. If the shooter has large hands they may even bump the slide stop up or down during the firing sequence. An extended slide stop is a no go in the Combat shooter's repertoire.

Extended Controls on other Combat Autos:

Extended slide stop

Probably the most efficient problem causing extended part on any weapon is the Glock extended slide stop. This part is a huge malfunction inducer. Here is what happens. A shooter with big hands uses the extended slide stop and their thumb extends all the way to the extension portion of the slide stop. As they fire the weapon, they put pressure on the top of the extended slide stop, not allowing the magazine to push the slide stop up and lock the slide to the rear as you fire the last round in your magazine. This also

13.25 1911 with beavertail grip safety and extended ambidextrous thumb safety.

happens frequently to Sig shooters, but there is nothing they can do other than degrade their grip to ensure they do not let their thumb sit on the slide stop since the slide stop is in a poor location.

The next problem caused by the extended slide stop on the Glock pistol is premature locking of the slide to the rear. If the shooter has large hands, or allows the left hand for a right handed shooter to creep up, the edge of the hand will apply pressure to the bottom of the extended slide stop and lock the slide to the rear before you actually run out of ammo. What is the quick fix? Take it off and replace it with the standard version. I have also seen more spring breakage with the extended version.

It is normal to see Glock shooters cussing their pistols for malfunctions, when it is actually their hand placement that causes it. When they shoot my Glock, without any extended parts, they immediately have a better go of it.

Extended Magazine Releases

Extended magazine releases are normally something that is added to allow a shooter a slight crutch during magazine changes. Competition shooters use extended magazine releases because reloads are critical to having a quick time in the make believe world of IPSC or IDPA. Shooters want to be able to release the magazine without changing their grip on the weapon. This is a good thought, but not necessary; you can just as quickly move your hand to the magazine release, and re-grip before the fresh magazine is ready to be inserted. I would not have a problem with extended magazine releases, but here is what happens.

A shooter installs the extended release, they place the weapon on their nightstand, and they go to pick the weapon up in the middle of the night, in the dark. As they grab the pistol, unintentionally they push down on the nightstand, slightly pushing in the magazine release. Now what is going to happen? As soon as they fire their first round, they will have a malfunction or the magazine will fall out of the weapon because the magazine has been unseated. It may only require a tap, rack to fix the problem, but every second counts in a gunfight.

The other issue I have seen with the extended magazine release is the premature release when a soldier is wearing their weapon on their chest, against a hard ballistic plate. They crawl over a wall, or bump into someone, and their magazine falls out or slightly unseats.

13.26 Glock extended slide stop.

13.27 Thumb on extended slide stop.

13.28 Hand pressed against bottom of extended slide stop.

13.29 Slide prematurely locks to the rear.

13.30 Extended magazine release, Glock 34.

Lastly, if your support hand hits the magazine release during the firing sequence you may release the magazine. This is both annoying and can cause the magazine to drop from the weapon.

If you still decide to put a slightly extended magazine release on your weapon, make sure you don't have these issues; push the weapon against a table to see if the magazine release is too long. If that doesn't cause the magazine to come unseated, you should be fine. Train as much as possible to ensure you won't have this issue.

Magazines

As was stated earlier, magazines are part of the weapon system. If they won't work, nothing will. Other than for the 1911, I would only use factory magazines in my weapons. The 1911 has a plethora of after market magazines that work relatively well, most are better than the factory magazines. Some factories have even started to sell their 1911's with high quality, after market magazines.

As far as all others go, I would only use factory magazines. There is no reason to buy after market magazine goodies, other than replacement base plates that do not add additional rounds to the magazine. There are a few versions of enhanced base plates available which may make your magazines even more durable than the original design.

If you are a competition shooter you are probably upset with this statement, however, ask yourself, would you really trust your life to your extended magazines?

13.30 L-R: 10 round 1911 magazine, Glock 22 magazine with +2 base pade, 8 round 1911 magazine, stock Glock 21 magazine, stock S&W M&P 9mm magazine.

13.31 Obviously not an extra power spring, note how short the spring is.

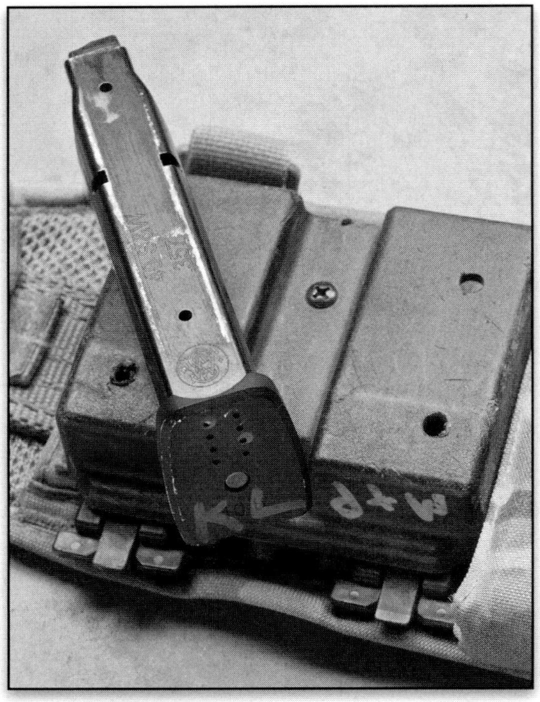

13.32 10-8 Performance M&P base pad.

Magazine Springs

Extra power magazine springs have started to gain ground in the past few years, because this is a product that simply works. There are several on the market; the companies I would recommend are Springco, ISMI and Wolff. ISMI and Wolff make the magazine springs, Springco makes high quality recoil springs for pistols and carbines. They all have great products and stand behind them with good service. Their springs can sometimes take a somewhat untrustworthy weapon back into good standing.

Magazine Well Extensions

Magazine well extensions have been popular for years on the competition side of the house, and recently I have seen a few making their way into the Combat Pistol world. For years we have used the SA Mag Guide, by Smith and Alexander, as it is a quality product, but it also required a gunsmith to properly fit it to your pistol. In the last few years, more and more magazine guides, or extended mag wells, as they are called, are becoming available for pistols, such as the Glock.

The difference between the SA Mag Guide and most of the available versions for the Glock is this: the SA version still allows the shooter access to the front lip of the magazine when it is in the weapon. The newer Glock versions do not. This is un sat. As a combat shooter you must have access to the front edge of the magazine in order to clear a stuck magazine. You also must remember that this will need to be performed with one hand. If you don't have access to the front lip of the magazine, you will be stuck with a magazine in the weapon, and no way to get it out.

Ultimately your reloads will not be significantly faster with a mag well either. Isn't it funny how that works out? Once again, a solution for a problem that didn't exist, at least in the Combat Pistol world.

Ultimately you will need to decide what your Combat Pistol of choice will be, just make sure you are doing it for the right reasons. Don't be steered wrong by the latest issue of Guns for Geeks, get out there and see what works for you. This is about fighting with a pistol, not impressing your friends. Remember, Ugly guns need love too...

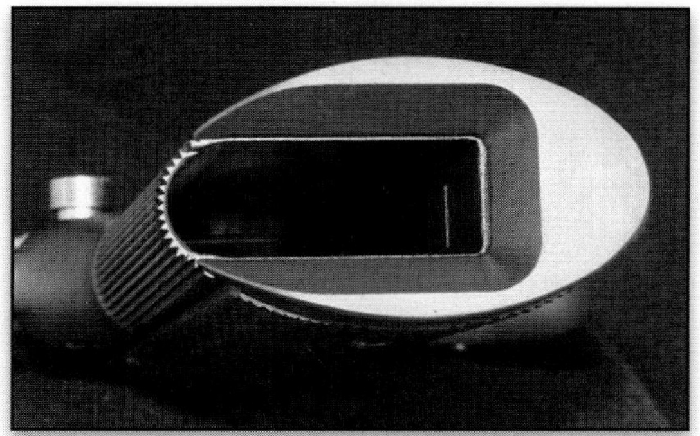

13.33 Smith and Alexander mag guide, courtesy of Clark Custom Guns.

13.34 Glock mag well does not allow access to the front of the magazine base pad.

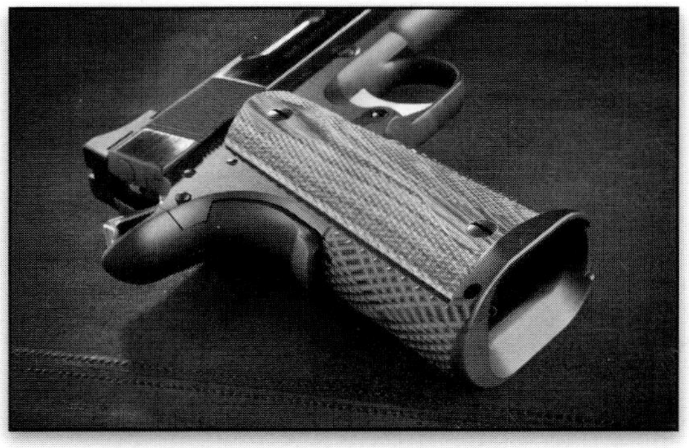

13.35 Stan Chen Custom 1911 with his custom magazine well.

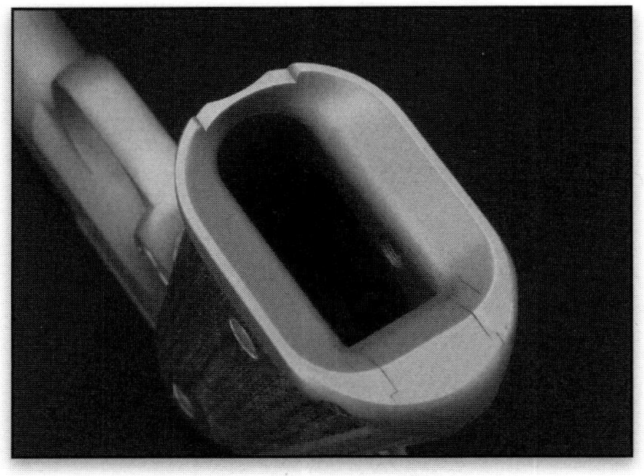

13.36-37 *Stan Chen Magazine Well with open front allowing instant access to the lip of the base pad on the magazine.*

13.38 Not pretty, but pretty effective.

Marking your gear and magazines.

It is extremely important to keep track of your gear. Not just to eliminate a barracks thief from absconding with it, but also to know what magazines are working and which are not. I always mark my gear with a special marking to quickly identify my equipment on a busy range or in the Team room. But on the serious side of the business, you need to mark your magazines, not only with your special mark or badge number, but with numbers to indentify which magazine is which. As you train you will notice that your weapon prefers certain magazines, or more than likely it just doesn't like a few of the older or damaged magazines. If you have numbers on the magazines you will be able to quickly Identify what should not be used for duty.

Chapter 14, Lights

14. LIGHTS

Bad things happen at night, yet we tend to train mostly in daylight hours when our focus should be hours of darkness. I prefer high noon, or darker than two feet up a coalminers... well you get the idea. Don't want to upset any folks from West Virginia.

14.1 Plenty of lights to choose from: hand held or weapon mounted.

Shooting in total darkness is sometimes easier than dusk, as dusk can be a bit tricky, but let's get back to the task at hand. You must have a primary light system as well as a backup. Just like everything else in the tactical world: Two is one, and one is none.

14.2 Surefire X-300 pistol light and Surefire VTAC handheld light.

Light Selection

There are tons of lights out there to chose from when selecting your pistol light. I don't want this to turn into an advertisement for everyone's lights, I just want to highlight the criteria that I use when selecting a light.

14.3 VTAC light sling.

Hand Held or Weapon Mounted

The absolute best way to shoot with a flashlight is with it attached to your weapon. Period. Anyone that says different has not spent time on the range or in the real world. Why would you not want a light solidly affixed to your weapon? One reason I often hear is this, "we can't point our weapons at innocent people." Roger that. Then use a handheld light up until the moment you need the weapon, simply release the hand held and go to blows with the weapon mounted version.

I use a VTAC Light Sling on my hand held flashlight so it stays put when not in use. No dangling, no leashes to become jammed in the magazine well during reloads; and you are still able to reload, clear malfunctions, and lay hands on someone if necessary.

If you absolutely cannot use a weapon mounted light, or don't want to purchase one, no worries, use what you have. But be aware that you will be more effective at stopping the fight if you have a full time, dedicated, weapon mounted light system.

14.4 Surefire G2 Nitrolon with incandescent bulb.

LED vs. Incandescent

What does this mean? Well, in layman terms, LED (Light Emitting Diode) has no bulb and throws more of a white colored light. Incandescent has a bulb and throws a more normal looking yellow light.

What is the best set up? LED or Incandescent? I would say this. If all you have is one light, then the selection process is easy, use what you have. If you don't have a pistol light, and are planning to buy, here are a couple things to think about.

I will tell you this up front. I now use LED lights on my pistols exclusively. Keep reading to better understand why.

14.5 Surefire Z2 Smith & Wesson M&P with Crimson Trace lasergrips.

Incandescent

Incandescent lights have a couple things going for them. They are normally relatively reasonably priced lights. You can get an incandescent light from almost any manufacturer out there. Theses lights also throw a very natural looking light, which I like. Most of the time, this type of light allows you to see a little bit better and have nice throw to the left and right of the main beam. So why wouldn't you use an Incandescent light?

The downfall of the Incandescent is the lack of durability. Since the light is coming from a conventional bulb type system, they are more prone to breaking during recoil. The pistol is especially hard on incandescent bulb systems, not only with the recoil, but muzzle blast as well. Lighting systems protruding past the end of the muzzle cause huge blast to the side of the light head. When shooting an incandescent light on your pistol, be absolutely sure that you have a replacement bulb for your light.

LED: Light Emitting Diode

When LED lights hit the market, in general, I was not impressed. The reason I didn't initially like the LED was because of the beam focus. Most LED's had beams that were either way too wide, causing the target you wanted to engage to be difficult to see. Or the opposite, the beam was too focused, causing you to only see the target and not the surrounding area. This was especially evident if you had 4-5 targets, and by targets I mean real people. You can't test a light on paper because it gives you a false read as to the true capabilities of your light system. When 4-5 suspects were lined up, then hit with the light, the LED failed miserably because of the improperly focused beam. If the LED was too focused and you wouldn't see that the suspects on the flanks had weapons; too much dispersion and you couldn't see anyone clearly.

Since these early days of the LED, things have changed drastically. The focus on these lights has been improved, not only giving you a good hot spot to use for engaging the threat, but excellent dispersion of the light to help detect threats that come from the outer edges of your light beam.

LED Durability

When I say LED Durability, I am talking only about the Diode itself; I am not referring to the rest of the light system, e.g. mounts, battery boxes, etc. The LED is almost indestructible when mounted on a pistol. I have shot one particular Surefire X-300 for almost two years and never had any issues with the LED. This is not a pistol that stays in the holster; this pistol is used for all my classes and also passed around to students to try their luck with. LEDs will keep working, at least if you have a light from a reputable manufacturer. Don't get me wrong, you can have issues with LEDs just like any other piece of kit, but the LED itself should be very durable. Shooters who mount incandescent lights near the muzzle of their rifle won't get but a few shots from the weapon before the bulb is toast, whereas with the LED the bulb will stand up to the torture. LED type lights do not need to have any shock absorption built into the light either.

Train with the Light

The LED is a very white light. This is hard to explain, but if you have ever used an LED you understand. The extreme white of the light does take some getting used to. I now have no issues with the light color, just had to train a little more.

Battery Life

The LED has great battery life as these lights don't seem to burn through batteries like other incandescent lights seem to. This of course is partly due to the head or bulb configuration that is on your light. The bottom line is you will need fewer batteries with a comparable LED when compared to an Incandescent.

IR Covers

For those of you who are fortunate enough to have NVG (Night Vision Goggle) capability, you won't be able to use your LED light through an IR Light Cover. The wavelength of the LED and the Incandescent are slightly different, which will not allow any LED light to penetrate your IR Cover. This normally isn't an issue with a pistol, but the same is true for a Carbine mounted LED, so be aware.

Tinted Glass

One interesting capability of the LED light is its ability to burn through tinted windows better than an Incandescent light source. For some reason you get less reflection when using an LED to look through tinted glass; this is a big deal if you are the Soldier or Officer making a car stop. This isn't just a slight difference; it is the difference between seeing and not seeing. Try it out for yourself, I know I was impressed.

Quality of the Light

When you select your light, the lamp is not the only part of the light that requires durability. All parts of a weapon mounted light should be able to withstand the rigors of thousands of rounds of ammunition. An important aspect that requires special attention is the type of spring system used inside of the battery box. If your battery box has leaf springs this may be a weakness. I have not had any luck with light systems on pistols that incorporate a leaf type spring. The coil spring seems to do much better with the heavier recoil. This is something you should always check before purchasing a light. Someday there may be a pistol light with leaf springs that work, but up until now I have not seen it.

Weight and construction are important as well. If the light is too heavy it can help to induce stoppages on your weapon system, and you have to carry this weight all day long as well. Ounces make pounds.

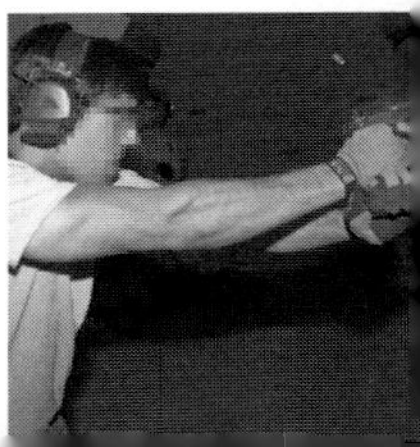

Plastic or Aluminum, I don't think it matters. Just check the durability. Will it withstand being carried every day, and shot a lot?

Mounting Options

If you do decide to use a weapon mounted light, there are several options that may interest you. Speaking from experience, I have favorites. I prefer a light that does not require tools to mount on the weapon. Even something as simple as a need for a screwdriver is a non-starter for me. The only caveat to this statement would be if the light also has laser capability. The screws are a must to get the light/laser to lock up for accuracy and repeatability of zero with the laser.

I prefer a light that allows you to easily slide the light into position, or off quickly as missions might dictate. This can be true in several scenarios, one of which is when you carry a concealed handgun. If the weapon is truly concealed, a light may not fit with the weapon inside your pants, or where ever your favorite concealment location may be.

I also prefer a light that works for both left and right-handed shooters. I don't like to see Arms Rooms having to stock left and right hand lights.

Whichever mounting option you chose, it must also work well with your holster. The quest continues for the perfect, universal, light gun holster. So far it has not been delivered. The downfall of most light holsters is retention. Once the weapon is in the holster, retention can be a little lacking, especially if you are a Policeman who is required to have a Level III retention type holster.

14.6 Insight Technologies light top, Surefire X-300 bottom. Both with tool-free mounting systems.

14.7 M&P with Blade-Tech WRS holster.

When you do make the call on the selection of your weapon mounted light, don't forget the backup. You must always have a backup light system on your person.

Switches

Normally, not much thought is put into the operation of the light switch. I try to think through all of the scenarios that I may encounter and what the light switch will be required to do.

Can the light be easily activated when you draw the weapon? If you are shooting a light that has a tail cap switch, can you easily reach this area of the light, or does it require you to completely change your shooting grip? If you must change your grip, this is a non starter. What if you are getting engaged or you have to conduct a reload? Does that light automatically shut off when you release the switch? This should also be a thought process you follow for your hand held lights. Too often, shooters start to reload or move and they have difficulty turning the light off. We all laugh when this happens on the range, but in combat, it is not a laughing matter; especially if you are a member of a team. Teammates will definitely be pissed if you attract attention or worse yet, bullets start flying in your direction.

Can you activate and deactivate the light switch with one hand? With your support hand only?

I prefer to use a pressure switch for my pistol lights. The switch should be positioned so that, if necessary you can draw and carry the weapon without turning on the light. White Light ADs (Accidental Discharges) will quickly make

14.8 Surefire X-300 with DG pressure switch.

you lose all of your cool guy points, so be aware of where the switch is at. I also like to be able to use my normal grip, so a switch that is activated by the middle finger of my shooting hand is perfect.

Tricks of the Trade

When you purchase your weapon mounted light system, ensure that you use thread locker on all screws. If you don't, it won't be too long before the light falls off the weapon. Definitely time to turn in more cool guy points.

Some light mounts can actually be adjusted to fit snuggly on your rail. Ensure to check out the instructions and see where you need to apply thread locker. This is one time you don't want to be the normal "guy" who thinks he knows how to operate and install a piece of kit without the instructions. Read and heed or you may lose your light when you least expect it.

Do not apply thread locker to the cross screw if you have a mount that is attached by the use of a thumbscrew. I am referring to all of the other screws on the light.

Use Lip Balm. Keep your Lips Supple During Night Ops

Whoa! Do I have your attention now?

This may sound completely crazy, but if you apply a very thin coating of tube type lip balm to your Pistol light, you will be able to wipe the carbon off easily. I heard this from my good friend, Johnny "Dead Eye Dawg." I thought it was goofy, but he has never steered me wrong. It works great and should be re-applied about every 400 rounds.

Rub a little on your finger, smear it in until you really can't tell it is there, and go to shooting. It will not degrade the performance of your light either.

If you plan to be in an extremely dusty environment, I would not use the lip balm as it will pick up dust.

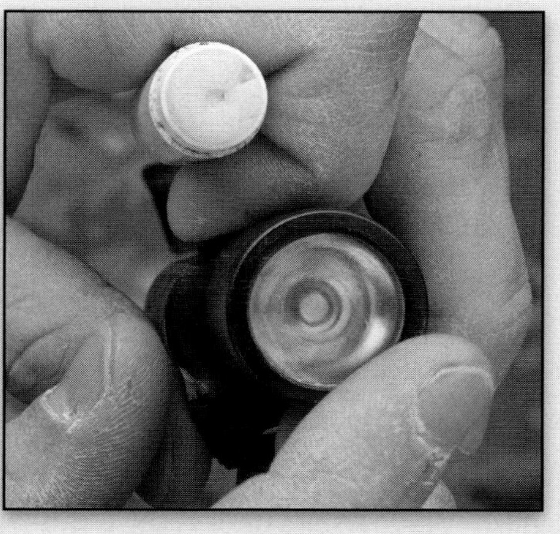

14.9 Just a touch of lip balm will allow easy removal of carbon and dirt from the light.

Chapter 15, Lasers

15. LASERS

Before I get too far down the wrong path, please understand that there are two types of lasers. Visible and IR. Visible, usually usually red or green in color and IR (Infra Red), invisible to the naked eye but visible with Night Vision Devices.

IR Lasers

IR lasers are an absolute must have if you plan to shoot your pistol with Night Vision Goggles. You can't see your iron sights, at least not quickly. You can't rely on point shooting because we all know that doesn't work. So now we are in need of a device that tells us when we are on target. Oh, and did I mention that the threat won't see it coming? That is the absolute best result of the use of Night Vision Goggles, as the 160th SOAR Special Operations Aviation Regiment says, "You will own the night."

If you have an IR laser on your pistol, you should always double check to see what has happened to the zero periodically, as most pistol IR lasers leave a little to be desired. You also want to have the utmost confidence if you have to shoot your pistol with NVG's.

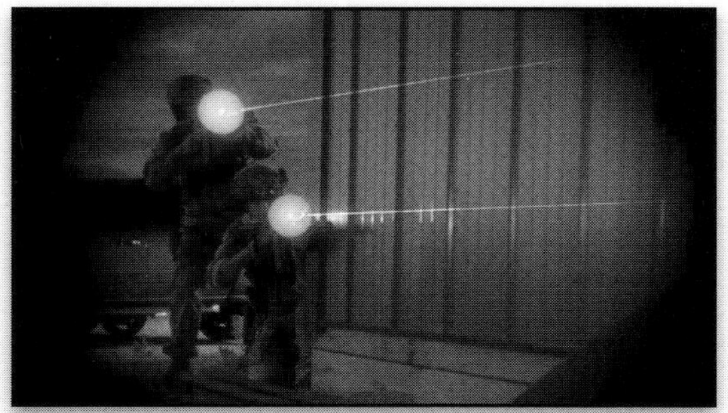

15.1 IR lasers are a great tool for the war fighter.

When engaging with the IR laser, attempt to shoot from your normal stance. Don't shoot from the hip or Position 3 if it can be avoided. You will shoot much quicker and have no issues if you present the weapon in the same manner as you would during daylight. This practice is also much safer, because you will not be covering someone in front of you or accidentally shoot an obstacle to your front, such as a vehicle or wall.

Visible Lasers

One of the latest fads in the pistol world is the visible laser. I say fad, because some folks are treating these devices as though they are the end all, be all, for your marksmanship and night fighting problems. This is absolutely incorrect. They are a tool just like an extended magazine well or new holster. Will they enhance your combat effectiveness if used correctly? Absolutely. But if used incorrectly, they could be the difference between life and death.

If you are using a visible laser on your pistol, do not rely on this device, use it as an enhancement. What does this mean? The point I try to get across to students is this: Use your sights, if the dot also happens to be there great. If not, you can still shoot your iron sights. If you are in a situation where you may be shooting from a difficult position and having a hard time acquiring your sights, then use the laser.

If you go into a situation, relying on these devices, they will fail. Who knows what will happen? What if it is day light, the threat is wearing light colored clothing? How about falling in the mud or having blood on your hands covering the laser device?

15.2 Visible laser works great, but can you ID the threat?

Threat ID

If you decide to use a laser on your pistol, ensure you also have a light source that will allow you to identify if the person you encounter is a threat or friendly. As you can see, as soon as the light comes on to ID the threat, you lose sight of the laser dot. This is especially true if the suspect is wearing light or bright colored clothes.

15.3 You can now ID the threat, but the laser has become almost invisible.

In the perfect world the laser would always work and we would all go skipping home with two gallons of Vitamin D milk. We are not in the perfect world, but for an instant, let's pretend we are. Step up to the line and use your laser, shoot as fast as you can acquire the laser dot. Now try it with just your iron sights. I think you will be surprised. Well over 75% of the shooters we conduct these drills with shoot faster with their iron sights.

Ok, time to get off the soapbox, the point is this:

Visible lasers work, iron sights work better, use them both as fast and as often as you can.

Chapter 16, Compensators and Porting

16. COMPENSATORS AND PORTING

The subject of Compensators and Porting shouldn't be discussed in a Combat Pistol book, however, since we see more and more showing up in the Tactical world, it deserves a minute or two.

Comps and ported barrels absolutely do help you be slightly quicker when delivering numerous rounds on target. Since the porting or baffles push gas in the opposite direction of the muzzle rise, you won't see the normal amount of sight movement. Compensators also can help to reduce felt recoil. This is obviously an advantage or you wouldn't see competition shooters using comps on their weapons.

Compensators and Porting for the Tactical Shooter

As you see there are many advantages to the comp/porting, however, I would not recommend either for a Combat Pistol. If combat shooting were simply about standing flat-footed in the middle of the day, with your pistol in the perfect position, then I would use one. But obviously this isn't the perfect world we live in.

16.1 Springfield XD with V-10 porting.

Malfunctions

Adding weight to the end of your barrel with the addition of the compensator will increase your odds of having malfunctions. This is normally caused simply by the weight of the comp, because it retards the ability of the pistol's barrel to move freely to lock and unlock. You may also notice a change in the velocity of the weapon's slide. This can be detrimental to function as well. Most compensators will cause the slide to move a bit faster, forcing the magazine to work differently than intended.

Zero Change

If you are using a compensator on your pistol, you have probably seen zero changes over time. The comp is famous for changing your zero as the carbon builds inside the system. It is just the way it is. Normally, the zero changes are not drastic, so this isn't a huge issue, but it is an issue nonetheless...

If you think you are going to be sneaky and drop the barrel in solvent to break up the carbon to ease the removal during cleaning, just be advised that you are also going to cause the compensator to loosen on the barrel. That is if it is held in place by thread locker or some type of epoxy. Although I don't see many of these out there anymore, if you are using a compensator with attached sights, when your comp loosens and twists, your sights are twisting too.

Night Ops

Bad things happen at night. Guns are needed at night. Compensators and porting are extremely bright at night. I guess what I am saying is comps and porting does not equal success at night. You are going to destroy your night vision with the use of a comp/porting, and once it is gone it will take several seconds to recover. This is an issue I don't want to have to deal with. It will also aid the threat in identifying your position, without a doubt they will know where you are at.

16.2 Very impressive blast at night.

Fast during day/slow at night

So the comp is intended to make you a faster shooter, which it will during the day. But at night the comp/porting will have diminished returns. You will actually have to shoot slower because of the huge flaming ball that erupts with each shot, distracting you from seeing your target clearly. Not to mention your sights.

Ear plugs required

When I am out and about, scampering from car to tree to store, I don't wear ear plugs. I don't know of anyone that walks around on a daily basis with their hearing protection in place. We all know that guns are loud, so we are ready for that, but compensated pistols are exponentially louder than normal pistols. If you must use your weapon without plugs, be ready for it.

Debris

When a comp/ported weapon is fired, there are small pieces of bullet jacket and lead that are pushed upward and outward. If, for some reason you have to fire the weapon from position 2 or 3, you will eventually catch debris in the face, and worse yet the eyes. I also don't wear eye protection at night when I am out on the town. If I need to use my pistol, I won't have time to stop and pull out the shades. Not all comps throw lead and bullet jacket fragments, but there is debris no matter the type of comp. Just the blast is bad enough.

16.3 Notice vented gasses and debris directed up.

This chapter is not meant to say compensators and porting do not work, they do. I am just not a fan of these devices when it comes to gunfighting. And that is what this book is about.

Chapter 17, Shooting with Gloves

17. SHOOTING WITH GLOVES

This book is for gunslingers, so I thought I would take a minute to address wearing gloves while shooting.

In today's market, there are endless amounts of tactical gloves as well as sport gloves that can give you some protection during your day and still allow you to be able to shoot extremely well.

If you are operating in a tactical environment, I believe you should always wear gloves. This is somewhat difficult for police officers, although my hero, Ponch, always wore gloves. I hope you know I am kidding by the way.

If you are a tactical operator with the Military or Law Enforcement, you absolutely should wear gloves. If you wear gloves, do not cut the fingers out; find gloves that fit well enough to give you the dexterity you need to be able to shoot as well as manipulate radios or whatever the task may be. Of course there are exceptions to almost every rule. If conducting explosive breaches for your entry team is one of your primary skill sets, you may need a little better feel to accomplish your tasks. This is acceptable since your team's failure or success is influenced exponentially by your ability to get them into the crisis site.

17.1 Trigger finger removed for dexterity, but all protection is lost.

When I select gloves, I try to find gloves that are easy to take on and off, since this is something I seem to do a lot of. I also want gloves that have relatively tight fingers so the material doesn't get caught under the trigger as I shoot. I also look for gloves that do not have a tight web between my thumb and trigger finger; this always seems to be the place they wear out, so the less stress to that area the better.

17.2 Great fit is important when choosing tactical gloves.

17.3 No matter the quality, tactical gloves wear out.

Flame Retardant

If you are a Military or Law Enforcement Operator that works around things that burn, such as explosives, bad guys' houses, or IED's (Improvised Explosive Devices), I would ensure that you always have gloves that are flame retardant. Cheaper versions of tactical gloves, as well as sport or driving gloves are normally not flame retardant. You may not consider this important now, but if you meet a Soldier or Marine who has been badly burned, you will immediately see the need for these mission specific gloves.

Chapter 18, Training Mentality

18. TRAINING MENTALITY

Several folks have asked me to try to put into words the Mentality that we strive for during our classes. I think this may take a chapter or two in order to get the points covered. I will start with Training Mentality and work towards the Mindset and Visualization in their own chapters. They all work together, but it will take a good bit of discussion to get the points covered. If you get bored, look ahead to the topics and skip around. They should all stand on their own. If you have the attention span that I do, you will have to read them in manageable chunks anyway.

During VTAC's Pistol and Carbine courses we continually push speed, a key element of the Gunfight. We also try to use realistic targetry to enhance student's skills. If you constantly use Bullseyes for your training, you are not preparing yourself or your students for the type of scenarios they will be exposed to in a real confrontation. Slow aimed fire is a great tool for enhancing Combat shooting skills, but we must push shooters way outside of their comfort zones if we expect them to perform well during a real fight. I constantly push shooters until their wheels fall off, and then we slow down until they are consistently able to perform at extremes in comparison to the normal shooter.

18.1 Push shooters 'til the wheels fall off.

System

I often hear the term "system" when discussing training ideologies. What system do you use? This didn't make sense until I started to get more exposure to total systems. What I quickly realized was the fact that these systems did not work as a total fighting, so called, system. Fighting and shooting were two different entities, and that is wrong. Everything you do should dovetail nicely with every other technique you use. Are your techniques easy to learn and is instinct taken into account? Not intuition, but instinct. Intuition is the goal of our

18.2 Instinct tells you to take cover near your vehicle, intuition is the ability to stay low and successfully engage a target.

training. My friend, Ken Good explains this well in his article entitled "Who is training Whom." We must learn intuition, intuition changes as we gather more data from training experiences.

Instinct vs. Intuition

Instinct is a God given ability. You may jump when you hear a loud noise. You may tighten your muscles when struck with any type of object. When you receive fire in a hallway, you do not just stand there, you move to one side or the other. This is instinct.

Intuition is not something you are born with, life experiences will change your intuition. Training will change your intuition; training will make you react differently than the untrained individual that is relying on instinct.

Ken Good explained this with a simple example. If you wake up in a stock car going 180 MPH into turn one at Rockingham Motor Speedway, what would happen? The untrained driver would use their intuition, which would be to slam on the brakes, going into a skid, lose steering control due to the skid, hitting the wall, the car bursting into flames, more than likely a quick trip to the hospital or morgue. The trained individual would use their intuition, which would be different than the person with no training. The trained driver would

18.3 Low ready or no ready should not be part of your system.

18.4 Train like you want to fight.

18.5 Four inches of more exposure is a big deal in a gunfight.

realize that he needed to bleed off speed by threshold braking, find the apex of the turn and drive through the corner, exiting the turn with a foot quickly getting on the accelerator.

Hopefully this drives home the point that we can teach intuition.

If your techniques do not work well with each other, streamline your training. I often see Law Enforcement Officers engage a threat, and then lower their muzzle with arms locked. This is not part of the draw stroke; wouldn't it be more efficient to go back to Position 3 (Retention Position) than to a totally altered position that does not allow for quick target acquisition if need be.

The bottom line is that everything needs to work together. You may have a great speed holster, but if the weapon has fallen out when you need it, what is the good of the speed holster.

Targets-Steel or Paper

Before I get too far down the road with the Training Mentality, I need to cover the basic needs for successful training. Targets are a key ingredient in the building of a better Combat shooter. If you find the term Combat is too hardcore for you, replace that with Tactical shooter. That does sound nice doesn't it? Every shooter must start with the fundamentals of Marksmanship. While working on basic marksmanship skills, the Bullseye target is great to dial shooters in. However, once they get dialed in, they absolutely must have a good selection of targets to enhance their skill set. If you get stagnant with Bullseye targets you will never know what is really possible with your weapon system. When you select a silhouette type target, it should have easily scoreable areas to allow for penalizing the shooter who isn't quite as accurate. We designed a target with this in mind; the VTAC Double

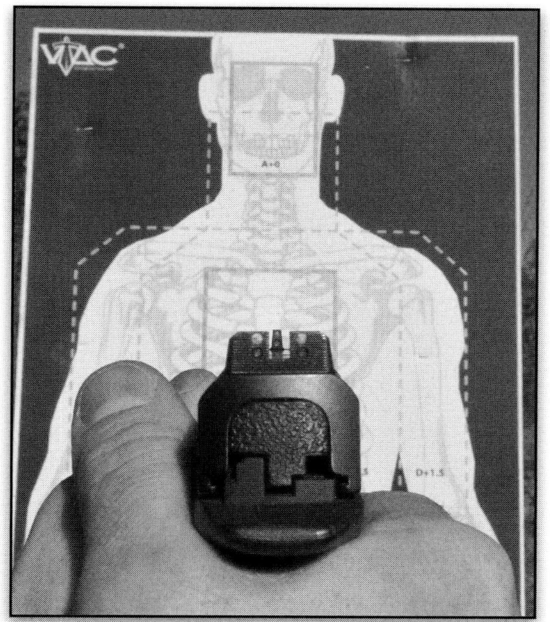

18.6 VTAC humanoid side of target.

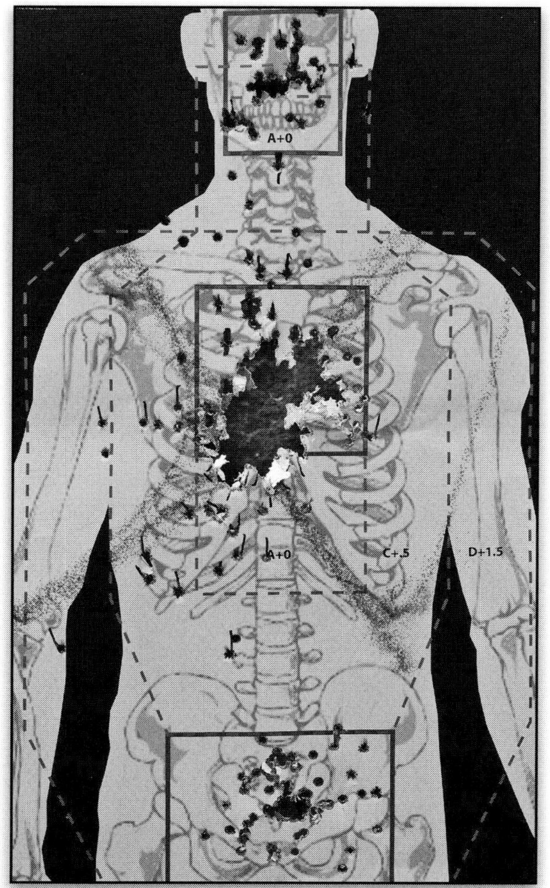

18.8 Use targets that teach. This target gets the point across of where we shoot to hit vitals.

18.7 This target is great if we are ever attacked by bowling pins.

Sided Target. The back of the target has four bullseyes for basic marksmanship skill building. The front of the target has a humanoid type silhouette that not only has scoring rings but shows a slight trace of the human anatomy so you will better understand what your target truly is. Head, heart, or pelvis are all effective targets.

Steel

Shooting steel is very gratifying as well as you receive the instantaneous feedback that you need. This will help to give you and your mates the confidence that you are in fact hitting what you are aiming at. Paper should always be used to enhance accuracy and help with proper shot placement, but once you are dialed in, use steel to push the speed, distance, and increase the amount of good training time for your range session. I also work with students as well as myself to help call my shots, if I call a bad shot on steel, I make it up before hearing that I did or did not hit the target.

Calling your Shots

When shooting a drill that involves hits and misses from peculiar positions, the ability to call your shots will be the difference between a mediocre score and a truly great score on one of these events. If you are able to call a good shot before you hear the report of the bullet impacting steel, this tells me you are in fact watching your sights throughout the entire firing sequence.

When you have a chance, start with the steel targets at a comfortable distance from a VTAC barricade, pistol 15 yards, rifle 50 yards. As you run through the 9-Hole Drill (see the VTAC Rifle and Pistol DVD's for more info on VTAC Range Drills) practice calling your shot, knowing that you hit or missed. If you call a good shot, quickly move from one port to the next, after awhile you will know when the shot truly was a good shot and when it isn't. Practice makes perfect with this drill, you must get the confidence built that you in fact know what you are seeing as you fire the weapon.

Call your shots with confidence; this directly applies to Combat Shooting. As you engage a threat you must constantly assess your sights, make small corrections, and re-engage as necessary.

If you have the ability to train with steel targetry on your range, you are very lucky. Some folks are not allowed to use steel to enhance their training regimen. Or they may just not have the financial ability to afford steel targets. In the long run, steel will pay for itself; this is especially true for departments or units that would normally go through thousands of paper targets in a short period of time. If you can't convince your leaders to buy steel, show them the figures on paper, it may change their mind.

If you do get the approval, buy quality steel. Cheap is exactly that, and you will not be happy with substandard steel targets. Worse yet, making your own can be dangerous to other shooters as well as yourself.

When buying steel targets, here are a few things I would absolutely say are a must.

18.9 VTAC Steel by MGM - AR 500

18.10 Quality steel is a great training aid.

18.11 No welds on targets and a slight angle down.

AR 500

The targets should have a hardness rating or steel type that we call AR 500. This steel will last forever with most pistol calibers and will also survive extreme abuse from rifle calibers such as 5.56. If you go softer, pits will develop that can shoot bullet fragments back at you as fast as they went down range. If you go harder, you will have plates that will crack and fall apart after limited use.

No Welds on the target

I try to use targets that don't have welds on the back of the target where bullets will impact. The welds will break after minimum use and that will require you to stop training and seek out a qualified welder. Years ago we had a set of targets that were bought from a sketchy manufacturer that told the military that 9mm would not harm the targets. Of course when I showed up for the training I said otherwise, but who knows better. As I guessed, by the end of the week, we had cracked a weld on every single target. This is unsat for the amount of money they had spent. I use targets from Mike Gibson Manufacturing which have a bolted hanging mechanism. Angle iron and bolts, not welds. Yep, bolts do break and sometimes come loose, but I can fix those in a jiffy with a crescent wrench or socket set.

Angle

If you can get targets that are angled towards the ground you will also be better off. You want the angle to cause the bullets and fragments to bounce into the ground, not back in your direction. This is not always possible, but if you have a choice I would go for the safer system.

Safety

Lastly, ALWAYS wear eye protection when shooting steel. No matter what, do not shoot steel without proper eye protection. This protection should wrap around to eliminate fragments from the side as well.

18.12 Instructors step up and put your money where your mouth is.

18.13 ALWAYS demonstrate to your students.

Never shoot steel closer than 10 yards with your pistol. Even at this range there will be splash back in your direction, so keep those glasses in place at all times.

Pushing your speed

Once shooters feel they can shoot relatively fast, we start to open up the scoring zones or decrease distance. The point needs to be made that we are not preaching "Spray and Pray," we are trying to push shooters past believed limits. Once they surpass their previous comfort zone we back them down to a comfortable speed level with increased accuracy, and low and behold they will shoot much faster with the needed degree of accuracy. Ultimately we are trying to get a shooter's 80% to be 25% faster than the threat/suspect's abilities.

Instructors who do not push speed are setting their students up for failure. Speed equals pressure, which normally equals failure or learning. We repeat this process until we get the learning. This technique will build unbelievable confidence in your abilities.

Stupid Students

"I would like to do that with my students or my officers, but they are stupid." How many times have you heard instructors say this? This is incredible. What you are saying as an instructor is that you are not up to the task of tackling difficult training. So who is the failure? You are. Get over yourself and train your people. Not everyone will be at the same level, but the goal is to train folks to win their next fight. It may be tonight.

Structure your training for each individual. There is no, "one size fits all," in Combat shooting.

Dealing with Disabilities

If a shooter shows up on the range and has anything from arm to eye trouble, we must work to overcome that disability. If your instructors can't help you, look for another instructor, someone will be able to help.

18.14 Get dirty, shooter demonstrates shooting under vehicle.

Realistic Training

Time to get Dirty

If you don't like to get your hands dirty, as well as pretty much every other part of your body, don't show up on the range to train with me. Your training should reflect the real world, and in the real world you will be required to sweat, roll on the ground, crawl, run, and close with and destroy the enemy. Train as though your life depends on it. If your training becomes stagnant you will not improve. Moving onto the next level should be the goal. Training in awkward shooting positions, such as seated in a car, are not only what you will need, it is a blast. This is a good time to find out if there are positions that will or will not work for you and your gear.

18.15 Give shooters a scenario to make training interesting.

Scenario Based Training

Put yourself in the situation you are training for. Don't get in the Bullseye mentality. Movement, vehicles, barricades, plastic barrels, whatever you can add to the training will increase your survivability in the next fight. What about night training? When was the last time you shot with your night sights or a flashlight?

Stay in the Fight

Most of my students get to hear this mantra many times, but I mean it. You must stay in the fight until it is over. If you are shooting a drill and you start with an unloaded weapon that is on you, not on me. Your time will be running until you load up and finish the drill. Don't lose focus on what you are training for; you are training to fight someone in the middle of the night. Things will not go perfectly, so treat every trip to the range and the line as a test. I hate when shooters get pissed during a drill and just quit, they drop their weapon to the side letting it dangle dangerously, not cool. Then they

18.16 At night, support hand only

laugh about it. I love to have fun on the range, I like to laugh and joke, but this is no laughing matter. Fix your mess and get back in the fight.

Shooting on the move

Shooting on the move is not an advanced skill; this is a basic skill that must be incorporated into your training if you are to have a good program. You will be a harder target to hit if you can move quickly out of the gun fire, and be much more effective if you can shoot will moving. Don't over think this skill, just do it. You also must be ready to flat out run for cover; there may be a time where this is necessary. You must also practice how you will effectively shoot from a covered position. There are tricks that can be learned with some basic shooting on the move and use of the VTAC barricades.

Use of the Shot Timer

Competition breeds success. The more you can use a timer to evaluate your training and those around you, the better you will be. You should also keep track of your times during the conduct of basic

18.17 Shooting on the move is extremely important.

18.18 A simple but effective set up to shoot on the move.

18.19 The shot timer does not lie. CED7000 pictured.

18.20 Pocket Pro II

and advanced drills. A lot can be learned from the shot timer. How long does it take you to reload? How fast can you get your weapon out of the holster? You must have a quality timer if you are going to assess your progress and run timed drills. The stress from the shot timer is what we want, it is what we need.

Don't get bored

Is your training boring? If it is, change it up. In order to improve you must have a drive to make the changes needed to improve. Attend training, it doesn't matter which trainer you chose if they are reputable. Even if you don't agree with everything they teach you can always pick up something. Get a training partner that can help you to track your progress and be your competition.

Use Video

Video doesn't lie, most of the time anyway. Get a cheap camera that you can use for range sessions. You will be surprised at what you will learn by watching yourself and others on video. Be safe with camera placement; don't get

18.21

18.22

too fancy unless you don't mind shooting cameras. Not that I have ever seen this happen....

Now back to our Training Mentality. Train as though your life and others depended on it, because they do. Look around at your normal day-to-day activities and build shooting scenarios based on this assessment. Once you are confident that you are prepared for the next confrontation, conduct all of the same scenarios with your strong or support hand only.

Fight through every problem you can come up with, or your trainers can throw at you.

Stay in the Fight!!

Chapter 19, Mindset

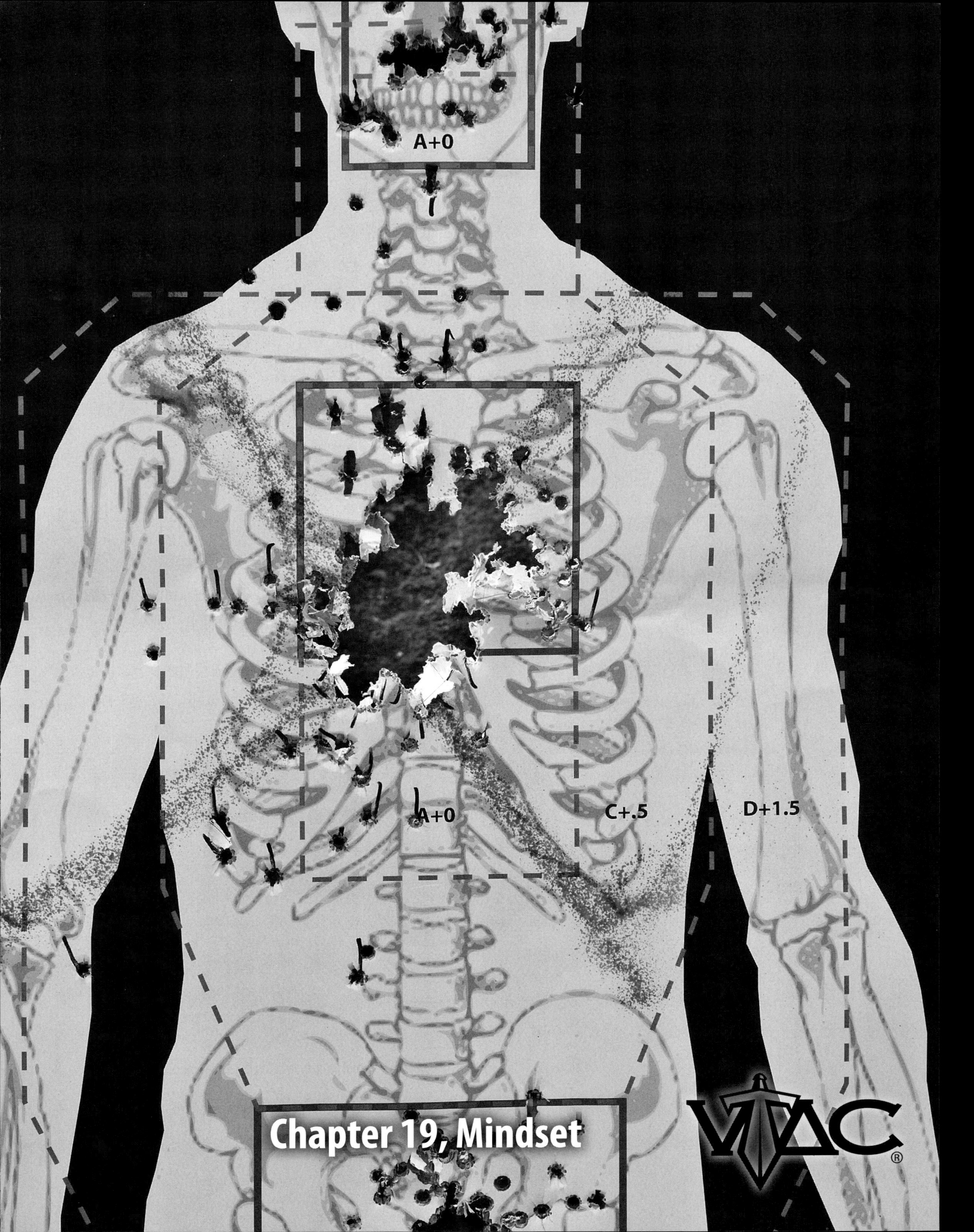

19. MINDSET

What is the Warrior Mindset? For me, this mindset is being prepared. Being ready for whatever the bad guy throws at you. Beyond the internal workings of the mind ,you must also have the skills to perform with your Warrior Mindset. How can you perform if you can't shoot or you are not physically fit? And physically fit doesn't mean you are a tri-athlete, but you must be able to get to your tools and do your job.

What do you think about when you get out of bed? Are you worried about going to Fourbucks to get your Orange Mocha Frappuccino, or are you thinking about how you will deal with a deadly confrontation? Get your mind in the game and stay in the game. Every day holds the possibility of getting to use your tools to eliminate a threat.

"Carrying a weapon is hard work."

I heard Clint Smith say this once. "Carrying a weapon is hard work." How true is that? Every day, in and out, if you are to be armed and ready, it entails some hard work. Concealed pistols hurt sometimes, but bullets hurt more. Just remember that when you are thinking about ditching your weapon because you are in a situation that would never require a weapon...

19.1 Train smart, train hard, be prepared for the worst.

They want to Kill you

Get it through your thick skull that bad guys want to kill you.... They want to kill your wife and kids, they want to drag your body through the streets and cut you into little pieces..... This is a fact about our enemies. Get used to it.

Offensive vs. Defensive

Go hide, call the Police? Lock yourself in a room and wait? Sorry, not for me. Is there a time for this behavior? There may be, but not in every situation.

This is not the way we will operate if we have an Aggressive and Offensive mindset, the Warrior Mindset. I can easily back off, but if I have never trained to be Aggressively Offensive, how will I do it when the time comes? What if you can't call the Police, because you are the

Police? What if someone is trying to do harm to your children, your spouse, your neighbor, a fellow American, an innocent person in the street? Take it to the bad guys; be prepared to perform on the Offensive. If it isn't needed you can easily back into the Defensive, but during a fight is not the time to start figuring out how to be Aggressive and Offensive. Even if you are in the defensive, you must be able to use your weapon, and that can quickly turn into the offensive.

19.2 Aggressive and Offensive.

Aggression

Aggression will get you through most things in life, whether you are playing sports or working as a commando, aggression is what has brought a lot of Moms and Dads back home to their children. An aggressive attitude will also show to the public, and if you are a tool bag punk who wants to find a victim, are you going to choose the aggressive, aware individual, or the timid, unaware person? Think about the Mom protecting her children. You want to see aggressive and offensive, Mothers are the textbooks of whom we should strive to emulate. Mothers do this naturally, the good ones anyway.

Survive or Win?

Are you preparing to survive a gunfight, or WIN a gunfight? You need to have the mental preparation and mindset to be the Winner. Warrior Mindset is being ready for every situation that you may be forced into, against your will. But you are there to react if necessary. We don't want to react slowly, the difference between slow reaction and an aggressive reaction is this: Slow reaction and you will find yourself in a gunfight, quick pro-active handling of the situation and you will find yourself involved in a shooting. Shooting or gunfight? Gunfights are too fair; I want to destroy the enemy before they have a chance to react, which I would call a Shooting.

19.3 Vigilance: Be prepared to kill everyone you meet.

Where do you live? Alert and prepared?

You simply cannot let down your guard. When will a threat present itself? It always seems that things go wrong when you least expect it. Do you flounder through life without a clue of what might be around the next corner? Unaware that bad guys like to operate at night, near poorly lit areas, parking garages? Wake up and be prepared, force yourself to get hold of your Warrior Mindset.

Chapter 20, Visualization

20. VISUALIZATION

Visualization is one of the more misunderstood concepts that apply to Combat shooting and marksmanship in general. "Practice makes perfect," at least that is what every coach I have ever had has told me. So is this true? Absolutely, the more we can train the better we will be when the game rolls around. What about Perfect Practice? Of course, slow down and execute everything absolutely perfectly. On the range this can be a trying event, but you should be able to make your Visualization an absolutely Perfect Practice.

Why wouldn't we want to get as many dry fire sessions completed as possible? Why not use visualization for your dry fire sessions?

If you have ever watched top athletes go through a sequence before an event, eyes closed, mimicking their performance without actually performing the task, you have witnessed visualization. How about sky divers, eyes closed, going through their pull sequence to ensure they don't bobble as they reach for a rip cord or throw-out pilot chute to save their own life.

Some shooters feel that visualization is somehow voodoo, mumbo jumbo that is reserved for those that are of feeble mind or body. This is a misconception that you need to get over.

The Process

Before you can successfully visualize, you need to accept the fact that you will look like a total idiot when going through this process. It is extremely funny to watch if you don't know what is happening.

Get comfortable, but not too comfortable. You don't want this to be a sleeping process; you need to be absolutely alert to the complete process. I think visualization requires more work than actually live firing your weapon.

Once you are in a position that is comfortable, close your eyes and start the visualization process. Where do you start? I always start at my toes and work my way to the muzzle of the pistol. This is up to you, but as you begin learning this process you need to focus on ever little detail of the shooting process.

Starting with my feet, weight on the balls of my feet, knees slightly bent, good fighter's stance. See yourself going through the process; try to feel what it will be like when the stance is correct. Head upright, looking straight forward, deep cleansing breath to get the needed oxygen to my eyes. Pistol held firmly in the firing hand, but not over gripped. 30-40% of the grip will be with the firing hand, web of your firing hand pressed as high as possible to gain the mechanical advantage on the pistol. Support hand, 60-70% of the grip, support side thumb pressed forward towards the target, but not pressing against the pistol's frame. A slight touch is ok, but no pressure. As I press the weapon towards the target I see my sights come into view, my focus is on the front sight. I can see every serration on the front sight. If I have a safety on this pistol, I am disengaging the thumb safety as I press the weapon towards the target. I place my finger on the trigger as the sights become aligned with the target. I prep the trigger as I finish the presentation of the pistol to the target. I check for proper sight alignment. I pull the trigger straight to the rear. The weapon fires.

Was it the perfect shot?

Perfect Practice

When using visualization you must have perfect practice. You cannot accept anything other than perfect performance during this process. Why is this? Why would you want to train yourself to fail or do something incorrectly? Doesn't really make sense does it?

So with this in mind, let's walk through the perfect shot.

As the pistol's sights align with the target it must be perfect, absolutely perfect. This means that there is a perfect sight picture aligned with the exact point you want the bullet to impact. When I work on basic marksmanship visualization I use a bullseye target. I guess I should say I visualize a bullseye target. This target has a small X and that is where I want the sights to be perfectly aligned. As the weapon fires, I visualize the muzzle blast, the circular flame that you will see as you shoot more and more. I will also visualize the sparks that fly from the ejection port as the weapon fires. I will see the bullet go through the center of the bull, through the center of the X. After the firing sequence, I will slowly release the trigger until I feel the disconnecter click, this is correct follow through. This is what I see when I visualize the perfect shot. So what did I forget?

Skip the Negativity

I did not visualize recoil. Why would you not want to visualize this, it happens every time we fire the weapon? The reason for the skipped step is that it is negative. We don't want recoil to be part of the visualization process. Negativity should not be included in any visualization process for the firing of the weapon. Of course there will be recoil, but we don't want to see it. Anticipating Recoil is a key cause for numerous marksmanship issues, do not build this into the process. Yes, there will be recoil, but if you have the correct support hand grip, aggressive stance, and are prepared to follow through, recoil will be nothing noticeable. Call a perfect shot on the target.

Follow through, prepare to repeat as necessary. Follow through is unbelievably important. Most shooters seem to be in a hurry to bring the weapon off the

target and back to the retention position. Why? Follow through is the process of watching where the sights were, and where they now need to be. It also involves slowly releasing the trigger until the disconnector clicks and you start to squeeze the trigger for additional shots on target. I constantly remind shooters to follow through. What if the sights were not on the threat when the weapon fired? This is a possibility and the threat is still a threat, follow through and re-engage the threat.

All portions of the firing sequence must be visualized.

Bad Shots

When you are going through the visualization process there shouldn't be any bad shots. If you see something during visualization that is not correct, start over. When I first started using these techniques, my goal was to fire one perfect shot. Sometimes it would take me 10 minutes to work through that perfect process. After a few weeks of working with this technique I was able to get through one shot easily, and then the goal became two then three to five shots. Visualization can be more work than you think if you are going to do it correctly, and it must be done correctly.

Advanced Visualization

Visualization is a great way to shake out new techniques. If you rehearse the techniques in your mind, you will find more efficient ways or possibly flaws in the new technique. It will also allow you to safely learn what you are trying to accomplish. A good example of this would be a new reloading technique, perfect practice and dry fire before attempting the new procedure on the range. This may not make sense now, but you will see if you try the visualization technique just how easy the first live fire session will be. These visualization techniques will also work well when thinking about barricade positions or tactics.

Option Analysis

Quickly analyzing options during a confrontation is not preferable, this is why we train. You could very likely be put into a decision making cycle by the actions of the threat. If you have previously analyzed your options you will be one step ahead of your adversary, and that is what we are after. Once again, this is accomplished through visualization, and it isn't restricted to shooting. You can use this to enhance performance no matter your skill set.

Chapter 21, Driving the Weapon

21. DRIVING THE WEAPON

Need for Speed

If you feel the need for speed, there is really only one way to get there. Drive the weapon faster from target to target. Anyone can shoot fast splits between shots, but it takes work to shoot fast splits between targets. This being said, double tapping does not work, because you have no idea where the second round will impact. As a Law Officer or Military shooter, you must account for every shot fired. Accomplishing this is a tricky training evolution, but once you get it, you will be able to aim every shot fired and improve your speed immensely.

There is nothing bad that will happen between targets, however, shooting fast can have consequences. If you shoot fast, missing is a possibility. If you drive the weapon as hard as you can from one target to the next, nothing bad can happen as long as your finger is only on the trigger when you have a target in your sights.

Take your time shooting; and do everything else as fast as you possibly can. Hopefully one of these statements starts to make sense as you continue to read.

Eyes Leading

Throughout life you have been looking and pointing at what you see. This is a very natural movement that we continue to practice religiously every day. You see something and point at it; you look at something then grab it. Why should you change the way you conduct business just because you have a pistol in your hand? No reason that I can see. You don't hear a noise, point at it, and then look. So do not do this with your pistol either.

When you decide to shoot multiple targets, this technique is by far the quickest way to improve your times on multiple target drills without a detriment to your accuracy. What you must envision is that your eyes move to a target, after the eyes have acquired the target, your weapon is pushed as aggressively as possible to become aligned with your eyes, thusly aligned with the target. If your eyes are on your sights the whole time, you will not know when to stop the weapon until it is too late. By that time the target will have passed by and it will be too late to make the shot without adjusting your eyes and sights back onto the target. Or you will fire as you see the center of the target pass in front of your sights, resulting in a poor shot. If you do this again and again, the time wasted will be huge. Lastly and most importantly, your effects on a threat target will not be impressive.

21.1 Eyes on sights.

21.2 Eyes lead to next target.

21.3 Drive weapon to catch up with eyes.

Target Discrimination

There are several reasons in the tactical world to lead with your eyes. Obviously the shooting is a large part of the equation, but there are other factors that are extremely important in the environment you operate in. Target Discrimination, determining which targets need to hold onto your bullets, is an important factor. You are the good guy, so accidently shooting an innocent has just reduced you, your team, and the mission to a failure. You save 300 and kill one innocent, you are a failure.

Leading with your eyes gives you the additional time needed to determine if the individual is a friendly or threat. This will also allow you to quickly move your weapon past non-threats to those that need a little lovin'. During training we shoot several targets at one time, and some are offended by this training because they say it is unrealistic. But this training allows us to practice the shooting and weapon driving that we need to be successful in a real world confrontation.

Flock Shooting

Some think the same end result is possible using a flock shooting technique. Flock shooting is really not the correct terminology, but that is what I call it when a shooter squeezes the trigger as the sights are coming across the target. Not allowing the sights to settle before the final squeeze of the trigger will result in

rounds not impacting consistently where you want them to. If this is a consistent problem, it can be remedied by shooting 3 rounds on the target. If you shoot one round you can fake the funk. If you shoot two, it may still not help you with this issue; but three rounds will keep you from flock shooting the target.

Be Aggressive

When you are shooting a pistol or a rifle, aggression is a good thing. Remember to do the following.

- Be aggressive
- Fighting Stance
- Weight on the balls of your feet
- Knees slightly bent
- Drive with your legs

21.4 Be aggressive.

21.5 Maintain a fighting stance.

21.6 Weight on balls of feet.

21.7 Don't reach for the target.

21.8 Watch your sights.

21.9 Drive with your legs.

21.10 Lead with your eyes.

21.11 Drive aggressively to the next target.

Drive with your Legs

Throughout this process it is important that your legs are doing the work. Moving your body this quickly can only be done with the legs; if you try to use your upper torso you will not have the power and precision needed to be successful. I often see shooters shift their feet as well; this is only necessary when you must swing over a large area. This movement should be jerky. You should jerk the weapon from one target to the next, if it is a smooth, easy motion, you will not be as quick as required to quickly neutralize multiple threats.

21.12 Aggressive stance.

21.13 Note shooter drives with legs.

21.14 Aggressive stance.

21.15 Shooter drives with abdomen, losing power and speed. Also ends up in a very upright stance.

Over-swinging the Target

Another problem that is often encountered is over-swinging the target; this is caused by not leading with your eyes. It is very common for shooters with tube sights, especially if there is any amount of magnification. Red Dot sights will usually help you with these drills, or simply use iron sights to get the point across for this particular movement. Magnified scopes make your eyes work harder to go from the target plane, to looking through magnification and having to refocus to that plane. Since you are using a pistol, you now have no excuses. Use the iron sights, lead with the eyes and drive the weapon as hard as you can. If you are looking at the target, the weapon will stop on the target. If you have difficulty understanding the drill or getting your eyes to lead, a good way to get the point is this.

Place your eyes and sights on one target, now look to the next target, but do not move your head or your pistol, only your eyes. Once your eyes are on the next target, drive the weapon as quickly as possible to that target, once the weapon stops, fire the shot. Ensure you have proper sight alignment as this process takes place. Once the shot, or shots have been fired, stop. Leave your weapon pointed at the target you just engaged, now move your eyes to the next target. Once you are there, drive the weapon and take the shots as necessary. Continue with this drill until you can flow from target to target with no issues.

Move your Eyes, not your Head

It is normal for shooters to want to turn their head to see the next target. If this is required, fine. But if you can see the target in your peripheral vision, you don't need to lift or move your head. Move only your eyes if possible. If the target is not easily viewed in your peripheral, then by all means, move your head.

21.16 Eyes on sights.

21.17 Shooter moves head when it is unnecessary.

21.18 Weapon catches up to eyes.

This is Important

This is by far the easiest way you can quickly become a better tactical shooter. This applies to all areas of your tactical movement and target engagement sequences. You must move with a purpose when it comes to drawing the weapon, driving the weapon to the threat, engaging the threat or discriminating shoot/no shoot targets and finally driving the weapon to the next target. Snappy movements will result in only positive results, quickly.

After all, Gunfighting is a RACE.

Testing your stance

Shooters get lazy as they shoot more and more. In order to test your stance, place several targets at varying distances. Start from near to far and engage each target with three rounds. I usually start with the farthest target 15-20 yards away and the close target 5-7 yards away. Feel how the weight shifts as you shoot near to far, now reverse it and shoot far to near. Shoot the close target quickly and notice where you are standing at the end of the drill. Are you still aggressively on the balls of your feet or are you slightly back on your heels? Always apply positive pressure forward; we want to keep you on your toes. Not literally, but weight forward is the key.

Chapter 22, Turns/Facing Movements

22. TURNS/FACING MOVEMENTS

When things go bump in the night they normally won't be to your front. We must be able to quickly face this threat and engage. While doing so, we want to have a stable shooting platform.

How can we successfully turn to a threat and have stability to engage that threat?

When I teach turns, I push our students to always turn towards the threat. What this means is the following: Step forward, always step forward. If you start to step to the rear, you will trip and not be able to catch yourself. If you trip going forward, there is a good chance you will be able to catch yourself or at least not completely crash to the ground.

During our normal day to day routine we rarely walk backwards. At least where I live it hasn't really caught on. So it is safe to say you don't move to the rear much either. So as you train to shoot, use aggressive movements to the front as you make these turns. Hopefully this will all become clear as we discuss the techniques.

Safety

As you practice these techniques, be very careful where you point your weapon. It is extremely important to always know where the muzzle is oriented. We conduct turns with students to test their ability to know at all times where they are pointing their weapons.

22.1 Keep muzzle in a safe direction until facing down range.

Lead with your eyes

Before you turn, you should lead with your eyes. If your head and eyes can lead, your body will tend to face the target once you stop. The exception to seeing the target before you turn would be with a target directly to your rear. In this case, you will start to turn your head, leading with your eyes, and your body will start to turn. Once you have began to turn you will then see the target, your eyes will stop, and your body will catch up.

22.2 Lead with your eyes.

Turning to the Right 90 Degrees

If you assume a standing position facing to the left of the target to your front we will discuss the correct procedure for making the turn to face and engage the threat to your front. Starting with your weapon at Position 3 will be the easiest to begin with. If you are attempting this task with other shooters on the line, be very muzzle aware as you face the shooter to your left or right. At no time should you cover yourself or your fellow shooters with the muzzle of your weapon.

Make certain you are facing the left side of the range, as though you are planning to shoot in that direction. When you decide to make the turn, first turn your head and eyes to the target as this is what will happen if you hear a sound and look to check it out. Now step towards the threat, do not present your weapon to the threat until you have made the facing movement and are facing directly at your target. As you step you should be stepping with the left foot. This will allow you to rotate on the ball of your right foot as the left foot moves into position. If you bend your knees as you turn you will be able to engage threats as soon as your muzzle comes up on the target. Once you are finished engaging the threat, move back to Position 3 or the Holster and repeat until you are comfortable.

22.3 Face as though you are shooting to the left.

22.4 Turn your eyes and head towards the threat.

22.5 Eyes ID threat.

22.6 Start stepping with left foot.

22.7 Be aggressive.

22.8 Step towards the target.

22.9 Drive weapon to the target

22.10 Engage.

22.11 Weapon in holster.

22.12 As eyes and head move, hand goes to the pistol.

22.13 Keep driving left leg forward.

22.14 Turn complete, weapon coming out of holster.

22.15 Drive weapon to target.

22.16 Steady shots.

22.17 Engage the threat.

Turning to the Left 90 Degrees

If you plan to turn left, face to the right of the target to your front. All of the same rules apply. Once you decide to turn, move your head and eyes into position and then make your turn. When turning to the left, step into position aggressively with your right foot. This is the forward movement we are talking about. If you stepped with your left foot you would be stepping back and this can cause issues. Continue working these simple turns until you are comfortable, and then move on to the 180-degree turns below.

22.18 Face as though you plan to shoot to the right.

22.19 Eyes move to the target.

22.20 Eyes lock in on target.

22.21 Eyes on target, stepping forward with right foot.

22.22 Driving weapon to target.

22.23 Engage threat.

22.24 Aggressive stance.

22.25 Push with right toe, rotate on left toe.

22.26 Step far enough to turn body.

22.27 Feet planted.

22.28 End up with weight on balls of feet.

Turning to the Right 180 Degrees

Turns to the rear are more difficult than the flanking turns. They do require a little more aggressiveness to get turned all the way around quickly. Start facing away from your target; place your feet in a stance that allows you to shoot up range. Don't cheat by turning your feet until it is time to start the turn. When you initiate your turn, start by turning your head as you start to step. Unless you are an owl, there is no way you will be able to see the target until you have started to turn. Twist your head to the right as you step with your left foot. If you step aggressively, the momentum will spin you into the correct position to engage. You should not have to take two steps. It is very common for shooters to make two steps but it is inefficient. Do not drive the weapon to the threat until you are facing down range. Not only is this safer, it is much quicker as well.

22.29 Face away from the target.

22.30 Eyes and head start to move.

22.31 Eyes drive to the threat.

22.32 Body follows.

22.33 Rotating on right toe.

22.34 Bend knees to stay aggressive.

22.35 Fire weapon.

22.36 Back to targets.

22.37 Head moves.

22.38 Eyes to threat.

22.39 Rotate on right toe, aggressive step with left foot.

22.40 Bend knees.

22.41 Sights on threat.

Turning to the Left 180 Degrees

Face to the rear again, now prepare to turn to the left. This entails stepping with the right foot aggressively. Do not confuse the fact that you will end up slightly farther from the target with stepping to the rear. You are still stepping forward, and if you were to catch your toe you would more than likely not fall down. Lead with your head and eyes, step across with your right foot, and drive the weapon directly to the target as you complete your turn.

22.42 Facing away.

22.43 Head moves as does hand to holster.

22.44 Body following head.

22.45 Turn on left toe, right foot stepping across.

22.46 Pistol straight up and out.

22.47 Pistol driven to alignment with eyes.

22.48 Eliminate the threat.

22.49 Weight on balls of feet.

22.50 Twist on ball of left foot.

22.51 Right foot steps across.

22.52 As foot contacts ground, bend your knees.

22.53 Weight on balls of feet. Ready to fight.

22.54 Aggressive stance.

Drawing your weapon as you turn

Drawing your weapon as you turn will make you much quicker than waiting to face the threat before initiating your draw. That being said, you should start the draw, but not finish the draw during your turn. The draw should finish as you come to face the threat. Start your draw, moving the weapon quickly to Position 2, making sure the muzzle is in a safe direction. Once you have stopped and are facing the threat, you should be in Position 3 ready to drive the weapon to the threat as stated in the descriptions above. I always think straight up and out with the weapon during turns, up from the holster, out to the target.

22.55 Movement starts.

22.56 Eyes lead.

22.57 Shooter steps backwards.

22.58 Good way to end up on your butt.

22.59 Definitely not aggressive movement.

Alternate Positions

Another option is to simply twist your body and engage. The downside is that you are not able to lower your silhouette or engage multiple targets. You will also be limited in your ability to move quickly if need be. This position will work well if you have to hang on to something as you turn, such as a ladder while climbing a wall. Other than a few rare circumstances, you will be better off and just as fast to make the turn, leading with your head and driving your body to face the threat as you draw. Try this with your timer on the range and see what your times are.

Chapter 23, Shooting on the Move

23. SHOOTING ON THE MOVE

When it is time to shoot we must shoot immediately. You may not have time to stop and plant your feet firmly and attain the perfect stance. You may not be afforded the opportunity to simply run to cover and then engage the threat. For those of you operating as a team, you may need to continue your movement for several other reasons. Continuing to move may be your only security when quickly entering a room, as the bad guy attempts to get sights on you, the moving target. Or, you are able to engage a static bad guy while on the move. Which end do you want to be on?

Stopping movement while entering a room to engage a threat could also be catastrophic. If you do not get out of the door, also known as the "Fatal Funnel" to those of you in the tactical team arena, the suspect will have an easier time getting sights not only on you but your teammates as you are silhouetted in the doorway.

Some shooters believe that truly shooting on the move is witchcraft, which will result in missed shots. Absolutely untrue. With proper practice, you will quickly attain the proficiency that will allow you to shoot effectively on the move.

Shooting on the move is not as difficult as folks would lead the layman to believe. In order to quickly cut to the chase, here is what we teach:

- Bend your knees
- Take shorter steps
- One foot directly in front of the other
- Heel, outside edge of foot, to toe
- Squeeze the trigger
- Do not time your shots

How hard does that sound? Not difficult at all with a little practice.

23.1 Bend your knees to absorb shock.

23.2 Heel is planted, not slammed, into the ground.

23.3 Outside edge of foot.

23.4 Roll onto your toe.

23.5 Don't time your shots.

23.6 Try to place feet directly in front of each other.

23.7 Heel to edge of foot.

23.8 Roll onto toe.

23.9 Heel.

23.10 Edge of foot to toe.

23.11 Keep on rolling your foot.

23.12 Shoot when your sights are aligned.

Bend your knees

Bending your knees is so easy, yet some don't feel comfortable with this particular stance. If you are planning to shoot straight ahead, you may be able to get away with less leg bend. But when shooting straight down range while moving to the left or the right, you will need to bend your knees. Bending your knees will allow you to swivel your body a bit more, which in turn takes the stress out of your back. This is especially true when wearing body armor or other tactical gear. Bending the knees also helps to quiet your sights down (sights will not bounce/move as much) as your feet hit the ground. If you are short, you may not need to exaggerate the knee bend, but if you are 5'10" and taller, you will benefit greatly from more knee bend. A lower center of gravity will also give you more control of your body if you have to stop abruptly, or if you run into an obstacle. The bent knees will also help you to be free from injury if you step off a ledge or into a hole. I have seen shooters trip and wrench their backs, simply because they were not bending their knees.

23.13 Bend knees to quiet bounce in your sights.

23.14 Step across, placing lead foot.

23.15 Try not to let foot hit hard, absorb shock with knees.

23.16 This technique will help you to twist towards the target.

Lower silhouette

Bending the knees also helps to lower your silhouette. In a gunfight, why would you not want a lower silhouette for the threat to aim at? Bend the knees, lower your silhouette and see what you think.

Take shorter steps

You will help to quiet your sights if you take smaller steps than normal. You don't have to take baby steps, but somewhere between baby steps and full steps, you will find the sweet spot. If you start to take the shorter steps you will see your sights stop bouncing up and down on the target. As you lengthen your stride you will see the sights start to bounce every time your front foot hits the ground. This will cause you to hit low, and may cause you to start jerking the trigger to attempt to get the round to fire before the sights are disrupted by the impact of your foot on the ground. Don't get lured into this bad habit.

To increase your speed, take faster, short steps. Do not lengthen your steps to increase speed. As you speed up your short steps, you will see the sights bounce right in the area of the target that you want to hit. The amount of movement should not get bigger, but just bounce in the same area that you want to hit the target.

One foot directly in front of the other

Sounds confusing, but it is not. Picture yourself walking down a 2x4 wooden plank. You would want your feet one in front of the other to ensure that you did not fall off the board. This is also true when shooting on the move. What happens when you walk with your feet one in front of the other is this: You start to slightly cant your feet so they are off camber. This allows the roll from heel to edge of your foot to toes to take place. This should be the same motion you would use if you were trying to sneak up on an animal, or sneak out of a room. Do not let the heal slam into the ground, place the feet one in front of the other. For females this is especially important. The good Lord designed all of us a little different; women have larger hips and will need to exaggerate this movement to quiet the movement in their sights.

If your sights are bouncing left and right, it is caused by the lack of alignment of your feet. One foot in front of the other should solve this issue.

Heel, outside edge of foot, to toe

This is important so let me reiterate. You should attempt to place the heel, then roll onto the outside edge of your foot. This edging procedure should not be uncomfortable or cause you to walk ridiculously, just enough that you feel the difference inside your boot. Lastly, roll onto your toes.

23.17 Lower silhouette with bent knees.

23.18 Take shorter steps than normal.

23.19 One foot directly in front of the other.

23.20 Concentrate on placing your heel.

23.21 Absorb shock with bent knees.

23.22 Heel

23.23 Outside edge of foot.

23.24 Roll onto your toe, repeat until threat is eliminated.

Squeeze the trigger

You must let the weapon surprise you if you want to be successful with shooting accurately on the move. This is the end result of squeezing the trigger. You cannot make the gun go off, it must happen as a surprise. This is especially important as distance is increased. Shooting while moving from 25 yards with the pistol is easy, if you do not jerk the trigger. As you close the distance with the target, you will be able to press the trigger more aggressively without disturbing the acceptable sight picture.

Do not time your shots

Some instructors teach shooters to time their shots as one or the other of their feet comes off the ground. This may be something that works for competition shooting, but will not work in a real world encounter. The threat will not wait until you have attained the correct foot placement to shoot. The threat will be engaging you no matter your foot location. Watch your sights, squeeze the trigger and let the weapon go off when the sights are in an acceptable area of that target. Do not time your shots.

23.25 Squeeze the trigger, do not time your shots.

Taking a hand off the weapon

Some shooters like to take their support hand off the weapon when they are moving towards their support side. They feel that they are more agile with the weapon in the strong hand only. This is a viable option, if you are competent and confident with the strong hand only. It does work well for those that are great strong hand only shooters.

Practice

Practice dry until you are confident in your moving ability. If you can maintain the acceptable sight picture as you dry fire, live fire should not be an issue. I always practice every angle, head on charging the threat is easy; shooting as you are moving left or right, ninety degrees from your target is a little trickier. This is a good time to video your practice to see if you are getting the movement as smooth as you would like.

Once you have figured this out, start adding movement and turns, as well as reloads and varying speeds. Check out our DVDs which have several drills to help with your shooting on the move.

Don't cross your feet

If you grew up as a ballet dancer or a football player leave the fancy footwork at home. Do not cross your feet as you are shooting on the move. This will cause you to get twisted up and start to fall. If you are faced to the rear as you trip you

23.26 First step is good.

23.27

23.28

23.29

23.30 Now shooter steps unnaturally behind leg.

23.31 Crossed legs - this is an accident waiting to happen.

23.32 If you trip here, there is no catching yourself.

23.33 Don't cross your feet.

23.34 This sequence shows the strength of one-handed shooting on the move. This works well when shooting with excessive gear.

23.35

23.36

23.37

23.38

23.39

23.40

will not be able to catch yourself. Keep moving with a slight crab, this is not crossing your feet, this is simply twisting. Keep practicing and bend those knees. This will give you the additional twist to keep from stepping to the rear.

Don't Stop

When practicing your shooting on the move, never stop to fix malfunctions or reload. Continue with your movement. At the very least, run for cover if your weapon is down. Seek cover, fix it, and then get back in the fight.

Chapter 24, Drawing From Concealment

24. DRAWING FROM CONCEALMENT

Drawing from concealment must be taken seriously if you have decided to carry a concealed weapon every day of your life. Most shooters do train, but when they train it is with less than realistic props. For example, how many of you have drawn your weapon while in your vehicle and shot? More than likely, not a lot. This is why we must practice the scenarios that will most likely hit us when we least expect them. Secondly, we must wear the type of garb that we would during our day-to-day activities. If this means you will carry different types of weapons and holsters, you must train to develop the muscle memory to quickly take cover, draw, and eliminate the threat.

Concealed carry is exactly that. I don't want any good or bad guys to know that I am carrying a weapon. I want it to come as a total surprise to a slack jawed hoodlum when he or she decides to take my truck for a test drive. If you have decided to place your weapon in a briefcase or purse, will that item be with you 100% of the day? If the answer is yes, you are good to go; but more than likely you are not able to carry your accessories with you all day. Carrying a weapon concealed on your body is much more relevant to what we are talking about here; and yes, it leads to discomfort at some points, but no one ever said carrying concealed would be easy.

24.1 Concealed to the casual observer types of carry.

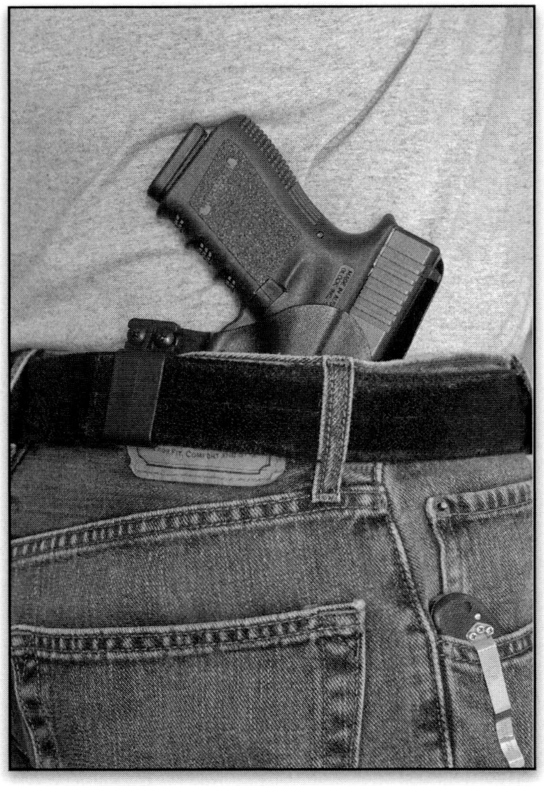

24.2 Inside the pants carry, Blade-Tech Razor holster.

24.3

24.4 Appendix carry, Blade-Tech Appendix holster.

24.5

24.6 Outside of pants carry, Blade-Tech Eclipse holster.

24.7 Appendix carry holster with slot that allows for flashlight carry as well.

Chambered or Not

This question always comes up. Do you have a round chambered when you are carrying concealed? Absolutely. Let me caveat this by saying one other thing. Only if you are carrying in a safe holster that will not allow the weapon to accidentally discharge. If you plan to shove the weapon into your britches and go with it, you may want to rethink the loaded chamber. I prefer a holster to save the embarrassment of dropping a weapon down your pants leg or into a third world toilet hole…..not that this ever happened to me in Saudi Arabia in 1991.

Types of Carry

For simplicity, I want to cover the 3 most relevant types of concealed carry.

(1) Outside of your pants, meaning a holster that is normally worn on the belt and covered by a jacket or shirt.

(2) Inside the pants, same scenario with the exception of the holster being tucked inside of your pants.

(3) Appendix carry, the weapon is carried in the slot between the front of your hip and the belt buckle; this being my favorite as well as normally the most concealable technique, although comfort is usually a thing of the past when carrying in the Appendix area.

Drawing from Concealment with Hip Holster

The basic rules that I follow when drawing from concealment are as follows.

- Knife cutting edge with the strong hand middle finger placed against the sternum
- Drive the hand back until the strong hand is directly above the holster
- Drive the hand down your side rotating from a knife cutting edge to using the thumb against your rib cage

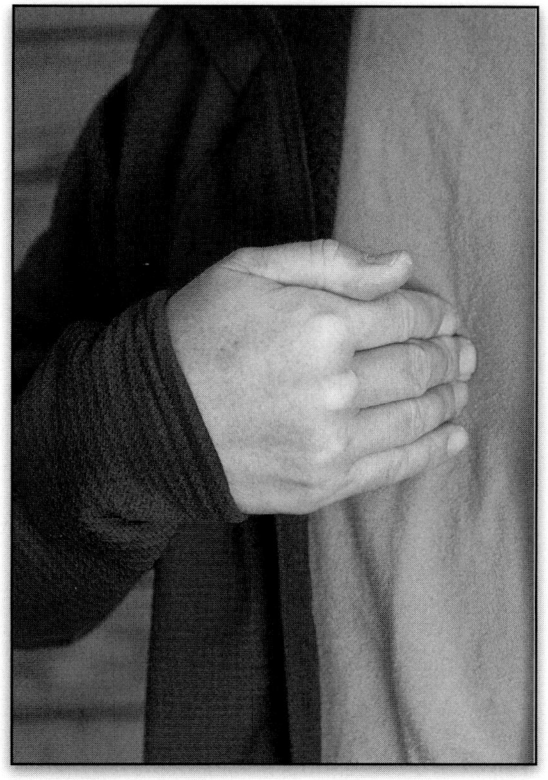

24.8 Knife cutting edge.

- Drive the hand directly on top of the weapon
- Pause to ensure that you have the firing grip that you prefer
- Draw the weapon
- If clothes end up under your pinky or ring finger continue with the draw and the clothing should pull free
- Repeat over and over until you don't have to think through the process

I have seen folks who modify all of their clothes with weed eater string in the edge of their jacket to make the jacket move quickly out of your way. This is an interesting concept but I don't have the patience or sewing skills to customize all of my clothing. I have also seen folks ensure that they have a fully loaded magazine in their strong side jacket pocket so they can fling the jacket out of the way. Once again, this briefs well but in a struggle you may not be able to fling anything. What if you are on your side or belly?

Knife Cutting Edge

When I say, "the fingers will be extended and joined to form a knife cutting edge," you are probably confused. I started life as a Paratrooper in the 82nd Airborne Division and this terminology is used all the time when referring to activating your reserve parachute. By knife cutting edge, I specifically mean placing all of your fingers, as well as the thumb, together and touching your middle finger to your sternum. This finger should be at 90 degrees to your sternum. This sharp edge will be used to pull the jacket out of the way quickly, but more importantly, consistently pull the jacket out of the way.

Drive the hand back until the strong hand is directly above the holster

Another key point is how far we push the strong hand back before we start the downward movement to the weapon. It is paramount that you continue this sweep until you are directly above the weapon. This action will aid in clearing the jacket out of the way regardless of shirt or jacket type.

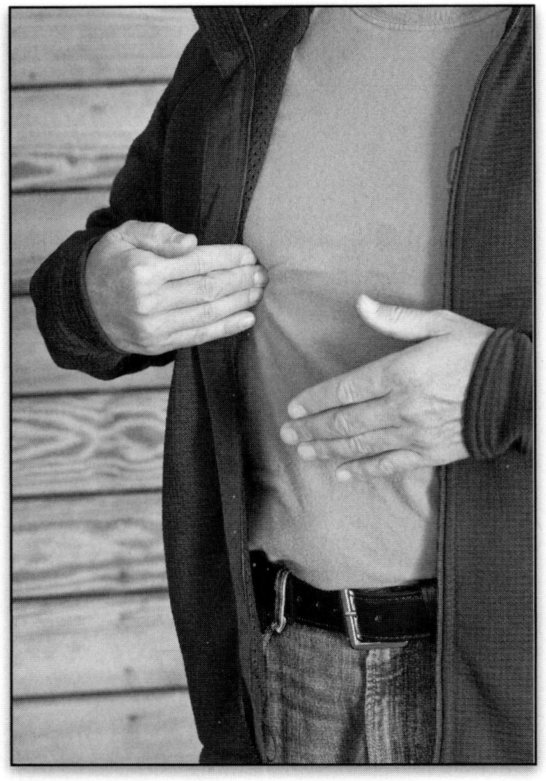

24.9 Push firmly with your fingertips.

24.10 Drive hand back until it is directly above the weapon.

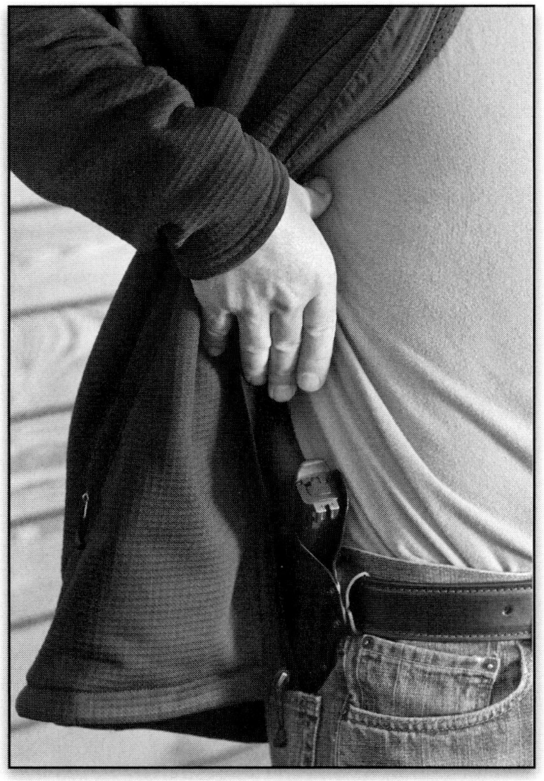

24.11 Drive your hand down your side, switching from a knife cutting edge to thumb against your rib cage.

Drive the hand down your side switching from a knife cutting edge to using the thumb against your rib cage

As you hit the point along your ribs that you should start the downward movement to the weapon, transition from touching with your fingertips to driving the hand down with the thumb pushed against your side. This will allow the clothing to continue to stay out of your strong hand's way and help you attain the proper firing grip on the weapon without the interference of clothing. Your hand should never lose contact with your body during this process.

Drive the hand directly on top of the weapon

You should press your hand back far enough that it will allow you to come straight down and in contact with the firearm. This position should be very close to the position that you would want your hand in for the actual draw.

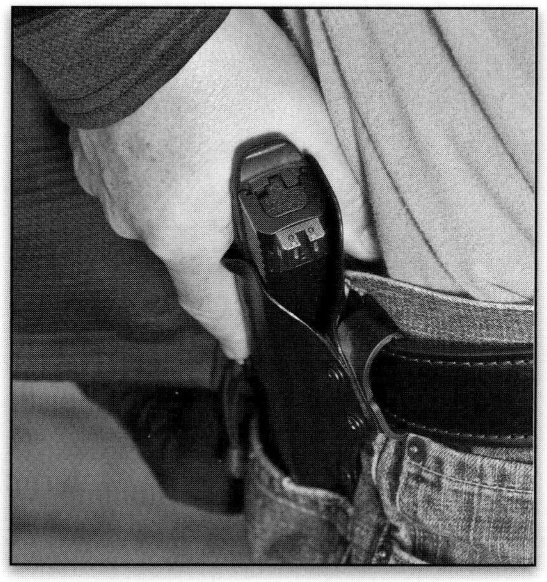

24.12 Drive hand directly on top of weapon.

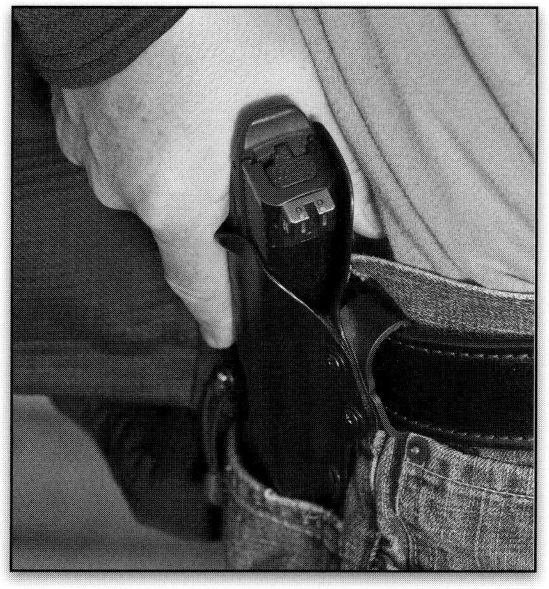

24.13 Pause to ensure you have correct firing grip.

Pause to ensure you have the correct firing grip

This short pause is important to ensure that you have the correct grip. If you fail to pause now, the poor grip will be seriously detrimental to your accuracy and speed as the draw continues.

Draw the weapon

If you have the correct grip, draw the weapon. Speed counts in a gunfight so be snappy about it.

If clothes end up under your pinky or ring finger continue with the draw and the clothing should pull free

This is a part of the concealed carry draw that you must experiment with. Will the clothing pull free if you only have it caught in your pinky and ring finger? What is your jacket or shirt made out of? If the material is not a stretchy, grabby, mesh fabric you should be fine. If you have a jacket with a mesh liner, I would look around for something a little more user friendly. Not only will this material catch on your pistol when you draw, but it will continuously be bothersome as a concealment jacket. Not to mention if you have any grip tape on the weapon, it will destroy the jacket.

The above technique should work well when using a belt or outside the pants concealment set up and an inside the pants set up when wearing an open front

jacket or open front shirt for concealment. If you are using an inside the waistband holster behind your hip, with a shirt that is closed and fastened in the front, you may have to change your technique slightly.

24.15 Start in somewhat of a normal position.

24.16 Knife cutting edge to sternum.

24.17 Drive fingers back along side.

24.18 Switch to thumb against body.

24.19 Get the perfect grip.

24.20 Snap the weapon from the holster.

24.21 Position 2.

24.22 Position 3.

24.23 Press towards the target.

24.24 Engage the threat.

24.25 Practice, practice, practice.

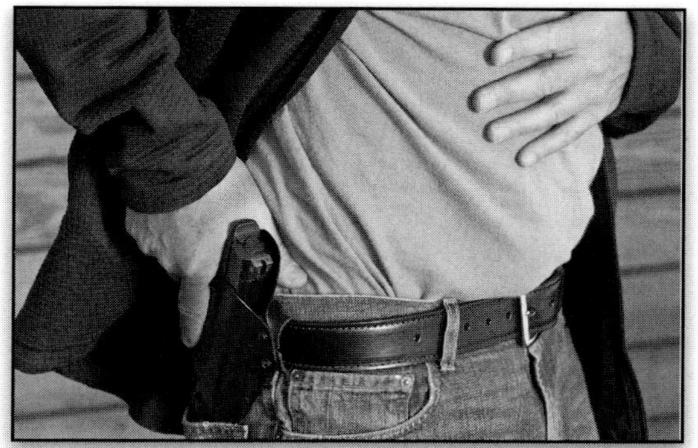

24.26 Good grip, but jacket is under pinky or ring finger.

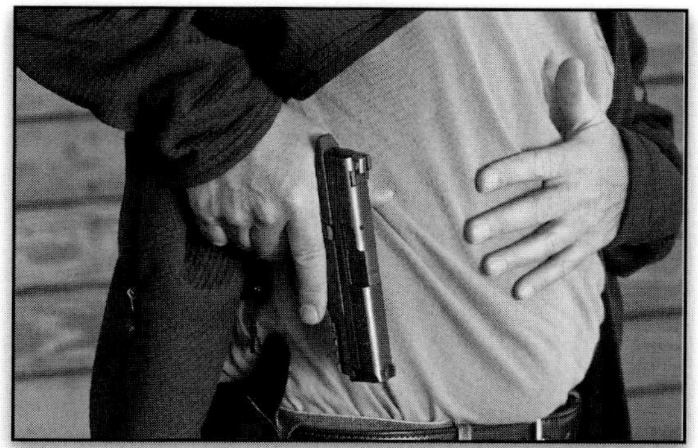

24.27 Continue with your draw.

24.28 Do not over grip.

24.29 Press weapon towards target.

24.30 At some point, the jacket will come free.

24.31

24.32

24.33 Engage threat.

24.34 Start in natural position.

24.35 Grip shirt and clear it out of your way.

24.36 Support hand holds shirt while thumb drives to weapon.

24.37 Get the perfect grip.

24.38 Snap weapon from holster.

24.39 Quick to Position 3.

24.40 Drive to target.

24.41 Eliminate threat.

Drawing from an Appendix Holster

As I stated earlier, this is my preferred technique. The reason being is that I can easily conceal a relatively large weapon without having to wear excessive clothing. If you are wearing shorts and a t-shirt, you will have plenty of clothing to conceal in this position. Always try to wear darker t-shirts to limit the amount of printing or see through of the shirt. You should also check yourself out in the mirror to make sure this technique works with your body type. I also like this technique because I have easy or relatively easy access with both hands, just in case I become wounded and must use my support hand. No issues, the weapon is readily accessible.

The Appendix Draw

- Support Hand grabs bottom of shirt or jacket directly below appendix carry holster
- Support Hand pulls shirt or jacket up and out of the way
- Firing hand thumb is pressed against belly well above holstered weapon
- Firing hand is driven down to the weapon with the thumb staying pressed against the body
- Thumb is driven behind weapon to ensure the proper draw
- Draw the weapon

The Appendix Draw is very dependant on the support hand making things happen; most draws are more dependant on the firing hand, but not the Appendix Draw. You must get the clothing out of the way before anything can happen.

Support Hand pulls shirt or jacket up and out of the way

The more you can pull the jacket out of the way the better. You don't want to have anything in the way as this draw takes place. Normally, parts of the jacket or shirt will want to still get in the way and the higher you pull the better.

Firing Hand Thumb pressed against body

Firing hand is driven down to the weapon with the thumb staying pressed against the body. Thumb is driven behind the weapon to ensure the proper draw.

It is important that you drive the thumb against your body and continue to drive this thumb down to the backside of the weapon. This allows for a much more positive and consistent draw.

If you are attempting this draw with one hand, strong or support, it is still paramount that you drive the thumb behind the weapon to attain a decent grip for shooting or for simply getting the weapon free from the holster.

24.42 Try to start in a natural position.

24.43 Support hand grabs bottom of shirt.

24.44 Support hand pulls shirt up and out of the way.

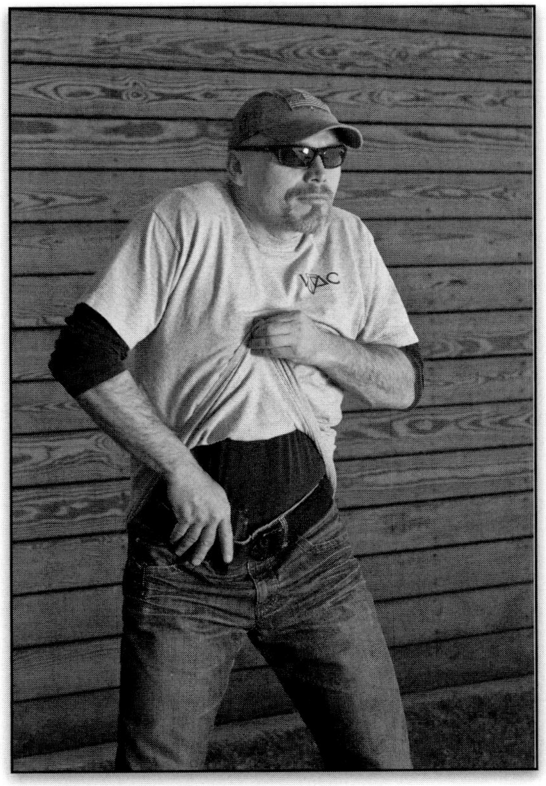

24.45 Drive thumb down behind holster.

24.46 Drive thumb down behind holster.

24.47 Snap weapon from holster

24.48 Position 3

24.49 Prep trigger as you drive weapon towards threat.

24.50 Squeeze the trigger.

24.51 Appendix carry with hand held light attached to holster, very convenient.

Prepare for the Worst

When using the appendix carry technique, I always prepare my clothing for the draw when getting situated in a vehicle. This simply means that I have the t-shirt or cover shirt laid over the seatbelt, not pinned under the belt. This allows for less pulling and fighting with clothing to get to the weapon, and once again, every second counts.

Train, train, train

I attempt to practice my concealed draws every day. I do this simply due to the fact that I am always wearing different clothes. Once you figure out what to wear, dry fire your draw to see if you can make it happen. Luckily I have never been a slave to fashion so the concealed pistol is the priority not the after thought. Snap shirts work well and allow you to practice without destroying buttons, luckily cowboy shirts are back in style.

You must also practice within the surroundings you live in on a day-to-day basis. The most often overlooked is your vehicle. You may not have the ability to live fire from your car or truck, but you can most certainly dry fire these techniques.

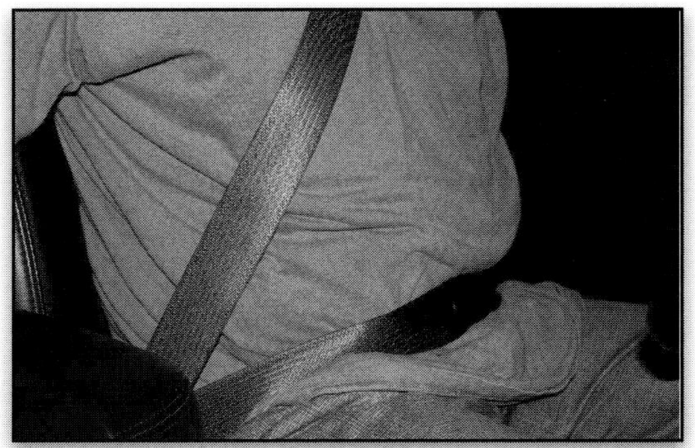

24.52 Normally this is how we would wear our seat belt.

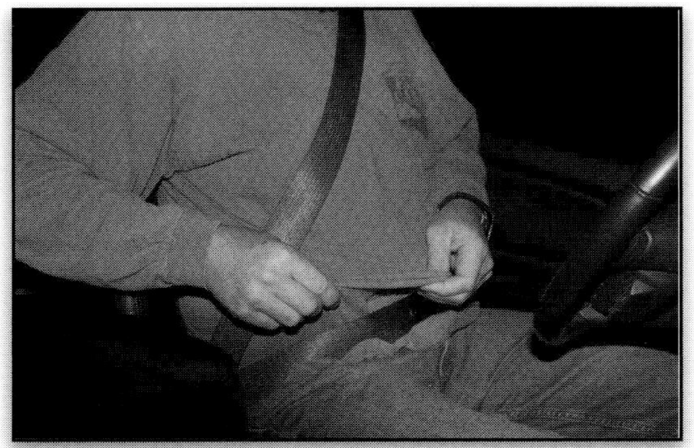

24.53 Take a few seconds to prepare.

24.54 Ensure you have access to weapon.

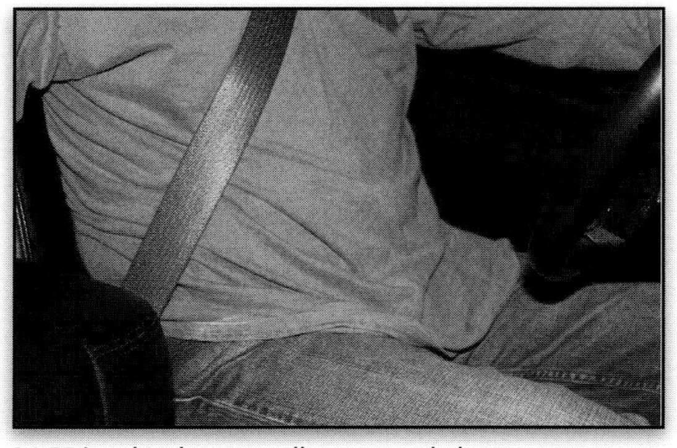

24.55 Let shirt lay naturally over seat belt.

24.56 When it is time to draw, grab shirt with support hand.

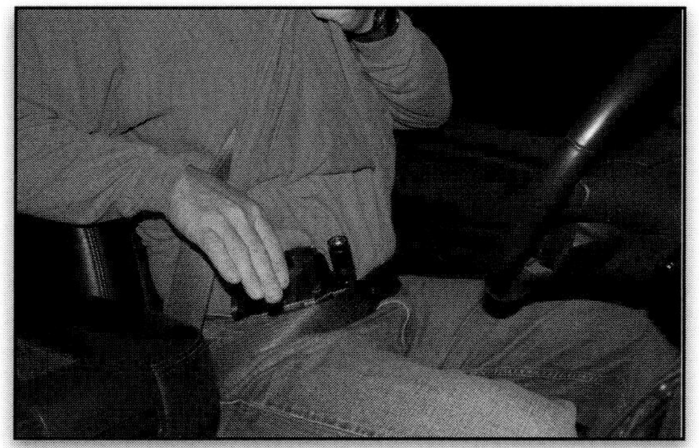

24.57 Pull shirt up.

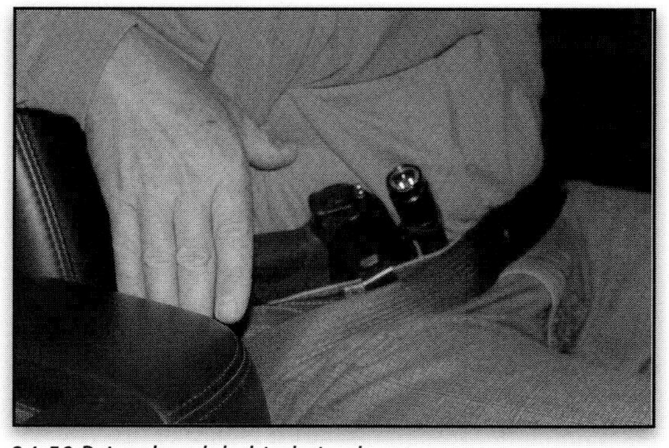

24.58 Drive thumb behind pistol.

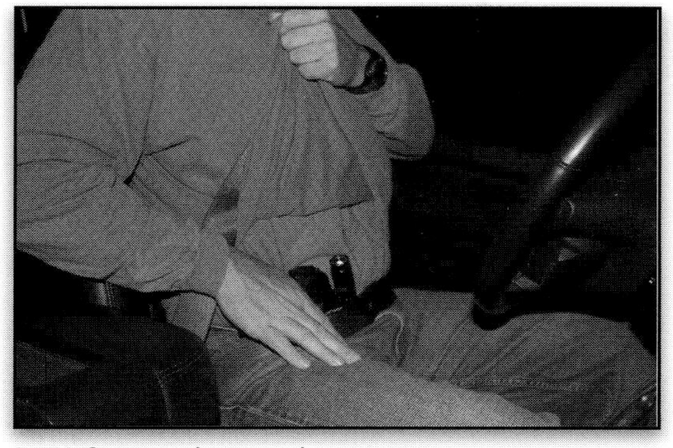

24.59 Get a good grip on the weapon.

24.60 Pull the weapon up to a good retention position and be aware of where your muzzle is pointed.

24.61 Present the pistol.

24.62 ***Car jack this!***

Holstering your Weapon

There are not too many scenarios I can think of in which you are required to speed holster the weapon. I am sure we could come up with a few, but not a place I would spend a lot of time practicing. Holstering absolutely, but not speed holstering. Be very careful when holstering your weapon during concealed carry scenarios. A few things have changed, clothing can get in the way, jacket pull cords and zippers can get in the way and all it takes is one wrong pull or push and things could get loud. You are also pointing the weapon extremely close to valuable body parts when using certain concealment rigs. The Appendix Holster is a recipe for disaster if you are not extremely careful during the holstering process. If you have decided to carry a 1911 type weapon that is single action, always ensure the thumb safety is activated before holstering. This is a common mistake with this weapon. The safety is there, please use it.

Chapter 25, Strong and Support Hand Only

25. STRONG AND SUPPORT HAND ONLY

What is normal or flat range specific and what is realistic are probably two different animals when it comes to one-handed shooting techniques. We must always remember what we are training for. Are you training to win the President's Hundred Tab, or for a combat situation? When, where, and why will you employ one handed techniques?

An injured Law Enforcement officer had found himself in the fight for his life. He had received injuries to his strong side arm that would not allow him to fire the weapon with his strong hand. Luckily, he had trained to shoot with his support side, so no issues here. After exchanging gunfire with the suspect, he found himself taking cover behind his patrol car and shooting until his weapon was dry. No worries, he had trained for support hand only reloads. He calmly dropped the dry magazine and reached down to secure a fresh, fully loaded magazine. What he found next was unnerving. The suspect's gunfire had hit not only one of his spare magazines, but both. He had two inoperable magazines on his hip. As he grabbed the first magazine and tipped it up to load it into the weapon, the remaining contents fell into his hand and onto the ground. He quickly dropped the destroyed magazine and grabbed the next magazine; it too was destroyed and dumped the remaining ammo on the ground. What would he do? He reached down and secured a couple rounds of loose ammunition. He quickly figured out how to load a few of these life saving rounds into the magazine, seat the magazine, cycle a round into the chamber, and be prepared for the final chapter of this story. The suspect, sensing that there were issues, advanced on the officer's position to finish what he started. To his surprise he came face to face with this brave officer who placed the sights where they needed to be and eliminated the threat. This is a crazy story with an unbelievable outcome, train for just this predicament. Murphy is always there…

I prefer to think through the scenarios that I will need to use one hand only. I would not choose to shoot with one hand, but sometimes you will have to play with the hand you are dealt. Are you shooting with one hand due to a wounded opposing arm, or is it because you are on a ladder and must keep one hand touching the ladder, or do you just rely on your unbelievably keen night vision and have exceptional balance?

The reason I try to stir a little thought into this process here is this: Most tactical shooters will draw the weapon and then blade their body to the extreme to fire the weapon with one hand. This is a great technique, but in the situations I have encountered, or my mates have encountered, they were forced into a slightly different stance. A squarer stance is more realistic and harder to shoot from.

Now if you happen to be a Cavalry man, which means holding your horse is required, by all means, blade your stance. We don't want Trigger running away.

Stance

The square stance is a good place to start with regard to strong and support hand only shooting. It will allow you to still have sufficient control of the weapon as well as good balance and quick mobility if needed. Practice from any stance you can think of that will possibly apply to your situation.

Just to be absolutely clear, if you want to shoot the best you can with one hand, the bladed stance is the way to go. But think of the real world, and practice the way you will be required to fight.

25.1 Square stance which you may have to shoot from.

25.2 Bladed stance with strong foot forward preferrable - if possible.

Grip

Grip is a key ingredient for shooting well with one hand. There are a few tricks to success with one hand shooting. First, grip the weapon as high as you possibly can without affecting the function of the weapon system. Ensure the web of your hand is as high as possible on the back strap of the pistol. This has several downstream effects with regard to not only accuracy, but also the proper function of the weapon.

If you have a poor grip on the weapon, you may induce a stoppage. Some weapons require decent grip due to heavier springing for high recoil rounds.

25.3 Grip as high as possible.

An example of this is the Glock 22 in 40 S&W caliber. You must hang on well to these weapons to ensure they function correctly.

Another reason for the high grip would be the fact that you don't want the weapon to have a mechanical advantage against you. The weapon gains leverage as you lower your grip, do not allow this to happen. It is very noticeable for follow up shots.

Thumb Safeties

If your weapon is equipped with a frame mounted thumb safety, you can use this for additional leverage against the weapon. With weapons such as the 1911, it is advantageous to have your thumb on the safety as you fire the weapon. I usually keep my thumb in this position no mater the type, old habits are hard to break.

25.4 Thumb not pushing on safety.

25.5 If the weapon has a thumb safety, use the safety for additional leverage against recoil.

Thumb to Middle Finger

If you are having issues with your grip, a technique that is widely used with American Special Forces Instructors when training shooters to use the Beretta 92/M9 is a thumb to middle finger grip. This is just the opposite of placing the thumb on the safety, well not really the opposite, but the M9 does not have a thumb safety mounted on the frame to give you a ledge. The technique requires you to rotate your thumb down until it touches the middle finger, then apply positive pressure. This works well for some, it may or may not work for you, but it is worth trying if you have issues with your one handed shooting.

25.6 *Try pressing your thumb to your middle finger.*

Arm Straight or Bent

Shooter's choice, what will work for you? I personally prefer to keep my arm closer to my natural two handed shooting position, therefore the arms are slightly bent, but not over exaggerated. Many great shooters bend their arms significantly. Try it to see what works for you. There is no one way that works for everyone.

Folks often want to know which technique is superior for recoil control. I do not feel that you can control recoil when shooting with one hand; you just have to use the recoil of the weapon to carry you to the next target, or drive the weapon back down to the current threat. If you over grip while attempting to manage recoil when shooting with one hand, accuracy normally suffers.

25.7 *Arm slightly bent.*

Draws

Strong Hand

Strong handed draws should not be significantly different than your normal draw. You should still be able to quickly get the weapon released from the holster and drive it to the target. I am not saying you should not practice, but you may want to place focus on more difficult movements such as support side draws.

25.8 *Place support arm against chest.*

25.9 *Establish perfect grip.*

25.10 *Release retention device and snap weapon from holster.*

25.11 Prep trigger.

25.12 Fire the weapon.

Support Side

Too often, the support side is overlooked. Not just the shooting portion, but how do we handle basic maneuvers with the support hand only? These basic movements are critical to Winning and Thriving in a gunfight, not just surviving a fight.

Before practicing these support side techniques, please ensure that you are using an unloaded/clear weapon. These techniques are advanced and should be treated as such. Plenty of dry fire training will prepare you for live fire on the range.

Gear placement is crucial to allowing you to actually gain access to your weapon with just the support hand. If you have a front mounted rucksack (belly), figure out how you will slide the holster to the proper location to make the required draw. So far I have never had a student that couldn't figure it out. It may take a little analytical work, but you must be able to get to your gun, no matter the situation. If you have a drop leg holster, pulling the holster to the front of your leg will help. This, along with slightly twisting your body and you should be in business. Some shooters are actually better off going behind their body to grab the weapon.

Along the same lines, you must figure out how you will activate the retention mechanisms on your holster. There are a few tricks to making this work. Be careful if you are grabbing and twisting with the weapon, ensure that all your fingers stay clear of the trigger mechanism of the weapon.

25.13 Stay aggressive from your support side, step forward and lean into it.

25.14 Do not try to control recoil, learn how to manage it.

25.15 Dry fire these techniques before going live.

Using your knees

You most likely will not be able to get the weapon into your shooting grip with the first grab. Normally shooters will grab the weapon however possible, pass the weapon to a position between their knees, and then simply transition their hand into the shooting grip. This is the safest, as well as the most secure movement for me, that is unless mobility is needed (the ability to run for cover). If your situation dictates that you need to find cover, your choices are simple. Run for cover while attempting to draw, or just run for cover and sort it out when you get there.

25.16 Reach across or behind and deactivate your retention device.

25.16 Pull the weapon from the holster, keep fingers clear of trigger.

25.17 Keep weapon pointed in a safe direction.

25.18 Place weapon between knees.

25.19 Attain firing grip.

25.20 Ready to fight.

Rolling the weapon on your chest or gear

When attempting to draw the weapon on the move, be absolutely sure that the weapon's muzzle does not cover any part of your body. You may choose to either roll the weapon across your chest or slide the weapon under an arm and conduct the transfer to the grip of the weapon. Do not try to flip the weapon in the air and catch it in the proper grip, save this for the made for TV action heroes.

25.21 Start with your gear rigged the way you normally carry it, don't cheat.

25.22 Release retention device.

25.23 Safely secure weapon.

25.24 Bring the weapon to your chest.

25.25 Watch your muzzle as you roll the weapon across your chest.

25.26 Keep trigger finger clear of trigger until you are in a safe poistion.

25.27 Prep trigger as you present to threat.

25.28 Fire!

Laying the weapon on the ground

If you find yourself on the ground behind cover, just set the weapon on the ground and re-grasp with the proper shooting grip.

25.29 Practice for all situations.

25.30 Release retention.

25.31 Secure weapon.

25.32 Safely draw.

25.33 Keep muzzle in a safe direction.

25.34 Lay weapon on right side so you can simply pick it up.

25.35 When you grab the weapon, keep finger clear of trigger.

25.36 Attain perfect grip.

25.37 Engage.

Rotating the weapon in the holster

Some holsters may allow you to pull the weapon then twist it and place it in the holster backwards. If your holster will allow this maneuver, use it. Make sure it is absolutely secure and will not drop out onto the ground. I normally run with a pistol light in place and my holsters will not allow this maneuver. Check your gear to make sure it works.

I can't stress this enough, BE CAREFUL when conducting these techniques. It is also advised that you place the weapon back in your strong hand to re-holster during your practice sessions. Do not overlook having to place the weapon in the holster with the support hand only though.

Reloads

Reloading the weapon is a necessary evil with one hand. It takes practice and patience, but with a little of each, you will become completely confident.

Strong Hand Reload

Conducting a reload with just the strong hand is not nearly as difficult as the opposite; however there are a few techniques to discuss. If you have to conduct a slide lock reload, you should first drop the magazine. Don't worry about recovering it because you can take care of that after you have inserted the fresh magazine. If you press the magazine release and the magazine sticks in the magazine well, use the front edge of the magazine to pull the magazine out of the well. I prefer to hook the leading edge of the empty magazine on my holster or magazine pouch and give it a tug. If you are not wearing a holster, such as during a house invasion scenario, use the edge of a nightstand or door jam to pry out the magazine. Once the empty magazine has fallen free, the next issue is to figure out the best method to hold the weapon while inserting the fresh magazine.

25.38 Use edge of holster to pull stuck magazine from weapon.

Using your holster

If you have a drop leg holster, or a stiff belt holster that allows easy insertion of the weapon, simply slide the weapon back into the holster. Once the weapon is secured in the holster, reach across your body, grab a magazine and seat it in the weapon. If the weapon is not completely secured in the holster, don't over-seat the magazine; I have seen shooters knock their weapons out of the holster. Using the holster is the best technique for me because I want to be able to run and move and not have to worry about losing the weapon. As you conduct the strong side reload, continue to glance towards

25.39 *Weapon is empty.*

25.40 *Rotate weapon slightly to reach magazine release.*

25.41 *Release magazine with weapon vertical.*

25.42 *Magazine drops free.*

25.43 Once magazine has dropped.

25.44 Drive weapon back to holster.

25.45 Glance at holster if necessary.

25.46 Safely place weapon in holster.

25.47 Reach across body for fresh magazine.

25.48 Ensure you have a good grip

25.49 Grip magazine for reload.

25.50 Once magazine is seated, grip weapon.

25.51 Let slide slam forward using slide stop or alternate technique.

25.52 Prepare to engage threat.

the area that the threat may come from. Do not get tunnel vision during this reload.

Using your knees

If you do not have a holster that will allow you to safely re-holster with one hand, you will need to find alternate methods. I prefer to use my knees, if mobility is not an issue. It is somewhat secure and does not make you point the weapon at yourself like some other techniques might. After dropping the empty magazine, rotate the weapon inboard with the muzzle pointed towards the ground, and clamp the weapon between your knees exposing the magazine well. After grabbing the magazine with the strong hand, seat it firmly, pull out on the magazine's base pad to ensure it is seated, grasp the weapon and move on to the next step below.

This technique also allows you to somewhat keep your focus towards the threat. All techniques should allow you to use sound tactics while safely conducting your reload.

25.53 Release magazine.

25.54 Place weapon between knees, magazine well forward.

25.55 Grab full magazine.

25.56 Slide magazine into magwell.

25.57 Secure weapon.

25.58 Ensure you have a good firing grip.

25.59 Shooter hooks rear sight on gear.

25.60 Release slide to slam into battery.

Under your arm

If the holster and knee options are out of play, you may want to try placing the weapon under your incapacitated arm. This technique is not preferred since you will be covering your body at some point with the muzzle of your weapon. This technique does allow for mobility and that can be the matter of life and death in some scenarios. Do not be overly aggressive when seating the magazine; the slide may slam forward which could catch on your skin or clothing, inducing a stoppage. As with the two previous techniques, read on for slide release procedures.

25.61 Release magazine.

25.62 Place weapon under arm.

25.63 Secure fresh magazine.

25.64 Slide magazine into weapon.

25.65 Seat magazine.

25.66 Secure weapon.

25.68 Shooter using holster and rear sight to release slide.

25.69 Let slide slam forward.

25.70 Back in action.

Behind your knee

For years I watched shooters reload with their weapons in the crook behind their knee. The only issue was that the muzzle was pointed at their other knee, foot, or leg. There is a better way to use the behind the knee technique and do it safely. Once it is time to reload, turn the muzzle away from your body and slide the weapon behind your knee with the muzzle remaining away from your body. Sit back on your leg to clamp the weapon firmly in place. Ensure you release your magazine before placing the weapon behind your knee. Grab a fresh magazine, seat the magazine and remove the weapon from behind your leg before letting the slide slam forward.

25.71 Weapon dry.

25.72 Press magazine release.

25.73 Release magazine.

25.74 Without pointing weapon at body, place weapon behind knee, barrel pointed away from your body.

25.75 Place weapon in crook of knee.

25.76 Hold weapon in place.

25.77 Press body weight against pistol to hold in place.

25.78 Grab fresh magazine.

25.79 Seat fresh magazine in pistol.

25.80 Keep fingers clear of trigger.

25.81 Once magazine is seated, get good grip on pistol.

25.82 Let slide slam forward.

25.83 Drive weapon to threat.

25.84 Engage!

Releasing the slide

Once the magazine is seated in the weapon, pull the weapon from the holster, from between your knees, or from under your arm, and allow the slide to slam into battery. This can be accomplished several ways. The first way is to simply let the slide slam forward by using the slide release. This works fine as long as you do not have to adjust your hand on the weapon to make it happen. If it requires shifting of the hand, there may be a better technique.

A faster and more positive technique that works with both strong and support hands is the following. Grab the weapon from the holster, same as the previous technique; next rotate the slide of the weapon inboard so the rear sight is aligned with the front of your holster, your pants leg, or your belt. At this point, be absolutely sure the weapon is not pointed at anything you do not want to destroy, in particular, your own leg. The weapon should be parallel to your leg and pointed safely at the ground. With your finger off the trigger, quickly drag the rear sight across the holster, pants, or belt. This will allow the slide to be released and slam forward. Do not let the slide ride forward slowly, this may induce a stoppage. Let it slam forward and you will not have an issue. Now you are back in the fight.

25.85 Releasing the slide using slide stop.

25.86

25.87 Releasing slide by hooking rear sight on body armor, then pushing weapon away from body, letting slide slam forward.

25.88

25.89

25.90 Releasing slide by hooking rear sight on holster or magazine pouch and letting slide slam forward.

25.91 Push weapon away from your body.

25.92 One fluid motion.

25.93 Slide slams.

25.94 Releasing slide by hooking ejection port of slide on magazine pouch, letting slide slam forward.

25.95

25.96

25.97 Weapon pointed in safe direction.

25.98 Let slide slam.

Support Hand Reload

When it comes time to reload with only the support hand, some thought needs to be put into the process. First and foremost, you want to be safe while conducting these movements. As with the strong-handed one-hand maneuvers, you will need to practice several techniques to see what works.

If you need to quickly reload, placing the weapon back in the holster with the magazine well facing forward is an option. You should first check with an unloaded weapon to see if your holster will accommodate the pistol in this manner. I almost always have a light mounted on my pistol so the holster I use will not allow me to rest the weapon as I could without the light. Test your specific gear to be sure. If the pistol does fit, as you seat the magazine, be careful not to knock the weapon out of the holster. If you decide to use your knee or under the arm technique, this procedure is relatively close to the strong side technique. If you are attempting to release the slide with your support hand, be very careful. It is more positive to use the technique we mentioned above and slide the rear sight along your pants, or belt to release the slide.

25.99 Dry weapon

25.100 Move hand on grip if necessary to reach magazine release.

25.101 Release magazine with weapon vertical.

25.102 Place weapon between knees.

25.103 Grab fresh magazine.

25.104 Guide magazine into well.

25.105 Seat magazine.

25.106 Secure weapon.

25.107 Hook rear sight or ejection port on belt or magazine pouch and let slam into battery.

25.108

25.109

25.110

Cycling the slide with one hand

If the slide accidentally slams forward before you are able to get the magazine in place, don't worry. Simply grab the pistol's grip and cycle the slide by using the same technique that you would use to release the slide, by using the belt or edge of the holster. You may need to be a little more aggressive to get the slide to move far enough to pick up the top round from the magazine. If this technique is not working well for you, it may be because of your sights. If the sights are too slick you may have difficulty. It can still be accomplished; you just might need to find a sharper edge such as a car door or edge on a piece of furniture. The best fix is to have sights that allow this procedure to be easily accomplished.

25.111 Hook rear sight on holster, belt or magazine pouch.

25.112 Push forward pulling slide to the rear.

25.113 Once slide is fully to the rear, let slide slam forward.

Locking the slide to the rear

If there is a reason for locking the slide of the pistol to the rear, it can sometimes be quite the undertaking. As you pull the slide to the rear using the rear sight against your chosen object, start with your thumb or trigger finger holding pressure on the bottom of the slide stop. When reloads are necessary, you should not have to lock the slide to the rear. Malfunctions such as a double feed more than likely will require the slide being locked to the rear though. I cannot overemphasize enough how difficult this can be. You must practice to ensure that you are able to accomplish this task. Try moving your hand around to gain the leverage that you need to get the slide pulled to the rear while holding the slide stop.

25.114 Hook rear sight on gear, thumb pushing up on slide stop.

25.115 Push down, pushing slide to the rear.

25.116 Keep steady pressure.

25.117 Continue pushing slide to rear.

25.118 Once slide stop moves up,

25.119 Release pressure from slide.

25.120 Slide now locked to the rear.

Malfunctions

If you have a malfunction that requires tap, rack, bang, you will first need to slam the magazine against your knee or some other firm surface. After ensuring that the magazine has been seated, once again rotate the weapon inboard and slide the sights against your leg or holster; quickly sliding the weapon will cycle the slide, clearing the malfunction. Ensure that your finger is off the trigger for this procedure. You should also try to keep some room near the ejection port to allow for any debris, such as a spent casing or live round to be ejected from the weapon.

If Immediate Action does not work to clear your malfunction, it is time to move on to Remedial Action. Remedial Action requires the removal of the magazine. If you normally lock the slide to the rear before removing the magazine, this is the time to change that method slightly. First, remove the magazine. If the magazine will not drop free, push the magazine release while hooking the front edge of the magazine on your holster or belt and pry the magazine free. Once the magazine has come loose, you may be able to rectify the situation by simply cycling the slide. If this doesn't work, use your best technique to lock the slide to the rear and attempt to clear the jammed cartridges from the pistol. As you pull the slide to the rear with your sights hooked on your belt or holster, use the thumb or index finger to push up against the slide stop. Repetition will help you to attain proficiency with these techniques. Don't give up on your technique, keep working and you will figure out ways to increase your leverage on the pistol's slide.

25.121 "Click" - no bang - initiate immediate action.

25.122 Tap magazine on knee with good force.

25.123 Hook sights on gear to rack.

25.124 Muzzle in a safe direction.

25.125 Rack aggressively.

25.126 Engage if necessary.

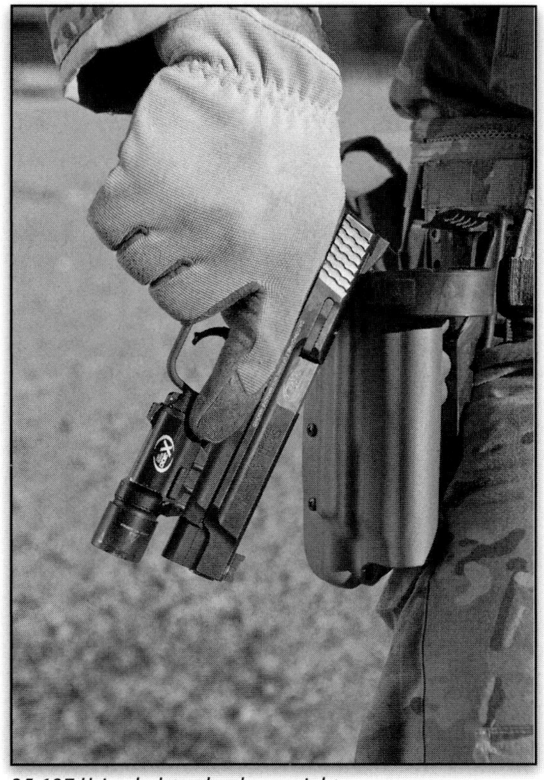

25.127 Using holster, hook rear sight.

25.128 Push down.

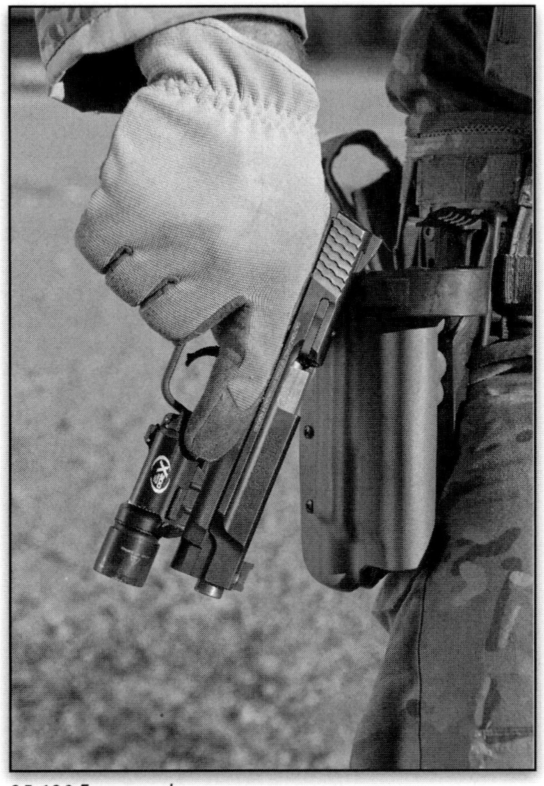

25.129 Even steady pressure.

25.130 Continue.

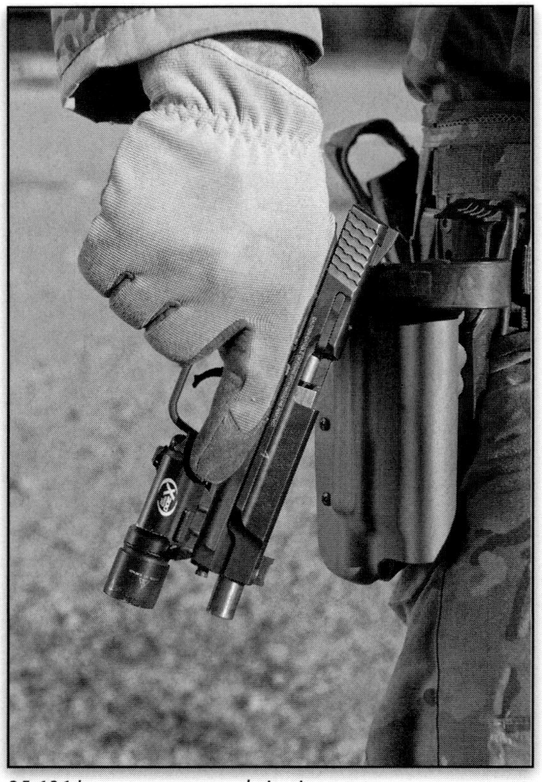

25.131 Leave space around ejection port.

25.132 Press slide all the way back to the rear.

25.133 Round Ejects

25.134 Remedial action.

25.135 Hook magazine on holster to pull free.

25.136 Apply even, steady pressure.

25.137 Slowly pull.

25.138 Pull magazine from weapon.

25.139 Rotate sight to holster.

25.140 Cycle at least twice.

25.141

25.142

25.143

25.144 Rear sight hooked on holster.

25.145 Once weapon is clear, place magazine in weapon, cycle and get back in the fight.

Firing the weapon with one hand

We have already discussed most techniques that will be used when shooting with one hand, but there are a few other ways to ensure you are able to hit what you are shooting at.

Most shooters will hit low left when shooting right hand only and low right when shooting left hand. This is from lack of trigger control. If you are not letting the weapon surprise you, you are more than likely jerking the trigger in the anticipation of the weapon's recoil. To get the rounds to impact where you are aiming, place the sights on the target, start a slow, smooth trigger squeeze, straight to the rear. If all goes well, you should see your sights lift from the target with the recoil of the weapon. If you are not seeing this, you are jerking the trigger. If you try to control recoil, your accuracy will not improve, so let the weapon recoil.

It ain't over 'til it's over.

There isn't a WEAK side.

If you are a firearms instructor or just want to be the best tactical shooter you can be, you must grab a hold of one thought process when shooting from the support side. Do not use the term WEAK. It will not help you or your students shoot any better, just the opposite. If you use the term SUPPORT side you are helping your students gain confidence in their abilities. Using the term weak will only cause your shooting and confidence to be weak as well.

25.146 Train for that "Murphy" moment.

Chapter 26, Weapons Retention and Contact Shooting

26. WEAPONS RETENTION AND CONTACT SHOOTING

As the Special Operations soldiers prepared to move detainees from one location to another, their training came into proper alignment with the real world. One of the detainees decided to attempt to cut the soldier with his handcuffs by bashing them into his face and head. He was successful in injuring the soldier, however, the soldier was successful in fighting through the pain and doing what he had been trained to do. As the detained terrorist grabbed for the soldier's weapon, the soldier pushed him away and drew his pistol. He fired the first round as the weapon cleared the holster, he fired one round from Position 3, and he fired twice from Position 4. This should help to drive home the point that you should always keep your muzzle in the direction of the threat throughout the presentation process.

How would you like to take my gun?

If I asked you this question, what would you say? Would you want me to hold the weapon at arms length, with a poor grip, and my wrist unlocked? Of course you would. Think back to the training you have had as a Ninja. As you stood there in your two toed socks, did they show you how to take guns away from someone as a last resort? Normally this is an intriguing part of any class. It usually starts like this, "ok, hold the weapon like this." The reason I say this is not to make fun of these drills;

26.1 Strong retention position ready to engage if need be.

however it is just puzzling that trainers do not believe that there are some retention positions that work better than others. I have never had anyone take my weapon from me while it was in retention (Position 3) that I could not have shot before they took my weapon. That is unless, of course, they came from the rear.

Contact shooting is pretty much what you would envision; you are so close to the threat that you are in contact with

26.2 Try taking his weapon.

them. Contact shooting normally will not allow you to get a good sight picture, or push the pistol out as far as you would like to comfortably shoot. Don't confuse contact shooting with point shooting, they are two different animals. Point shooting is firing without the use of your sights at distances beyond what we are defining as contact shooting distances.

Position 3 is an incredibly strong position, especially when someone goes to grab your weapon.

Try your gun take-away techniques with plastic training weapons, from Position 3, and see what happens.

As a reminder, if you choose to use Position SUL, just remember it is an admin position, not a retention position.

Shooting from Position 2

If the time ever comes where you need to shoot a threat from Position 2, it should not be the first time. You should practice this technique so you know what to expect. The blast can be exhilarating and the debris may surprise you. Before you practice with live ammo, ensure that you have dry fired the technique several times. This is not a basic movement.

If you are in a situation that requires you to shoot as soon as the weapon clears the holster and is aligned with the threat, here are a few basic principles to remember.

• Make sure the weapon has cleared your clothing and more importantly it is pointed at the threat and not at you or one of your partners. It is a good idea to slightly roll the weapon away from your body to ensure the movement of the slide is not impeded by any contact with clothing or your body.

• Try not to step back from the target, especially if you are already in physical contact with the threat. A hand to the face of your opponent (palm strike or hooking any part of your opponent's face) will help to make the fight less fair, giving you the advantage. Remember, we do not want a fair fight; we want to destroy the threat.

• If your eyes are on the threat, do not look away. Never drop your head so far that you cannot see your target. There is nothing wrong with blocking a blow to your head, but try not to look away from the threat. You must see where you are shooting, and if this is not possible, you need to feel where you are shooting. Soldiers or Law Enforcement Officers wearing kit, especially with a helmet, should attempt to keep their head on the gun side of their body. This will help to support leverage and ease of drawing and retaining the weapon in case the threat tries to take your weapon away. This must be an instinctive movement and rehearsed on the range.

Always remember there are more vitals then just the heart, lungs and brain. If you are not able to get a weapon oriented at the upper torso, go for the pelvis. The pelvis is extremely vascular and a gunshot wound to this area will take away the threat's mobility.

If you grab the target, do not shoot your hand. Ensure that the weapon is depressed far enough to safely engage and neutralize the threat.

26.3 Draw starts with support hand coming up for protection.

26.4 Holster retention device is released.

26.5 Attain perfect shooting grip on pistol.

26.6 Eyes on the target.

26.7 Snap the weapon from the holster.

26.8 Be prepared for the worst.

26.9 As soon as you are aligned with a part of the adversary's body.

26.10 Begin shooting first round to pelvis.

26.11 Second round close to spine.

26.12 Third round to chest, don't lower hand and eyes.

26.13 Fourth round to heart, keep eyes on throat.

26.14 Fifth round in heart. Shooter is still aggressive.

26.15 Sixth round in heart. Note brass in air, things move quick at this distance.

Shooting from Position 3

The difference between these two positions is minimal, but the accuracy range is increased from Position 3. If you need to eliminate a threat from 3 yards, and do not have time to push the weapon to Position 4, you will not have any problems. Some would call this technique point shooting. Point shooting falls in the area between using your sights and Contact shooting. I am not a fan of Point shooting, merely for the fact that it does not work in every situation and every distance. Using your sights will always allow you to hit the target; however, in this situation you don't have a choice. As you engage from Position 3 you should try to press the weapon towards the threat, as long as space has been created between you and the threat and there is no chance of a struggle ensuing for the possession of your weapon. If possible attain a sight picture to refine your point of aim allowing you to neutralize the threat. You may have been shooting around the edges of the threat. Remember, bad guys are not impressed until you place rounds in their vital areas.

Shooting from Position 4

26.16 Shooting from Position 4. Shooter realizes threat.

26.17 Starts to press weapon forward.

26.18 Almost to Position 4 and no shots have been fired.

26.19 Position 4, still no shots.

26.20 Finally a shot to the heart.

26.21 Much slower than shooting from Position 3.

26.22 Great shooting but we need to be quick at this distance.

26.23 "P" for plenty.

26.24 Shoot until the threat has been eliminated.

26.25 Shooting from Position 3. Shooter realizes threat.

26.26 Tightens grip and starts to squeeze trigger.

26.27 First round fires from Position 3.

26.28 Second round fires as weapon is pressed forward.

26.29 Continue to refine as you press to threat.

26.30 3rd round fired.

26.31 4th round fired.

26.32 5th round fired.

26.33 6th round fired (finally at Position 4).

Remember:

Create Space

If possible get the needed space to get to your weapon.

Get to your tools

Get that weapon quickly into the fight, in certain instances your pistol may not be the tool that you can get to……..

Be AGGRESSIVE!!

Compensators/Ported Weapons from Position 2 or 3

Be extremely careful if you have a ported or compensated weapon while firing from Position 2 or 3. The ensuing blast of debris and flash can be overwhelming if you are not prepared. Ensure that you rotate the weapon far enough to the side to eliminate the blast from hitting you in the face. These weapons sometimes throw small amounts of debris that can cause severe damage to your eyes if not protected. You must also be prepared if the situation happens during the hours of limited visibility. (That would be called Night for you civilians.) You will have more issues with flash than those using non-ported and non-compensated weapons. This blast of light may help or hinder depending on the situation. The large flash will degrade your night vision much more significantly than the lesser flash from a non-ported pistol.

Chapter 27, Combat Shooting Positions

27. COMBAT SHOOTING POSITIONS

Normal range days are usually occupied by shooters standing flat-footed, practicing draws and reloads, some multiple targets, but rarely the crazy positions that a gunfight may force you to shoot from. Unstable or irregular shooting platforms and obscure positioning is the cornerstone of the truly tactical shooter. You may or may not end up in these positions in the next fight, but having a Combat Mindset is being prepared for what will possibly happen in that fight.

If you have not developed the skills necessary to accurately and safely engage a threat from a normal standing position, then you must practice until this is second nature. But as soon as you feel that you are able to reasonably hit your targets where you aim, then change it up and add the new positions.

Prone

The Prone position is the most prevalent position that shooters want to practice even though it is normally not the most likely position you will engage a threat from; at least not from the normal flat out prone position, without the use of some sort of concealment or cover. Prone is also difficult for shooters who have previous neck injuries or have a larger gut than normal. There are tricks to the trade to make this position work for you, no matter your disabilities or body style.

27.1 Prone position.

Once you determine which prone position works best for you, practice. Most shooters have a slightly different impact downrange than they would from a more normal shooting position. It isn't the same for everyone, so try it on the range from several different yard lines to be sure you know where you need to hold.

Moving Quickly into Position

Getting into the position quickly is half the battle. I also like to recover from positions quickly and that really isn't possible from the prone unless you are a young fella. To quickly and efficiently move into this position without injuring yourself, you may want to try this technique. This technique works better the faster you can make it happen. If it doesn't work, you should get into the position by dropping onto your knees and rolling forward and down into the position while bracing with the non-firing hand.

If you think you want to get there a bit quicker, here is an efficient way. Squat quickly while placing the non-firing hand flat on the ground, between your legs. After you have placed the hand flat, a slight hop to get your momentum going is needed. Once your butt and back rise, kick your legs out into the push up position and then lower your body to the ground as you extend your firing arm towards the target. As I said earlier, this technique actually works better the faster you move.

27.2 Keep eye on threat if possible.

27.3 Squat into position

27.4 Place support hand palm on the ground.

27.5 Quickly spring with legs.

27.6 One fluid motion

27.7 Land on toes.

27.8 Lower body to ground.

27.9 Once on the ground,

27.10 Acquire sights and engage target.

Don't bend your elbows

Once you are in the prone shooting position, there are a few things to know. If you have a severe bend in your elbows and you are shooting a Glock 22, there is a good chance you will have a malfunction. These weapons are sprung pretty stiff and not having the needed grip will result in the malfunction. Try to extend your arms, they should not be locked, but they must help you to maintain an aggressive grip during recoil.

27.11 Good prone position, make sure not to overbend elbows.

Rolling to the side

Your level of flexibility will dictate which prone position you will have to use. If you have a bad neck, you may want to try slightly laying on your strong side arm. As you start to roll to the side, only roll as far as you need to, don't overdo it. If this is the position you choose, ensure that you maintain cover or concealment when rolling into this position. Rolling onto the support side will work too; it just isn't as stable for distant engagements.

27.12 Relieves strain on neck.

27.13 Rolling on your side may be a better option.

27.14 Practicing positions with VTAC barricade.

Elevating the weapon

If you have issues locking your arms out in the prone, or trouble maintaining the strong grip needed, you may need to try interlocking your fingers on the grip of the pistol to get the needed elevation and still maintain support.

To get in this position, I prefer to interlock the index finger of my support hand with the pinky finger of my shooting hand. As I interlock, I also place my support side thumb along the side of the grip, against my strong side fingertips. This added pressure will increase your torque against the weapon as it fires. This position allows you to get the elevation you need and add stability for extended periods from the prone firing position. This will also help tremendously with recoil management, especially for those finicky weapons we talked about earlier.

27.15 No support.

27.16 Using support hand for stability.

27.17 Interlock strong hand pinky finger with trigger finger of support hand.

27.18 Tighten grip with support thumb using strong hand finger tips as a ledge.

27.19 This technique may give you the elevation you need to take the shot.

Prone Issues

What should you practice from the prone? I am a fan of practicing everything you would from the standing position. You should practice shooting multiple targets and reloads, which may lead you to repositioning of your equipment. Once again, better to figure it out on the flat range than in an alley, at night. You should also work on your malfunction clearances; it is difficult and repetition is needed to hone this skill set. You should also practice drawing from the prone position, strong hand and support hand. You never know where you will end up in a fight. It would be nice to see if your holster selection will even work when you are face down in the mud, the blood, and the beer. You know it happened to a boy named Sue.

Supine Prone

Supine prone is as it sounds. You are lying on your back in the prone position. Supine Prone is a great position if you want to quickly roll out from cover to take a shot. This position also allows you to shoot at a greater angle upward if needed. For example, if you are rolling around a corner, you will be able to engage a threat that is in the standing position at close range. Be careful of your foot placement, you must be able to quickly shoot without worrying about shooting your toes. If you are in the correct position, you will also be able to quickly move behind cover if needed. This position is also a likely position that you may have to fight from. Getting knocked on your butt may happen, do not let the fight end there.

27.20 Supine prone under vehicle

27.21 Opposite side of tire.

27.22 Supine prone around corner.

27.23 Prepared high and low.

27.24 Supine prone allows for super elevation if needed.

27.25, 26 Supine prone.

Recovering from the Supine Prone

If you end up on your butt, how are you going to get up? I have seen several techniques, some of which require rolling around or doing acrobatics. Some recovery techniques also do not allow you to cover a threat with your weapon as you are standing up. I use a Jiu jitsu technique that Rorion and Royce Gracie taught me in the 90's. Place your support hand on the ground as well as the strong side foot. As you lift your butt off the ground, swing the support side leg under your body until your support side knee is on the ground. Once in the kneeling position, just stand up. You may be able to swing your support leg all the way through until your support foot is on the ground. This will be even more efficient. I like this technique because you can accomplish the task no matter what gear you are wearing and your weapon can maintain cover on a downed suspect or threat area.

27.27 If you end up on the ground, you need a quick way to stand up.

27.28 Come to a sitting position with support hand and strong side foot on the ground.

27.29 Lift butt off ground.

27.30 Swing support leg under body, coming to a knee.

27.31 Regain grip on weapon, keep eyes up throughout this process.

Kneeling Position

The kneeling position is usually the ideal position for taking cover, clearing corners, or almost any other tactical task. When you are using the kneeling position as a shooting position, there are a few things to remember. Try to keep one knee up, if you go down on both knees you will be slow to recover from the position. Also, you should use your elbows or triceps against your knee if the position allows. To get into the kneeling position, it is usually much quicker to step into the position, if possible. As you step forward, drop into the position. This act doesn't seem like much, but every millisecond counts.

27.32 Kneeling position

Leaning around corners

When using the Kneeling position to clear a corner, or to lean out from cover, you may need to switch knees to be efficient and safe. As you lean out from cover to clear or shoot, you should be able to catch yourself if you lose your balance and start to tip over. Sometimes this is easier if the outside knee is up. This allows you to use the knee closer to the cover as an out-rigger if you start to lose your balance. I use both techniques; it really depends on the way you get into the position. You must try every possible configuration to see what will work best. You may also have knee problems that will dictate which knee is used.

Get Low to Clear Corners

When operating in a tactical environment, it is important to stay low when clearing corners. Invariable, bag guys look at chest height, and if they are expecting trouble they will more than likely have their weapon up as well. If their weapon is up, it will obscure their lower field of view. So stay small, stay low, be aggressive and dynamic when clearing corners, don't slowly pie the corner, instead snap into the position to gain the tactical edge. The more you practice these low positions the better off you will be. Once you have built the muscle

memory, it will be a piece of cake. This isn't something I read about, I have seen this in the real world, and by the way, our boys won....

Barricade Positions

There is no doubt the previous positions can be used in conjunction with cover or concealment, which is the intent. Absolutely always use cover if you can. The next positions I discuss will lend themselves specifically to being used in covered or concealed positions. Demonstration will be done with vehicles and barricades to show the effectiveness of these positions. Our goal is to get you to think outside of the box. Try everything and use what works for you. All of the positions will work for someone in the crowd; it might be you.

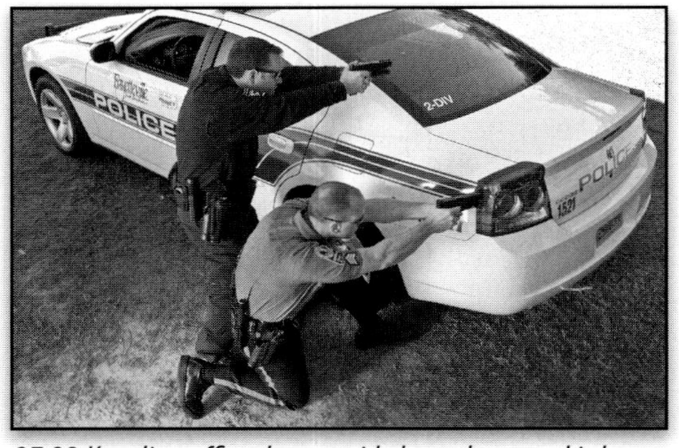

27.33 Kneeling officer has outside knee down and is bumped.

27.34 You will end up in a less than desirable position.

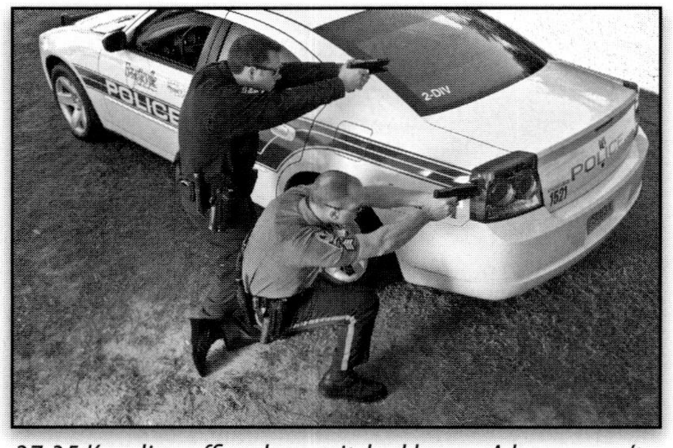

27.35 Kneeling officer has switched knees. A bump won't effect him now.

27.36 Don't rest hands on top of vehicle.

27.37 Back up and lower your silhouette.

27.38 Hands on hood.

27.39 Hands pulled back, lower silhouette.

27.40 Outside knee up allows you to quickly step, then slide out to engage threat.

27.41

27.41

27.42

27.43

27.44

27.45

Use the Cover for Support or Not?

This is an ongoing battle that must be fought. You are much steadier for long shots if you rest your weapon on the barricade or cover, but what are the downstream effects of this contact? If you are using a dust cover mounted flashlight or no flashlight at all, it is not a good idea to touch the dustcover of certain weapons to your cover. The reasoning behind this is the fact that the flex in the dust cover can impede the movement of the slide and other key parts. If you are shooting a completely metal weapon, or a weapon with a beefed up dust cover, this may not be an issue. There really isn't a reason to do this in the first place when we have techniques for working around the issues. You should also be careful about placing the slide on or against cover as this will cause all weapons to malfunction with enough pressure. Once again, no reason for this unneeded interference with the slide, there are ways around this as well.

Front Sight Destruction

The last issue I see with weapons coming into contact with the barricade is the front sight. Shooters love to slide their weapons into ports and start shooting, every time the weapon recoils the front sight is being driven into the top of the barricade port. It won't take long until that front sight is broken or missing. Slide back from the restrictive hole and go to blasting.

This is also true when shooting under a vehicle. Always ensure that you have the weapon at the correct angle to eliminate front sight contact with the bottom of the car's frame. This is very destructive to your weapon.

27.46 Be careful with the front sight of your weapon during recoil.

27.47 Recoil wil cause front sight to hit barricade.

27.48 Stay back just enough to allow front sight to clear.

27.49 Allow front sight to clear.

Using the Barricade for Support

After all is said and done, you can get some support with the barricade, you just have to be smart about the technique.

Press your knuckles into the barricade

As you press forward, use the knuckles of the support hand between your weapon and the barricade. This will allow the weapon to function normally and give the slight support that is needed. This will work over or around a piece of cover or concealment. Put heavy pressure against your cover if possible, this will help to keep your sights on target after you fire as well as to keep from having your hands slide around as you shoot.

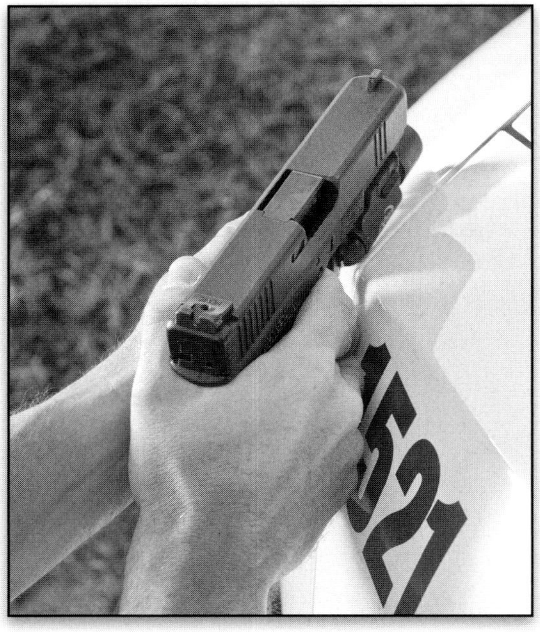

27.50 Use your knuckles.

27.51 Knuckles pressed against cover for added stability.

Using your Thumb for Support

If you want a bit of stability but there isn't a great place to place your knuckles, use your support thumb as a rest for the weapon. You will be surprised when you see how well this works. Just be prepared when you fire if your thumb slides off its perch, it is best to push the thumb against a flat surface if possible.

27.52 Thumb pressed against barricade for support, do not let your pistol slide touch the barricade.

27.53 Thumb pressed against barricade for support, do not let your pistol slide touch the barricade.

27.54

Lead with your eyes

You must still lead with your eyes when dealing with barricades. If you slowly pie the corner, the threat will definitely see you before you see them. Quickly lead with your eyes and drive the weapon to the threat.

This takes practice around barricades; you can't expect to learn this in one day at the range. Every time you go to the range you should be practicing your aggressive barricade techniques. Training your eyes is the key to success in the fight.

Prone with a barricade

If you use the prone position around a barricade, you need to be ready to move quickly in and out of position. This is sometimes difficult. If you start to roll over you can let your inside leg roll out and over your body to support your body weight. This will also give you a quick way to roll back behind cover by pushing with the extended leg. Be careful that the leg does not hang out too far giving away your position and giving the threat a decent target to shoot at.

27.55 May appear awkward, but works well.

27.56 Top leg is used to roll you back behind cover.

27.57 Push with back leg.

27.58 Back behind cover.

27.59 View from down range.

27.60 Ensure top leg is still behind cover.

27.61 Roll aggressively.

27.62 Back behind barricade.

Viking Tactics Barricade

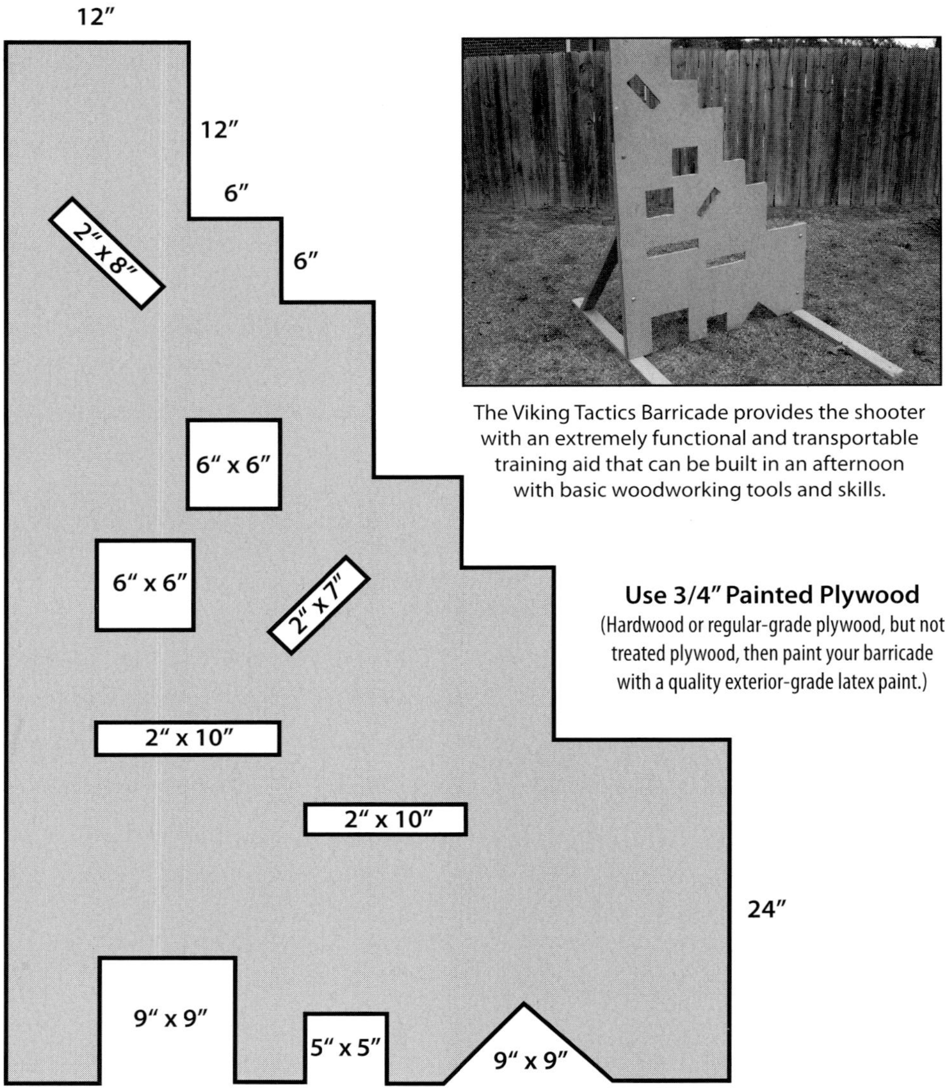

The Viking Tactics Barricade provides the shooter with an extremely functional and transportable training aid that can be built in an afternoon with basic woodworking tools and skills.

Use 3/4″ Painted Plywood
(Hardwood or regular-grade plywood, but not treated plywood, then paint your barricade with a quality exterior-grade latex paint.)

Base legs are 72″ long and have holes at ends so barricade can be staked into the ground.

Barricade is secured to base legs with 1/4″ bolts and wing-nuts. Barricade and legs are marked.

27.63 The VTAC Barricade

Seated

I like to make people uncomfortable when they shoot. One way this is accomplished is with positions that they have never shot before. One of those positions is the sitting position. Normally not a great position for the pistol but it is worth practicing, just in case. Sometimes the seated position will not allow you to easily view the target; this may get you in a very uncomfortable position. That is what we are after, concentrate on the sights, trigger squeeze and follow through, you can make it work.

27.64 Uncomfortable, but this may be where you end up.

Supine

Practicing the Supine position around corners of barricades is worth any time spent. You will see that this position works well, however it does take away mobility since you are sitting on your 4th point of contact. This is a great skill set to practice while moving in and out, also going back and forth from side to side around barricades. Lead with your eyes, you will see how effective this technique is after a few practice sessions. As you get more aggressive with this position, you should be on your back quickly moving in and out off position. Watch where those appendages are, stay safe.

27.65 Supine.

27.66

27.67 Supine, muzzle elevated.

27.68

Broke Back Mountain Prone

For those of you who have read my book, "Green Eyes and Black Rifles," this doesn't even get you breathing hard. For those of you who have not, please relax and listen in. Broke Back Mountain prone is a position where, as you guessed it, your head is down and your butt is up. Best part of the name is that you won't forget it. Several Police Officers from Santa Clara's Police Department jokingly called this Broke Back Mountain Prone. Well boys, it has stuck. This position is quick to get into and out of; it also allows shooters with a lot of gear to move efficiently. When you plan to go all the way prone with extra gear, you will be slower to recover from the position.

When shooting from this position, shooters will invariably turn their support side towards the threat. If this is the case and you are trying to keep both hands on the pistol, you will have a hard time feeling stable. You may feel like you are going to tip onto your head. If this happens it really isn't a big deal, but it may be distracting. There is a better way to attack this position though.

27.69 Strong side Broke Back Mountain

Using your forearm for support

If you have decided to reach across your body to engage the threat, you have a couple choices. Place both hands on the weapon and tip onto your head. This works but may be a little slower to get into and out of. It also hurts the noggin if you do this on pavement or concrete.

The next choice would be to hold your body weight with the support arm and shoot with the strong hand only, without any support. This works ok, but the weapon ends up pretty close to your face and is hard to shoot quickly.

Or lastly, press the back of your hand against your forearm to give the additional stability. This works really well. This is similar to using the magazine well of your carbine pressed against your forearm. This will allow you to slow your movement into the position with the support arm as well as allow you to keep your head from banging into the ground. Lastly it will give your weapon support to shoot quickly and follow through effectively on your targets. The added support may eliminate any limp wristed malfunctions as well.

27.70 Strong side Broke Back using forearm for support.

27.71 Support side Broke Back using forearm for support.

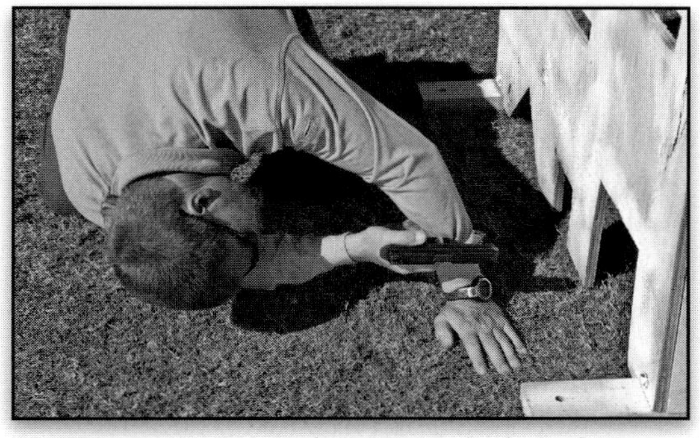

27.72 Using VTAC Barricade to practice Broke Back Mountain.

27.73 Broke Back using forearm next to vehicle.

27.74 Broke Back using forearm under vehicle.

Reverse your Position

If your covered position allows you to reverse the direction you are facing so your strong arm is next to your cover, you will be able to easily bend into position. You will also be able to use your support arm to lower yourself into position and be relatively stable. Once in position, you will be able to extend your arm away from your body giving you better recoil management. Maybe not better, but the weapon will recoil as though you are in the standing one handed shooting position. You will also have a clearer sight picture with the weapon away from your face a little. You should feel more stable and have better ability to shoot several targets quickly without your body getting in the way as it did when you shot across as we discussed above. This position works unless the barricade is very low to the ground, then you may have some difficulty. Try it, you will like it.

27.75 Unstable with sights close to face.

27.76 Officer switches to support side, better recoil control

27.77 Not a strong position.

27.78 Better position.

Under Vehicles

Quickly dropping into position behind a vehicle to eliminate a threat is something that must be practiced. If you are decisively engaged and the threat drops behind your vehicle or his, you may need to beat them to the punch and get down in the dirt. If you need to quickly get under and into the fight, you will be forced to fight according to the cover and concealment that is provided. You will not get to choose the position, place, and time that you are forced into this situation, but rather you will only have to play the cards you are dealt. If this happens to be on your left or right side, how will you fight? You also may have an extremely low vehicle that may be an obstacle as well.

27.79 Under-the-car view is quick transition.

27.80 Get comfortable shooting under vehicles.

Shooting from your side

To keep everything in perspective, I will discuss this for a right handed shooter, so keep that in mind. If you are forced to be laying on your right side, the strong side of your body, you can sometimes have issues getting the weapon low enough to actually engage a threat at the opposite side of the vehicle. This may force you to take the support hand off the pistol to get the correct angle on the target. Remember what we discussed earlier about not letting the front sight hit the bottom of the vehicle. So with the pistol laid to the side, you will engage with one hand only. Unless of course you have plenty of room to negotiate the problem without shooting one handed. If you are in a hurry to get down you may want to use the support hand to help you get into this position by grabbing a hold of the vehicle. This works especially well if you are able to grab the door or the side mirror of the vehicle.

If you are forced to get into a position on your support side, you may not be able to use the vehicle to help you get into position, but rather you will use your support hand to lower yourself into position. If this is the case and you end up on your side, you do not need to shoot with your support hand, but you may need to shoot with your support side eye. This sometimes baffles shooters, but if you are in a position as close to the ground as you can get on your side, you will not have a choice. Practice from this position so you are able to quickly adjust to the forced shooting position.

27.81 Officer decides to go low.

27.82 Drops to knee.

27.83 Lowers body to ground using vehicle as hand hold.

27.84 Officer drops into position, ready to shoot one handed.

27.85 Or with both hands.

27.86 View from the bad guy's perspective.

Shooting on your chest

Another option that is often overlooked is shooting from your chest. This position is extremely quick to build and there is not a lower prone position with the pistol that I have seen to date. This position will allow you to see farther than any other position with regard to angle under a low obstacle. There are downfalls though, first you will be forced to shoot with one hand, but the speed at which you can get your first shot off should negate that disability. Secondly, you are facing the ground, which puts you in a poor position to react to an advancing threat. Keep this in mind if there are multiple assailants to your front and flank.

27.87 You may need to get really low.

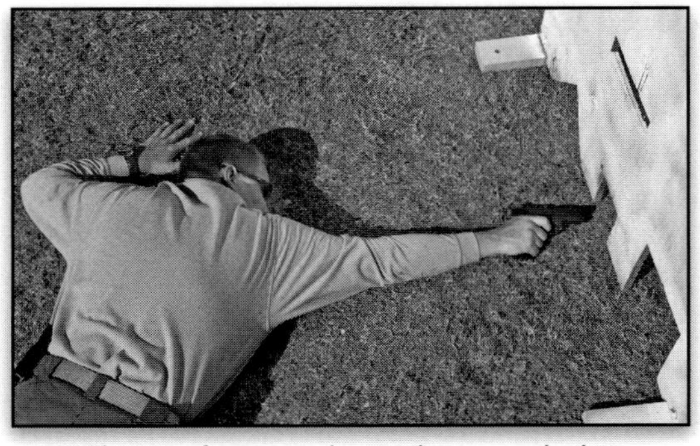
27.88 Shooting from your chest is the way to do that.

27.89 Note shooter is shooting right handed with left eye to get low.

27.90 Bad guy's view.

Play the scenarios out on the range and see what will work with your capabilities.

There are literally hundreds of positions you may end up shooting from. If you are forced to shoot from a new unrehearsed position in a Gunfight, you will be way behind the power curve. Develop your strategy now so that you have a plan that will actually work when the bullets start to fly. Get to the range and put it to the test. If the positions won't work on the range, they absolutely will fail you in the Fight...

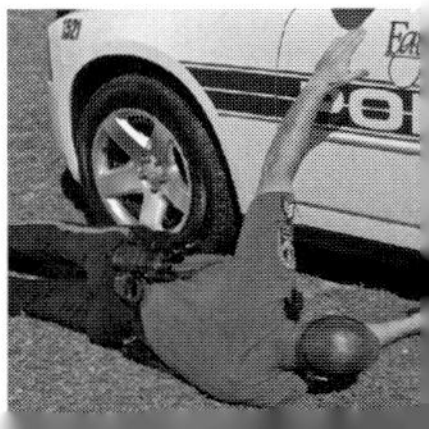

Chapter 28, Long Range Shooting

28. LONG RANGE SHOOTING

What is your definition of long range shooting? Is it 25 yards? Is it 50 yards? I would define long range shooting with the pistol as any distance that I need to adjust my sight picture to successfully get a hit on the target. From 40 yards and closer, I feel very confident in the weapon hitting where I aim. After this distance I may need to slightly adjust my hold to get the hits that will incapacitate a threat. A few edge impacts on a target should not be considered success. You should be able to shoot groups with your pistol all the way to, at a minimum, 100 yards. If grouping isn't possible, you should at least be able to hit a human size piece of steel or paper with a large percentage of the rounds that you fire.

This being said, the stated max effective range for the M9 (Beretta 92F) is 50 Meters. This does not mean that the bullet from your 9mm will magically stop at 50 Meters and fall from the sky. It simply means that the U.S. Military has determined that 50 Meters is the distance at which this set up becomes less than desired. Shooting at a threat with the pistol beyond 50 Meters is not the perfect scenario, however this could be a scenario that you end up playing a part in. Hitting targets at and beyond 50 Meters will build skill and confidence. Train for the worst, train for the extreme.

Don't Hold Over the Target

So if you don't hold over, how will you hit the target? Well let me ask a few more questions here. You are planning to shoot at people, not stationary targets. How can you successfully engage a paper target, let alone a human if you can not see where they are at? If you hold high you will not see the person drop their weapon thus becoming a non-threat. Or you may not see them take cover or move to a position of advantage to assault your position.

Front Sight High

When I engage at extended distances, I try to elevate the front sight in the rear sight notch. This will allow you to keep an eye on the threat and determine if this hold is enough after you fire the weapon. If you have a front sight with serrations, you can use the serrations as elevation markers to determine how much elevation is actually needed. If you cannot see serrations, you should still be able to judge how much elevation you are putting on the front sight. Try this the next time you go to the range to see if it

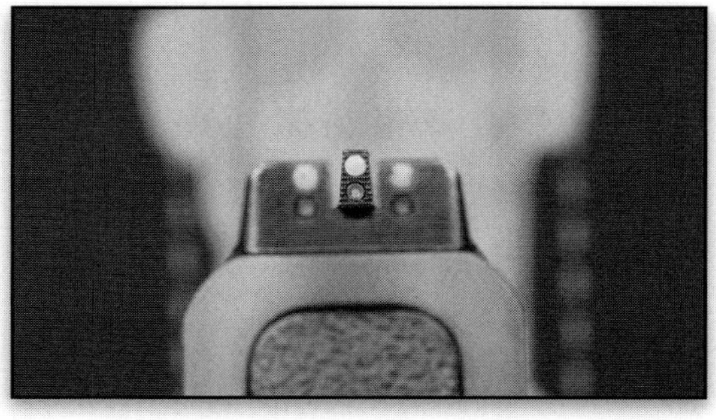

28.1 Hold front sight high so you are able to see the target at extended distances.

works for you. This technique will work on people, holding over will not work on real targets, at least not for multiple shots.

Stable Positions

At extended distances you must attain a better position than you would need within 25 yards. Any little bit of extra support or stability will help tremendously. If you decide to go prone, shoot groups to determine the correct hold because I would almost guarantee that your impact point will change with the position.

Refer to the previous chapter on Positions for a discussion on the specific techniques for making these shots.

28.2 Interlocked fingers with stacked hands will help to take stress off neck and be very stable.

Chapter 29, Flashlight Techniques

29. FLASHLIGHT TECHNIQUES

Lights and the selection thereof have been addressed in the Light Chapter. I do feel it is necessary to discuss the techniques that will enable you to quickly engage a threat at night with your light. Whether handheld or weapon mounted, you absolutely must have a light. If you have a weapon mounted light, you must always have a handheld flashlight as a back up. It is necessary to be able to use either technique without serious degradation to your accuracy and speed. If you have not taken the time to practice at night, you are really missing the point of combat shooting. Rubber meets the road at night, and bad folks like to take advantage of the darkness. Get out there and work through the issues that abound with the coming of night.

29.1 The best option is weapon mounted.

29.2 Appendix carry with hand held light option.

Hand Held Light Techniques

I am a cheater. I want to win. In order to win you must have a few tricks up your sleeve when the sun goes down. Part of the issue with weapon mounted light systems is finding a useable holster system when carrying concealed. If at all possible, attach the light to the weapon. If this is not an option then work with the following techniques to see which one works for you. Every one of the techniques is viable, see what works for you, and determine your favorite. No matter the favorite, practice all of the techniques.

As you practice these techniques, always turn the light on as you draw, or as you present the weapon to the target. After the engagement, always turn the light off. You have to be in control to quickly turn it on and off during a gunfight. This is especially true during reloads and malfunction clearances, which are times when you cannot shoot, so turn the light out quickly and move if possible.

Hands Crossed / Harries Technique

Developed by Mr. Harries in the 70's, the Harries Technique was designed for use with large bodied flashlights of that era. The technique works well with modern small body lights as well. This technique involves crossing your strong side wrist over your support side wrist. Crossing your hands to engage a threat is a good technique; the strengths of this position are that you will be able to quickly engage and you will be able to easily aim the light in the proper direction. The weakness of this position is that you will not be able to quickly re-engage. As you fire the weapon, your hands will separate from the recoil and this is not conducive to quick target re-engagement as well as it disrupts your normal follow through. When you use this position, ensure that you place the non-firing wrist below the firing wrist. This will allow the weapon to recoil naturally and will keep you from breaking your wrist. If the hands are crossed with the support hand wrist above the firing wrist, the slide will come back during recoil and cause you severe pain and possibly a broken bone. Not only that, but the weapon will usually malfunction.

29.3 Hands crossed/Harries Technique

Syringe Technique / Rogers Technique

The Syringe Technique is just as you guessed. You will hold the light as though it were a syringe. This works well for those who have large hands and can get the flashlight pointed in the right direction. Some lights are equipped with a grip ring to enhance this shooting position. You will also need to have a tail cap that is pressure activated to get this technique to work effectively. This position is quick, but the light may move as you engage, which does not allow you to keep the light where you want during the firing sequence. In the hands of the right shooter, this is an excellent technique.

29.2 Syringe/Rogers may require modified light.

29.4 Syringe/Rogers technique using palm to activate light.

"Shoot me in the face technique" / Neck Index

This isn't the actual name for this technique but it is where you are headed if you use this technique. This technique is accomplished by placing the flashlight to the side of your head or neck as you shoot. It allows you to quickly engage the threat one handed and lights your sights as well. Shooting one handed is not preferred and lighting your pistol means that not only will you see your sights, but the threat will have a clearer picture of where you are. As the threat engages you, they have a better chance of making successful hits if aiming at the light. I have seen several soldiers shot in the hands and weapon. All of these shooters were shot near their lights from the left or right. If the threat was shooting from the front it really doesn't make a difference, but when being engaged from the flank it is a sure sign to getting hit in the vitals… aka your Melon. Not a place to offer as a target.

29.5 Neck index - not my favorite technique.

One handed / FBI Technique

Shooting your weapon with one hand as the other hand holds the light is not a bad technique. This can also allow you to hold the light away from your body, which will hopefully keep you from getting hit in the vitals. Try to sporadically move the light around as you are shooting or moving to keep the threat confused. This technique will also allow you to swivel the light to search an area without having to turn completely to the right or left.

29.6 One handed light held well away from head.

Mouth Hold

At what point would you need to put a light in your mouth? What if you have an injured hand? Don't discount this technique. Not where I want to hold the light, but it may be all you have.

29.7 Definitely not preferred, but what if you only have one working arm?

Lamb Technique

The technique that I prefer is to place the light in my support hand with my thumb on the tail cap of the light. Very similar to the Harries, without crossing my arms, I then take the side of my pinky finger of my support hand and hook it behind the fingertips of the strong hand. I apply a lot of pressure as I fire the weapon for two reasons. First, the pressure will help with recoil, and secondly, the more pressure you apply the less likely the hands will separate as you fire the weapon. This technique will be even more effective if you can use one of our light slings to help hold the light to your hand. If you do not use pressure the hands will separate as you fire, and if that is the case you may be better off using a different technique.

29.8 Lamb Technique allows for some recoil control.

29.9 Pinky finger of support hand pressed against finger tips of firing hand. (VTAC Light Sling pictured.)

Reloading with the Light

As I said, if you have one of our light slings, you will be very efficient during reloads and malfunction clearances. If not, these techniques may help.

When attempting to reload with the light, you may want to re-read the Reload Chapter. If you use the flashlight like a magazine during the tactical reload you will be very efficient.

Grasp the light with the thumb near the tail cap. Hold the light with your ring and pinky fingers. As you reach for the magazine, use your thumb, middle and index fingers to get a decent grasp on the magazine. Once the magazine is near the weapon, release the partial magazine and let it fall, you can pick it up after the reload. Now seat the new magazine as you would during a tactical reload. If the magazine you are replacing is empty, it should have already been released to hit the ground.

29.10 Time to reload with handheld light.

29.11 Turn off light, tail cap is preferred.

29.12 Release magazine.

29.13 Regrip weapon/grip flashlight with ring and pinky.

29.14 Thumb, 1st finger and middle finger used to grip mag.

29.15 Light and magazine should be very secure.

29.16 A quick glance at the magazine well if it isn't completely dark. Guide magazine in with index finger.

29.17 Once you start to guide magazine into weapon, focus back on threat.

29.18 Seat magazine

29.19 Let slide slam forward.

29.20 Reassume shooting grip.

29.21 Reload with VTAC Light Sling. Ready to reload.

29.22 Rotate grip to reach magazine release, keep weapon vertical.

29.23 Release magazine

29.24 Regrip weapon while grasping magazine.

29.25 No need to grip light, only be concerned with magazine.

29.26 Attain perfect magazine reload grip.

29.27 Quick glance to magazine well.

29.28 Eyes back on threat while seating magazine.

29.29 Seat magazine. No need to hold light with the VTAC Light Sling.

29.30 Release slide.

29.31 Reassume shooting grip.

Weapon Mounted Lights

A weapon mounted light system is the way to go for a pistol as well as your carbine. If you have a weapon mounted light, don't give up practicing the above techniques. There will be a time when you will use them.

Pressure Pad

When I use a pistol-mounted flashlight, I prefer to use the Surefire DG switch. This switch not only allows you to quickly turn the light on, but it allows for one-handed pistol shooting with the light. It also turns off as soon as you take the pressure off the pad. I prefer this system since it sits under the knuckle of my firing hand, which allows me to have plenty of power to turn on the light. For those of you worried about accidental discharges with the light, it will take some practice to know how much pressure it will take to activate the light. It always comes back to practice.

Tape Switch

If you use a tape switch, place it in such a position that it will not disrupt the function of the weapon and also allows for one-handed manipulation. If you are going to have this type of switch you might as well do it right.

For years I used tire inner tube to hold a tape switch to the left grip panel on my 1911 for my work gun. It was effective, but the DG switch is better if available for your weapon.

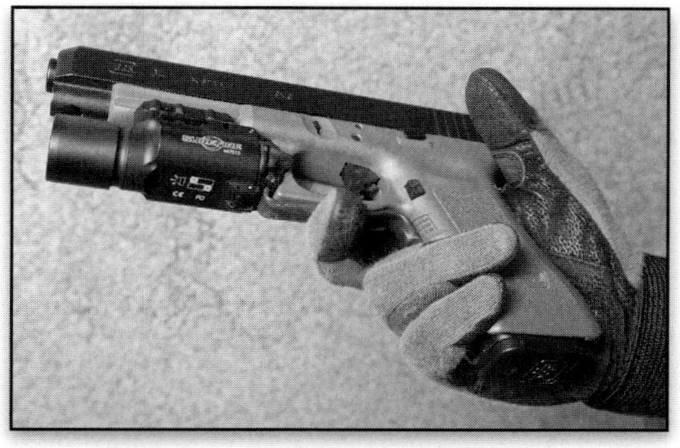

29.32 DG switch activated with knuckle of middle finger.

29.33 DG switch activated with knuckle of middle finger.

Using the switch on the rear of the light

If you don't have the DG or Tape switch, you will be forced to use the back of the light for activation. This works but is not as quick for on and off as would be preferred. Each light is different so practice with two hands as well as one to see what is necessary to activate the light. If you are going to shoot with one hand the switch on the rear of your weapon mounted light may get a little tricky, work out the technique during dry fire then head to the range and, you guessed it......practice.

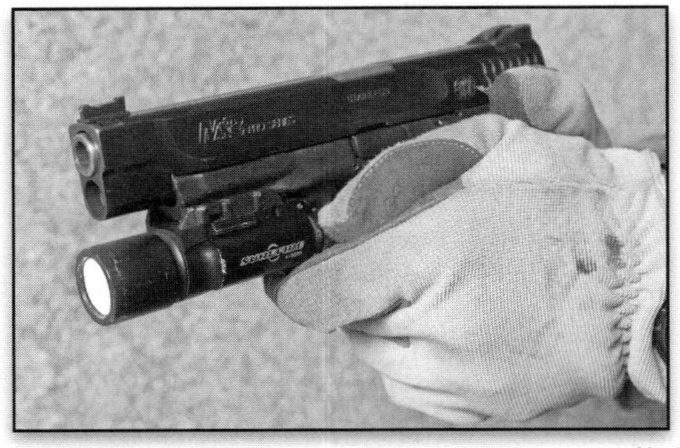

29.34 Using support thumb to activate switch on rear of light.

29.35 Bad things happen at night.

Not allowed to point weapons at bad guys??

I must begin my rant right here. Some Police agencies do not allow their officers to point weapons at bad guys. I know what you are saying, Lamb is confused, this really isn't happening. Well my gun-slinging friend, in parts of Oregon, you cannot point a weapon at a suspect during a felony traffic stop. Unbelievable that city managers, definitely not leaders, have taken rights to defend themselves away from their officers. So why is this important during a flashlight chapter?

All weapon mounted lights that I have seen are aligned with the weapon's sights and bore, therefore these officers are getting in trouble when they conduct a felony car stop at night with a weapon mounted light. As soon as they point the weapon with light attached at the felon, the felon runs to Mom and Dad and says Johnny picked on him. If this nonsense is permeating your city, do not get shot because of a ridiculous rule. Carry your handheld light, but

> *make sure you also have the weapon-mounted light. As soon as things do go bad, release the light (held by Lamb Light Sling) and transition to the weapon mounted light to engage the threat.*

If you happen to read this and are in a position of influence, please convince your leaders to give the rights back to the Officers on the street.

Ok, I am done ranting….

Chapter 30, Last Round

30. LAST ROUND

The importance of having the tools to fight at night and the training to be successful in this environment cannot be underestimated. Every single skill that has been covered in this book must be executed at night. Once that is achieved, you must work on these same skill sets with the use of only one hand. Are you prepared for the absolute worst-case scenario that you can imagine? Will you be able to successfully engage the enemy to your front with these tools at hand? Have you mentally prepared for what may happen when things go really bad? As an armed professional or civilian you must take this responsibility very seriously. No matter the situation, time of day, or the tools at hand, the most important thing to remember is that it ain't over 'til it's over, so...

Stay in the Fight!!